Will Randall was born in 1966 and educated in London. He taught languages in the West Country for ten years before going to live in the South Pacific. His first book, *Solomon Time*, was the story of his experiences there, and his second, *Indian Summer*, recounted his period as a teacher at a slum school in Poona. He continues to travel, teach and write, and is currently resident in the mountains.

Visit the author's website at: www.willrandall.co.uk

Praise for *Indian Summer*

'Many great writers have written about their time in the East: Somerset Maugham, E. M. Forster and Rudyard Kipling among them. Even if he never writes about India again, Will Randall should be added to this illustrious list'
DAILY EXPRESS

'*Indian Summer* is an engaging account of an India that most people try to ignore – an India of ramshackle huts, raw sewage, dire poverty and gnawing hunger. It is in this India that Randall found inspiring goodness – and with it the material for a fine and moving book'
DAILY MAIL

'Randall kaleidoscopically evokes his changing perceptions of the country's extraordinary diversity in a travelogue full of sensuous detail, humour and poignancy'
OBSERVER

BOTSWANA TIME

WILL RANDALL

ABACUS

First published in Great Britain in June 2005 as a paperback
original by Abacus
Reprinted 2005

A CIP catalogue record for this book is available from the
British Library.

ISBN 0 349 11777 2

Typeset in Palatino by Palimpsest Book Production Limited,
Polmont, Stirlingshire
Printed and bound in Great Britain by
Clays Ltd, St Ives plc

Abacus
An imprint of
Time Warner Book Group UK
Brettenham House
Lancaster Place
London WC2E 7EN

www.twbg.co.uk

Acknowledgements

During my travels through southern Africa I encountered far too many wonderful, kind and generous people to mention them all here. However, there were a number of people who helped to set my course and without their assistance I would never have made it to Kasane. In Cape Town, my friend Chef Didier helped me find my feet and Phil got them on the road. Tona Crookshank in Devon introduced me to Mark and Jane Bing through whom I met the Freeman family in Palapye, who provided me with a great insight into life in Botswana.

Many thanks too to all my friends and acquaintances, listed here or not, who made me so welcome in Kasane: the Rankin family, Heather Carr-Hartley and all my colleagues who made teaching at Nokya Ya Botselo School an unmitigated pleasure. Kibonye and Simon Healey were regular, generous hosts and I miss their delightful company greatly. Andy and Gay McGregor, and my godson Jamie provided me with one of the most memorable journeys of my life, plenty of hilarity and, finally, a very comfortable caravan on the Black Isle in which to write. Thank you.

In those rare moments that travelling loses its charm, it is a very great pleasure to be able to tramp down the drive to Exland where I am always greeted with the warmest of welcomes. My family, of course, continue to give me the most level-headed, big-hearted support. I consider myself very fortunate. Tanya again has produced beautiful illustrations.

Richard Beswick, Tamsyn Berryman and Kirsteen Brace at Abacus, and my super-agent Kate Hordern continue to supervise the turning of my wheels, and without their support, advice and great good humour the writing of this book might have been a less pleasurable experience.

Clearly, the main reason that it has been such a satisfying process is that it has given me the opportunity to tell the tale of the very remarkable boys and girls that I met in Botswana. I wish them all every good fortune.

The French Alps, February 2005

Author's Note

Setswana should be pronounced as it is written. Its 'e's are not silent – 'Kasane', for example, has three syllables.

This is a book for optimists.

Contents

BOTSWANA TIME

Prologue

Sliding slowly towards sleep, I closed eyes that stung with delicious heat-induced torpor. Of course, as so often happens, just as I was about to pitch towards that dark, comfortable chasm, I was awoken suddenly by obtruding noise. Above me the tin roof clattered and crackled.

The sound of fat, warm raindrops.

Pula!

Rain!

Had it come at last?

I pushed my wicker chair across the roughly sawn floorboards of the wooden hut, leapt up and turned to the window. My disappointment was acute as I realised that the African sun – surely the fiercest in the world – was still blazing down on the submissive land. As its morning rays warmed the galvanised sheets, they had begun to expand until they were fighting for room, bending and slightly buckling against each other causing this percussive rumble of sound.

Tantalisingly, away on the horizon in Namibia, I could see hill ranges of black, potent clouds rumbling and rolling, and spitting and glittering with spikes of electricity above the several hundred Brahman cattle and their ambling, stick-switching herders as they roamed across the river plain. Below me, 'my' village – a modern collection of neat houses, varied shops and grand safari lodges whose verandas extended to the river bank – was obscured by dust-dirtied acacia thorn bushes. From where I stood the plains disappeared into a misty infinity; a vista that had changed not at all since these tribesmen had first brought their livestock from the west and north countless hundreds of years before.

As I turned to sit again, my reasonably practised eye made out two familiar shapes away to my right. Like badly drawn 'M's etched on the side of the tan escarpment some few hundred yards away, the silhouettes of the mother and calf elephants, majuscule and minuscule, moved slowly across the clearing. Nodding with surprising synchronicity, they made their way down the shallow slope. Their serious, rather mechanical determination made me smile. Occasionally, hardly turning her head, the mother looked back to ensure her offspring was still following closely, for even in the heat of mid-morning predators prowled the forest of thick, shady thorn-trees.

Naturally the grey of cracked potter's clay, but dusted darker now with the black mud of the last dried-out pan that they had found on their long journey from the Chinamba Hills to the south, the animals lumbered on. Instinct guided them, with other unseen hundreds, onwards to the cool, deep brown waters of the Chobe River. Soon they were heading almost directly towards me but seemed oblivious, in their quest for water and green vegetation, to the shaky wooden cabin in which I was standing.

A fallen mopane tree had collapsed into the track before

them, desiccated and broken like a drought-stricken corpse; from its rib-like branches flitted a lilac-breasted roller, the glorious national bird of Botswana. Flashing its electric-turquoise wings and croaking *rack-kack kacker* in fright, it disappeared into the bush just before the cow elephant, with slow deliberation, slid her luminously white tusks under the main trunk of the tree and lifted the ton or so of wood off the ground, tipping it with a creaking crash out of the way. Ponderously she reversed a few steps and considered how much tidier things looked. Her calf raised his small trunk, curling its little pink tip, and poked the air in a demonstration of filial admiration. His parent allowed herself a slight affectionate smile before forging on.

Gusts of kiln-hot wind blew up eddies of dust around the two elephants' knees, which appeared to disorientate them and cause them to diverge from their chosen route. Now, it seemed, they had decided to take the short cut through the small beautifully tended and carefully watered garden that surrounded the building. Paying scant attention to the white wooden fence, the pickets of which scattered like spillikins, they proceeded, quite unaggressively, to crush or consume the bright patches of flowers and ornamental shrubs that had stood out in such colourful contrast to the sweeping beige and brown of the miles of bush. Young Gabamukuni, our cheerful if not overly industrious groundsman, would not be happy when he got back from the clinic, not happy at all.

Really, I ought to do something, I thought.

Shooing an Elephant . . .

There were various techniques. Some people always kept a noisy old aluminium saucepan and dented soup ladle to hand; others possessed November 5th quantities of pyrotechnics, strategically disposed, to deter these gentle but destructive creatures.

My method normally involved trying to stop breathing.

Despite the countless hundreds, no thousands, of these colossal, graceful beasts that I had seen while I had been living in Botswana, there was still, mixed in with the thrill, excitement and awe of watching them, a sizeable shot of stomach-gurgling alarm. As these two passed in front of me barely thirty yards away, I felt a double measure of fear float slowly up my throat. I could not help but back off. As cautiously as a retreating cat burglar, I stepped back as the shadow of the first elephant fell across the window. In doing so, of course, I collided with my desk and knocked a pile of reading books into a leaning tower that teetered and then fell noisily onto the wooden floor, where, half a second later, I joined them with a resounding, cabin-shaking crash. For a few seconds I sat there, listening hard, before climbing back as quietly as possible to my feet and peeping over the window-ledge. Sweat trickled into my eyes.

The mother elephant's ears were now spread wide. She had swung three-quarters of her bulk round to face me and instinctively raised one of her forelegs, shaking her tusks up and down as she did so. Her frightened calf pranced with surprising agility behind her and peered out at me.

I peered back.

Elephants are always pretending to charge. It's just show-ing off. Maternal instinct takes over. They didn't often actu-ally, you know, flatten things, I thought rather fancifully, as I glanced past them at the devastation of uprooted, smashed trees and crushed vegetation spread before me. This building was made of plywood, tin sheets and a few tacks – there weren't even any window panes.

Still, even if the cow did charge it would only be a little bit, just to show me who was boss – not that I really was in any doubt. Then she would just back away and the pair would meander off down to the river to drink their fill, eat a few leaves and wallow in the mud.

Wouldn't they?

Lifting her trunk high, higher than the roof of the hut, the mother woke me from my wistful reverie. Stamping the ground, she trumpeted sonorously enough to summon the dead. So loudly did she bellow that the teeth shook in my head and my eyes watered.

Of course, it was inevitable that at this noise pandemonium immediately broke out in the classroom. All fourteen children, who had previously been reading their storybooks in contented silence, had been shocked out of their fantasy adventures by my tumble. Now aware of our visitors, they abandoned their tasks, spraying pencils, rubbers and crayons about the floor, and racing under and over desks towards the window.

'Elephants, beautiful elephants!' squealed Stella, the thick braids of her hair bouncing up and down.

'Where is the elephant, Mr Mango?'

'What do you mean, where is the elephant?' I replied, astonished, but without demur, at my new African soubriquet. 'Where is the elephant?' I glanced nervously back at the huge beast outside. Then looking down, I realised that Blessings was much too short to see out of the window. Without thinking, I picked him up under the arms and he wriggled and squirmed to get a look. Bothle, normally lacking any semblance of get up and go, was energetically trying to climb up my right leg for a better view although he was much impeded by his rotund tummy. At the same time, Olobogeng was looking up at me imploringly and shaking my left elbow in an attempt to see what all the fuss was about.

'Sit down and, *ssssh*, for goodness sake, be quiet!' I begged in a curious half-falsetto, as I glanced over my shoulder. Obedient, as usual, the children returned to their places, a few even remembering to pick up their reading books on the way.

To my great relief, the elephants, probably put off by the commotion in the hut, had decided that they had made their point and were moving slowly away across the football pitch. I watched them go, nervously looking out for signs of second thoughts.

'Mr Mango, Mr Mango!' sang out the irrepressible Courtney, his blue eyes crinkled up with excitement.

'Yes, Courtney? Go on, get down off your chair. You'll only fall off again.' I felt weak at the memory of last week's bloodshed.

'Sorry, Mr Mango,' he apologised in a sing-song voice as, hands on the desk, he slithered down to the floor before shuffling his bottom back onto his seat. 'But, Mr Mango, can I play centre forward on Saturday, Mr Mango?'

'No, Courtney. We've already decided haven't we? Dolly and Olo are going to be our strikers this week.'

'*Ohhhh*, Mr Mango!'

'Shush, Courtney!' Elizabeth, our classroom helper, gently admonished, as she shifted comfortably in her armchair and continued to repair Blessings' torn shorts with a needle and thread.

Heaven only knew what would happen on Saturday. One set of goalposts had just disappeared into the bush on the back of an elephant.

1

Ding, Dong the Bells are Going to Chime

The Waterfront in Cape Town in the early months of a Southern Hemisphere autumn is a remarkably pleasant and sophisticated place to be.

Most of the numerous fish restaurants and bars have open views across the bay to Robben Island. Somehow the sharp corners of this prison penitentiary have been gently rounded as, in a surprisingly short space of time, it has developed the iconic status of Alcatraz and entered into a Hollywood-style retirement. The thousands of tourists, borne there on a number of sleek passenger ferries, wear down the paths of the former convicts, gradually eroding the brutal, horrifying reality of the institution and the regime.

Meanwhile, the near permanent sunshine, the range of wonderful smells and the sounds of cheerful, foot-tapping jazz bands that drift out from the quay across the sea create a safe protective bubble in which the international bourgeoisie can disport themselves.

Relaxing in a canvas chair on a teak deck, I faced on the table in front of me a no more challenging prospect than a fillet of snapper and a glass of Semillon Chardonnay, the yellow of Arcadian mead. The Victoria and Alfred Waterfront was a development that would not have been out of place in Miami, Nice, the Caribbean or practically anywhere on the coast of Australia. Altogether, it would be fair to admit, it was a fine example of what was described on one of the very helpful tourist signboards as 'modern living in a traditional setting'. The architects had cleverly constructed the boutiques of the shopping mall along the edge of old quays; jetties, which still preserved their massive iron bollards around which the Brobdingnagian hawsers of ocean liners had once been hurled, were dotted and splashed with some reasonably authentic-looking guano. A number of fishing trawlers were moored here now, some stained by patches of honest rust but most smartly painted in bright jolly-boating colours. For the main part, fishing nets and cases of slithering, silver fish had been replaced by wood-strip benches and emergency instructions. Some of the vessels' owners would not have looked out of place in the pages of Melville. One bristling fellow with a real Sou'wester and a pipe would, I was sure, have roared 'Billions of blue blistering barnacles' the moment a little white dog lifted his leg on his yellow Wellington boots. The majority of those who stood on the quayside, however, were now advertising in stentorian tones 'value' whale-watching trips along the coast rather than their daily catch or vacancies for harpooners.

Still, it was a very comfortable and, with the Rand at an all time low, a very cheap place to be, as I was now, amongst friends. We clinked our sparkling glasses and started to eat as a rather incongruous but by no means unappealing Santa Claus rollerbladed past. Dressed in economical terry-towelling hot pants, she whizzed along the smooth walkways, her blonde hair streaming out from beneath her red and white bobble hat.

'Delicious,' I mumbled to general assent.

Delicious, warm, pretty, inexpensive and friendly, but not at all how I had imagined Africa to be.

Indeed, much that I had seen to date on this, my first visit had proved disconcertingly familiar. Most of the architecture of Cape Town, particularly the more modern, could be found without difficulty in any European city. Even the townships, that old, disfiguring scar on the face of the new South Africa, could draw sad comparisons with the slums of India, where I had worked and lived only the year before; the juxtaposition of rich and poor was almost as stingingly shocking.

Wealthy suburbs along the coast were stunning; motoring along the corniches was reminiscent of the Adriatic Coast or the Côte d'Azur, the drive made all the more nostalgic by the hire of a midnight-blue Fiat Dino Spyder – a beautiful make of car and similar to one I had owned in my youth. Forays into the hinterland, for reasons oenological and gastronomical, to the vineyards of Stellenbosch and Paarl and the valleys of Franschhoek reminded me of visits to Beaune and Beaujolais, Alsace and the Loire; the cellars and restaurants familiar-sounding: Chamonix, La Couronne, Mont Rochelle, Haute Cabriere. We lunched in rose gardens on *foie gras*, stuffed partridge in champagne, *tarte au citron*, and any variety of cheeses. At one establishment, rather at the wrong end of the proceedings, I even engaged mine host in a lengthy conversation in schoolteacher French about the respective merits of *pinotage* and *cabernet franc*. I still remain a little unclear about the nuances of difference.

The purpose of my visit to South Africa was not simply one of hedonistic pleasure. I had been invited by Tim, an old friend from Australia. Tim had decided to get married and settle down which had surprised me mightily because he was a will o' the wisp, a flibbertigibbet and some might say, but only very kindly, a clown. With admirable single-mindedness and an acoustic guitar, he had played the troubadour over most continents. He had been a salesman in Uganda, rickshaw-driver in London, ice-cream salesman in Italy, pedlar, or possibly peddler, in the foothills of the Himalayas; all these for fun but none for too long. We shared a certainty that it would be not only a great shame but practically a crime if we didn't experience as much as we could of what lay beyond the shores of our home before it was too late.

Not one of his many friends overseas was quite sure what had brought about Tim's announcement that he intended to marry and settle down with his long-term Zimbabwean girlfriend, Tracey, in Cape Town. Perhaps it was his age; perhaps he was tired of always trying to keep one step ahead of the game, the rules of which had been laid down by his middle-class Australian background; perhaps it was a final need for the comforts of the hamster wheel – a desire to get back into the loop.

Adulthood pursues us all relentlessly and, more often than not (possibly for the good), tracks us down and scoops us up. Love, too, is certainly a beautiful life-changing thing, but what sent electronic messages of consternation whizzing through cyberspace between those who knew him well was Tim's declaration that he intended to work as a manager for his father-in-law in the latter's construction company. This was surely a role that he was, by any standard, quite ill-equipped and totally unqualified to fulfil.

Still, I suppose he was forty.

And, I realised now with a heavy-sinking heart, in about eighteenth months, so would I be.

Looking at Tim's situation more positively, it did mean

that there would be a wedding and, hence, a celebration – a party. Knowing the man as I did, I suspected it would be quite a party. So it was that from Adelaide (Tim's home-town) to Zwillingen (where Pete, his ski-instructor younger, wilder brother temporarily resided) holiday time was booked, flights reserved, gladrags bought and bags packed. My invitation was particularly gratefully received as a long winter in the UK came to an end. For once I had no hesi-tation in accepting. My finances, due no doubt to some technological banking glitch, seemed surprisingly, worry-ingly buoyant. Indeed I did not even have to consult my bank manager and intermittent friend – the splendidly but not always appropriately named Mr Jolly. Since I had returned from a happy time living and teaching in India, I had flipped and floundered as I tried to find a satisfactory niche back at home. No doubt because I still had high levels of a nasty travel bug pumping around my veins, I had bought an open-ended return ticket to Cape Town. Before I had left England I had resolved that this celebration would be a stepping-off point to explore as much as I could of the continent of Africa.

So future career moves again, with no little measure of guilt, put temporarily on hold, I had arrived in Cape Town a week prior to the Happy Day in order to take the oppor-tunity to catch up with other old friends. Many of us had met in the Solomon Islands some years before where Tim had been of great assistance to me during my chicken-restauranteuring days. Charlie and his Malaitan wife, the beautiful Gracie, had flown in from Honiara, and it was with them that I was relaxing at the Waterfront on the day of the ceremony. We chewed the cud about various South Sea adventures while Gracie, who had never left Melanesia before, looked around her, pop-eyed at the choice of treats available. Occasionally, she skipped off to one of the many colourful stalls to buy a toy here or trinket there for one of her sizeable tribe of children.

As the wedding was not until four that afternoon, it may not, with hindsight, have been a good idea to agree to meet at eleven in the morning. Charlie, who as best man was dressed in a grey morning suit complete with top hat, was almost as out of place as the roller-blading Father Christmas. He was also suffering badly from the heat. At both waist and neck his attire was coming asunder and his hat had lurched to a raffish angle normally only attempted by the most roguish of Dickensian characters. Quantities of cigarette ash, crumbs of fish and blobs of tartare sauce now bespeckled the front of what had been a pretty exotically patterned waistcoat in the first place. Patting his beaming forehead with Gracie's gloves, Charlie made a unilateral decision that we needed more refreshments.

Two more bottles of something white and delicious seemed to set my friend up for the duties he was to carry out that afternoon. Now, standing somewhat inelegantly, a task which would have been distinctly more arduous had it not been for the assistance of the sturdy table's edge and Gracie's well-practised supporting grip, he bid us pay the bill and follow him. The mathematical skill required to divide the amount owed between us seemed momentarily to have eluded us, so I shrugged and, as so often happens in these situations, blithely paid with a credit card that had been provided for me by the ever trusting Mr Jolly. Whatever needling feelings of guilt I certainly should have suffered seemed to be strangely dulled, and I made my way jauntily up a gangplank in the direction of the road. Charlie was already gesticulating rather wildly at a variety of vehicles that were quite clearly not taxis.

Soon after, the rest of our motley and slightly flushed group arrived at the roadside to find our best man engaged in a lengthy negotiation of price and route conducted in a complex mix of war-movie German, beginner's Afrikaans and English.

'*Ach ja, wunderbar*, Stellenbosch, *sehr groot*, let's go, mate!' He waved his hat out of the side door before sliding it closed with a flourish and collapsed back into his seat. 'Stellenbosch, here we come, "I'm getting married in the morning,"' he warbled as we pulled out into the traffic.

'Stellenbosch, you sure?' Jonny, another close friend, leant through the headrests, his normally cheerful face displaying a frown of puzzlement.

'Course it is! Didn't you read the invitation? Will, give us the invitation. Give us your invitation.'

'Charlie, I was relying on you. You were there yesterday for the practice. You must be able to remember where we're going?'

''Xactly, follow me, course I know where we're going,' he confirmed as we sped out of town.

But of course he was wrong. Kirstenbosch, not Stellenbosch, was our destination, but that was not discovered until we had arrived at the latter some thirty miles out of town. By this time we were running very late. 'Get me to the church on time!' Charlie sung lustily as he waved at bemused pedestrians.

Suffice it to say that the church was reached minutes if not seconds before the bride arrived, and the dash there involved a worrying degree of traffic-dodging and language not commonly connected with the sacred contract of marriage. Tim looked less than grateful and relieved as Charlie came lurching up the aisle attempting to get his shirt tails to finally stay in his not inconsiderable waistband. I slid into the back pew with Jonny, and buried my nose in the order of service rather than face out the stares of the bride's family.

After the ceremony, wedding photographs were some-what delayed by the disappearance of the best man and his wife backwards over a low, small wall. After a certain amount of flailing arms and a great deal of giggling they reappeared. Charlie's topper now looked more like some-thing normally worn by the Cat in the Hat. Thanks to Gracie's accidental elbow, his right eye was now a rich maroon. Afterwards, the chronology of the events of the evening could be charted photographically by the size of his swelling.

We all then proceeded to the reception. Having consulted the seating plan, I found myself on a table of strangers and prepared myself for an hour or so of unchallenging, incon-sequential small talk. So it was to my surprise when the gentleman on my left, gimlet-eyed and goatee-bearded, lifted off his half-moon glasses and fixed me with a stare.

'So,' he glanced at my place name. 'Will . . .'

'Yes, er . . . Neville?' I smiled, peering sideways at the small piece of decorated card in front of him.

'What do you make of modern Africa?'

'Well, blimey, I'm not at all sure. You see, I haven't really been here that long.'

'*Semper aliquid novi Africam adferre*. An educated man like you would agree?'

'Sorry, not sure I am quite with you there . . .'

'"Africa always brings us something new." Pliny the Elder, *Historia Naturalis*, Book Eight. Remember? How true it is.'

'Is it?'

'Where are you heading to from here? There's so much out there. Remember your Shakespeare? "I speak of Africa and golden joys," *Henry IV Part Two*, Act Five, Scene Three. Remember?'

Before I could even open my mouth, let alone think of

an excuse, he went on. 'Botswana. That's where you want to go. There is a country going places. It's not all ladies and their detective agencies you know.'

What the hell was he talking about? I smiled at an impassive, suet-faced girl sitting opposite me, hoping for rescue. None was forthcoming.

'We are looking at the formation of a modern democratic state, you know, with a genuine, operating social system.'

God, how dreary.

'What's your game then, Will?'

'I'm a teacher. Just sort of taking a bit of time off.'

'Teacher, eh? You better get up to Kasane, go and see my mate Graham. He always needs teachers – runs a little school in the bush. Now, that would be a tremendous experience. I don't know, he's probably got about sixty kids there. All sorts of different backgrounds, countries. Nice facilities and everything. What's so great about the school is its location in the bush, so you're surrounded by some of the biggest variety of wildlife in the world. Stunning. God what I wouldn't give to do that. You know, if I was a bit younger . . . God, yes! I'm sure Graham would take you on like a shot. You've got references and all that I suppose?'

'Right, Kasane. Good. Yes, I have got references and things. But I couldn't just turn up like that out of the blue, could I?' I tried to imagine just turning up at a school in England and presenting myself for duty. Then I thought of the endless offices and interviews and pointless paperwork. The form-filling. Grabbing my glass, I shuddered at the thought.

'Will, listen, this is Africa. We don't get hamstrung with all that bureaucratic nonsense that you do in Europe. All I need do is give Graham a ring and you just have to get yourself up there. Here is my card. If you're interested give me a call. Think about it.'

'So where exactly is Bots—?' But once he had handed
me his business card Neville turned to the guest on his left
and became engaged in a conversation that lasted the length
of the meal and seemed to revolve almost entirely around
lingerie.

Professor Neville Botting. University of Cape Town; I shoved
the card in the breast pocket of my jacket and set about
tackling a new bottle of Sauvignon which originated from
somewhere just up the road. Glancing at the girl opposite
me who was sucking Coca-cola cross-eyed through a straw,
I realised I was on my own.

Botswana.

Of course, I had heard of Botswana, but what did I know
about the country? Well . . . nothing really. To my embarrassment, I realised that I knew next to nothing about any
of the countries of the African continent. Apart from South
Africa, whose momentous political changes at the end of
the twentieth century had been the centre of world attention, and then the recently publicised sufferings of the
people of Zimbabwe, the rest of the vast land mass
remained obscure to me, its peoples and traditions alien.
Yet, I was intrigued by Professor Botting's brief description
and tempted by the slightly nebulous concept of the 'natural world'. More than this, though, I was surprised by how
appealing I found the thought of teaching in a little school
'in the bush'. As far as schools are concerned small is definitely beautiful. The vast inner-city establishments in the
UK where I had once taught seemed to lose the souls of
the children in their endless disinfected corridors, and
compared unfavourably to the warmth and succour of the
'large family' type of school in the Indian orphanage where,
not so long ago, I had been so happy. Some years back, I
had realised that I was a very poor tourist, and I secretly
loathed long tours of decaying buildings or sliding across

the polished floors of hushed museums. What I really enjoyed was the opportunity to get under the skin of a community, and to share food and drink, and conversation and humour at the table of people whose experience was vastly different to mine, but with whom more often than not I found I had a great deal in common.

Charlie, his church duties adequately performed, had delivered a speech which had caused only a few eyebrows to be raised and two champagne glasses to be dropped. He had then made himself comfortable at the bar. I made the life-transforming decision to join him. Fairly accomplished, almost by birthright, at the art of drinking, and certainly having put in a number of years of fairly regular practice, I had always considered myself, perhaps with a certain misplaced pride, to be something of a natural. Pretty quickly, however, I came to recognise that as far as Charlie was concerned, I was punching well above my weight. What astonished me was not only the quantities of alcohol involved but also the pace at which we were expected to progress. Varieties of blends, colours, strengths and smells quickly began to kaleidoscope in my mind, and the bound-aries of my vision began, in a wholly comforting and well-recognised fashion, to shrink to this warm and friendly little corner of the world.

As the evening wore on and the hired jazz band warbled away underneath some lime trees at the end of the lawn, the celebrations took a classic course. Initially, the guests had come together tentatively, the two camps shyly polite and occasionally bemused; exercising their well-honed small-talk skills, they had circled and introduced, sipped and nibbled. Later, as the champagne had given way to other wines and worse, the volume of the conversation had taken a sharp and noticeable turn upward, reaching its apex when pudding was finished and the band started its first boisterous set. Many of the more enthusiastic roisterers took to the specially laid parquet flooring and danced in a manner ranging from the fervent, almost zealous, to the downright inappropriate. Occasionally people reappeared from bushes and alcoves wriggling items of clothing back into their proper positions. At the bar, laughter was elicited in generous measure by anecdotes that more often than not did not merit it and which totally escape me today.

At least it was clear that everyone was having a good time – apart, of course, from those inevitable couples that were having rows and that strange minority who find that, after a few drinks, for some inexplicable reason, they have to burst into floods of tears.

The top of the festive hill was reached some time after midnight and slowly, imperceptibly, everything slowed down, became a little quieter, a little unsteadier, fuzzy at the edges. The lights blurred, hands crept to stifled yawns; jackets, handbags and discarded hats were sought out in corners where they had been either dropped or thrown; taxis were ordered, and thanks and apologies given. Everyone realised that the party, certainly a great success, had come to an end. Everyone, that is, except Charlie.

'Come on, Gracie, arise from that semi-recumbent posture!' he bellowed, a wild look in his eye. He lifted the coffee-stained cloth of one of the tables and peered underneath.

'Come on, old girl!' he called encouragingly as a rather frazzled, slightly crumpled Gracie crawled on all fours back into the swinging greens and blues of the disco lights. For the first time, she looked like she was wishing that she was curled up comfortably on the veranda of their little beach house back in the islands of New Georgia, being lulled to sleep by the breaking of Pacific waves.

Instead, she was invited, as were I and a couple of other

guests who had not yet managed to make good their escape, to go clubbing. Any resolve that I might have had to not overdo it, to call it a day at a reasonable hour, to get a good night's sleep, collapsed as we poured ourselves into a taxi and headed off to a place Charlie 'used to go to twenty years ago. Assolutely magic.'

To the surprise of us all, Rhythm Divine was still there, a place that was 'downtown and happening' – at least that was what I was told by Charlie shortly before he tripped over the doorstep and disappeared at speed into a large throbbing, leaping crowd of partygoers. The bouncer seemed so astonished that he hardly bothered to look at my ticket as he rubber-stamped my watch strap. I considered asking him when the last top-hat-wearing clubber had visited Rhythm Divine but the music was too loud.

'You'll never guess what, Will, mate,' Charlie had sought me out in a small yard behind the club. Gracie had curled up under a tree with my jacket over her head and I was considering the health benefits of another bottle of Castle beer after a rather hectic Mick Jagger impersonation on the upstairs dance floor. Much of the old magic of my performance was still there, I liked to think, and certainly people had stood back, although whether this was through admiration or self-preservation I was unsure. The only definite outcome was that I was absolutely exhausted.

'You know who this is, Will?' Mate, you know who this is?' Charlie had a rather shorter figure in a headlock that seemed to be applied partly in a spirit of camaraderie but also partly in an attempt to remain upright.

'This is Phil, my ol' mate Phil!'

He loosened his arm to reveal a wiry, deeply tanned, grizzled man of about my age. Shaven-headed, with a diamond earring and a tattoo of somebody naked wrestling with a snake on a solid bicep, Phil's appearance was piratical but his grin overwhelmingly friendly.

'How are you, mate? Charlie, mate. Having a good time? Good wedding?'

So many people that I had liked and sympathised with on the road over the last few years had proved to be Australian, and Phil was the right type of Aussie – the type who wasn't obsessed about being an Australian. Indeed, it seemed that he had made every attempt to flee that continent as soon as he was old enough and had been on the road ever since. Now, though, he had declared his never-ending love for Africa; this was where he wanted to stay.

'So, you seen much of the place?' he asked me as we leant against the wall of the yard and he stroked his neck trying to relieve some of the discomfort inflicted by Charlie's ministrations.

'Cape Town?'

'Nah, Africa, mate – all that out there.' He wafted his arm around him in a manner that suggested that he was not entirely sober either. 'You gotta get out there.'

'Yes, well, I have been to the vineyards and stuff, you know. Very nice.'

'Oh pssh, that's nothing, mate. That's just like Europe – no, I mean Africa. The bush, mate. Have another beer.' He was beginning to sound like a bladdered version of Professor Neville Botting and the curiosity that I had felt at dinner swirled to the surface again.

'Oh, no, I won't thanks. Got to head off in a min . . . No, honestly. Please!' But he had headed off to the bar leaving me with a beatifically beaming Charlie, who swayed slightly to and fro and muttered 'bloody brilliant' under his breath a few times.

What was distinctly not so bloody brilliant was my state of health, both mental and physical, when finally I met up with my friends for a late breakfast in leafy Green Point the next morning. A fried breakfast, the panacea, according to the cognoscenti, for all alcohol-related ills, snarled at me from the plate that had been placed before me in a trendy bistro. The thumping music didn't seem to be on my side either.

Charlie, who was putting a fantastic face on things – or who was not yet entirely sober – was appallingly chipper.

'Not eating your sausages, Will?'

I could not reply and watched listlessly as he scooped one off my plate and consumed it in one long sliding motion.

Phil smacked his lips as he wiped his plate clean and then took a slug from a brown beer bottle – an item that I noticed seemed to be an almost permanent accessory.

'Right, better be getting you fellows to the airport,' he announced briskly as he drained the last drops onto his tongue.

Charlie and Gracie were flying to Australia that morning en route for the islands. If Charlie felt anything like I did, which is certainly beyond my powers of description, then the trip must have been an appalling prospect but, without even the quietest groan, he stood up and gathered together numerous bags and the gently fading Gracie. Although I was almost overcome by the relief I felt at not having to embark on a long journey myself at that moment, I did also sense a slight panic at what my future might or might not hold. My eventual visit to the travel agent to book my return ticket to London would, I realised at that moment, be undertaken with a heavy heart.

'Right, I'll just get the truck,' announced Phil and disappeared into the car-park.

'You don't have to come, Will, you know, if you don't want to . . . Go back to bed!'

'No, no, I'm fine. Really. Fine.' I didn't see my friends often. It was the least I could do – I supposed.

With a groaning of air-brakes, a large yellow lorry drew up in front of the café. Phil grinned at us from the driver's seat. To my surprise, as I stumbled out onto the pavement, I saw that the truck had been converted into a heavy-duty charabanc with windows cut into the back section. A hefty door fixed into the side was swung open, and I clambered, like an alpinist suffering from lack of oxygen, into the back. Here I discovered carpeting and moderately comfortable bench-seating bolted to the floor. The cab was separated from the rest of the vehicle by a mesh screen; communication between front and back was by a white telephone affixed to a bulkhead.

We rumbled through the lunchtime traffic as I lapsed into a state just a few levels away from coma, disturbed only by the thumping and grinding of Phil changing gears and the occasional whining horn of a car as it flashed by on the motorway.

Our farewells were somewhat muted at the departure gate but I managed a small wave and a half-smile as Charlie and Gracie, using their trolleys as much for support as anything else, wandered off in the direction of the passport officials. It was surely touch and go whether they would be allowed onto the airplane.

Back on board the yellow machine, this time up front alongside the driver, I began to feel rather faint. Rolling down the window I leaned out for some fresh air.

'Here you go, mate!'

I turned slowly to discover that Phil had flicked up the lid of a small cool box that had been fitted between the seats. The rows of silver beer-bottle tops looked like bullets in a magazine. I shook my head as vehemently as it would allow but, unperturbed, Phil pulled a bottle out with a practised flick of the wrist. Placing it between his teeth, he bit down hard and twisted off the cap. His eyes never leaving the road, he spat it expertly into a small receptacle screwed to the dashboard. When he thrust the cold bottle towards me, I took it with all the enthusiasm of a man being offered a live hand grenade.

'Go on, then. You know it makes sense!'

I did not, I really did not. I lifted it to my lips as reluctantly as Socrates had his hemlock.

'So what do you reckon to the old truck?'

'Mmm, absolutely great . . . So, er, what is it? Er . . . I mean what do you do with it?'

'Well, Will, it's what we call an overlander. You know, get out there in the bush, in amongst it. Great, love it.'

'Oh, you mean a sort of safari truck?' I hazarded. The last thing on earth I felt like doing at that particular moment was getting 'in amongst it'.

'Well you're kinda right, mate, but you see this beauty's fully fitted out. We got the lot. Camping kit, all the spares you want, cooking stuff. Everything you need. We can sort out a trip for like twenty PAX. You know, passengers, punters.'

'Oh, yes. I've always wondered what PAX stands for. Do you know?'

'Absolutely no idea, mate. Anyway this beauty will get you halfway across the continent – fully ready to go for like a month before we need to restock.'

Five minutes more in the over-heated cab would be quite enough for me. I took a deep breath and a small sip of beer.

'Yeah, in fact I'm heading out tomorrow. Got sixteen coming in in the morning. Frenchies and Germans – new lot. Taking them through the Namib, Kalahari, through Bots, over the top into Vic Falls. Just a bit over a couple of weeks, you know? Should be great.'

'Oh, I see.'

More of an effort, Will.

'So . . . is that a long way?'

Or something.

I drank some more beer and battled with a resentful digestive system.

'Oh, mate, yeah, it's gotta be fifteen hundred miles. Yeah, good long stretch.'

Good? I hardly thought so.

'Yeah, I'll leave them there then get on up to Zambia, Malawi, Kenya. You know? Love it up there, you know? Gets pretty tough.' This seemed strangely to be a positive recommendation.

Just listening to Phil was enough to make me feel like going back to bed.

'You don't have to do everything for them, do you? I mean like cook and put up their tents and . . . well, talk to them.'

'Ah well, listen, mate, you know, they're supposed to muck in, help out, teamwork and stuff. And Janey comes along too.'

'Oh, yeah, who's she?' I slid up a bit in my seat, and to my alarm as I tipped the beer bottle again to swig from it, I discovered it to be empty.

'She's my girlfriend.'

'Oh, OK yes, right, I see.'

'She's great, does the cooking, barbies, you know what they call *braais* here. And she's a guide, so she points out all the interesting stuff on the way. Flora and fauna. She's flying in from the UK tomorrow because she's a Pom. Been staying with her Mum in Reading, so we'll all meet up at the airport. Bit of an early start – gotta be there about six-thirty.'

'Ha, ha. I think I'll still be firmly tucked up at that sort of time in the morning!'

'Yeah, don't blame you. Anyway, what do you fancy doing now then?'

There are moments in life, in my life anyway, when I am rendered quite incapable of coming to a decision. At given moments, rights and wrongs, pros and cons all seem to be mulched into an indecipherable mess. To do nothing and go nowhere is quite obviously the right course, and yet also quite the wrong one. Now was such a moment.

'Oh, I don't know. What do you suggest?'

'Well,' he paused and became quite thoughtful. 'I'm not going to be in town for a while. Might as well make the most of it. So, I dunno . . . how about going and having a few beers?'

'Ugggghh . . .'

'No, go on, mate. Hey, I know what. We can go up Table Mountain. Nice bar up there. My mate Christian is the manager of the tourist set-up there and I've got to go and collect a few bits and pieces from him that I'm going to run up to his family in Botswana. And you know what? The cable-car ride is great.'

'Uggggggggh . . .'

In fact, unbeknownst to Phil, I had been putting off a trip up Table Mountain since my arrival. As years have gone by I have noticed my increasing propensity to vertigo. Once, I would have hung off chair-lifts in Austrian ski resorts snowballing anyone below me with a reckless disregard for my safety or international relations. Although I had of course never contemplated anything quite as absurdly dangerous or inversely unnatural as bungee-jumping, I had even considered doing a parachute jump. This, however, had only been in a futile attempt to impress a very beautiful, but dangerously outward-bound young colleague. Fortunately, she had disappeared over the hill and far away before I was required to demonstrate my commitment to the relationship. Nowadays my world would begin to swim and my consciousness try to escape through the back of my head if I so much as peered out of a first-floor window. Riding a moving staircase had become a white-knuckle experience. And as for funfairs . . . a misnomer if ever there was one.

Strangely, aeroplanes presented no problem at all. Someone once told me that this was due to the fact that your body and mind believe you to be inside a room with your feet on the room's floor. My instinct is that it more likely had something to do with the generous contents of the miniatures of gin dished out from the trolley.

Captive now, and in a weakened state, I seemed to have little choice but to follow my leader. As Phil ground down through the gear-box and we climbed the narrow, winding road that led to the cable-car base station, I could only faintly cheer myself up with the thought that the ride to the summit was a marginally, but just marginally, better option than walking.

Masses of enthusiastic ice-cream-toting children fizzing with excitement were gazing up to the peak.

'I bet it breaks down, hey? Then we will have to be rescued by paratroopers and a helicopter,' said one hopeful boy to another.

'No way, man. If one of those cables snaps then the whole thing will explode and burn, and the mountain might even fall down. We would just have to throw ourselves clear and do a couple of ninja rolls,' replied his mildly more fatalistic friend as my scalp burst into a rash of hot sweat.

'Two tickets, mate, please.' Phil stuffed some notes under the glass. 'You're going to love it, mate. It's a really great ride. You'll see the whole city. Right down there that-a-way to Bloubergstrand. Over there, that's Lion's Head. That's Camp's Bay that side. What a beach, mate. Great surf!'

With that, he cheerfully made his way to the cable-car entrance, muttering 'shoudda brought some stubbies for the ride' to himself and 'how are ya, mate?' to most of the other passengers. If, as it appeared from his buccaneer swagger, Phil was still more or less under the influence of alcohol, then I, suddenly and dramatically, felt stone-cold sober. We were all herded into a large, circular, plastic and tin cabin which reminded me strongly of skiing trips. Thankfully, this time I would not be subjected to the steaming designer jumpsuits, the lumps of slushy snow that slithered along your neighbour's ski and cleverly down the back of your neck, the bad breath born of too much *Glüh-wein* and cheese fondue, or the anguish of watching drips hanging on the end of pink, sunblock-smeared noses.

Due to the random movements of the various people in the cable-car, like molecules in a bubble, I found myself shuffled over to the edge of the cabin, my face all but squished against the thin barrier between me and oblivion. With a jolt that seemed to rearrange the whole layout of my internal organs, we started to move upwards with surprising speed. To add to my general sense of disorientation, I realised that the floor of the cable-car was slowly beginning to turn and within a few minutes, where once I had faced the mountain wall, I was gazing out across Lion's Head, a rocky outcrop that to me, I thought as I clenched hard, looked in no way leonine. Beyond the headland I could see the enormous tidal clash of the seething waters of the Indian and Atlantic Oceans – the Cape of Good Hope – the spot where the European adventure in Africa had commenced. From here had set forth the great treks of discovery, missionary expeditions and the herding of thousands of cattle; from here had begun the rearrangement of ancient societies – a disruption of ways of life older than recorded history. The scramble for Africa had indeed been a messy mix of egos, greed, religious zeal and a plain old desire for discovery. Fortunately, the view, combined with this sense of the seismic nature of events in the continent over the past two hundred years, allowed me, briefly at least, to forget my queasy indisposition.

Even so, by the time we reached the top, I had little desire for anything apart from the miraculous discovery of a cheap hotel, but my companion seemed to have a cast-iron constitution and an unslakeable thirst.

'Castle, mate?'

'Ugh!'

'Coming right up! I'm just going to see if Christian is free. Should be coming up to his lunch-break.' He darted through the milling crowds leaving me gripping a shiny, black safety rail.

The exit from the cable-car had left us heading out for the other side of the mountain, and I unsteadily followed the guard-rail which, before I knew what had happened, had brought me dangerously near to the sheer cliff-edge that dropped away to the northern side of the summit. Away down to my right, the white lines of foaming surf ebbed and flowed across the bright sand of Camp's Bay.

'Here you go.' Phil held out the brown bottle as if it was nothing more sinister than a lollipop.

I disengaged one hand from the rail and took it with a grimace.

'Christian is just on his way. Look at all that out there, mate. Africa, mate.'

Thinking it probably a little uncharitable to point out to him the somewhat unoriginal nature of this last observation, I let him run – which he certainly seemed in the mood to do. Professor Botting's natural successor.

'Yeah, it's massive. Huge, and so totally unspoilt, mainly. It's not like here.' He waved extravagantly at the European city below us, at the skyscrapers and shopping malls, the ordered parks and the grey ribbon of the smooth coast-road.

'Go that way,' he pointed to our left, 'and you'll be going up through Springbok and into the Great Namaland; after that, it's the Dunes out of Swakopmund and Walvis Bay – from there on up, it's the Skeleton Coast. Go that way,' he swung to the right a little unsteadily I noticed as I shifted my gaze accordingly. 'Go that way and you'll hit the border at Simon's Drift, then you're into the Central Kalahari, where there are the diamonds, then on out of there into the Makalagadi Salt Pans – you can get lost for days out there. Looks the same as far as you can see. Push on and you'll get to the Falls – don't let anyone tell you they're not just amazing.'

As Phil talked on with a feverish sparkle in his eye, his stubble glistening with enthusiasm, I was swept up by his descriptions and, with my senses swirling with alcohol and the no doubt thin air we were breathing, I settled into a reverie. Rider Haggard and his heroes trooped across the valley below in search of King Solomon and his mines. Soldiers in red uniforms snaked in lines across the plateaux turning the continent pink from Cape to Cairo. The distant call of Tarzan mingled with the cries of weird and wonderful animals in distant jungles. There was so much more I wanted to know about this great land, its peoples, its history. What adventures there must have been, what dangers and excitements. Staring searchingly at the horizon, I made a promise to myself.

When I got back to London I was definitely going to buy one of those really thick books by Wilbur Smith.

'Hello friends!'

My reverie was broken by the appearance of a tall, genial man dressed in a crisply pressed, short-sleeved shirt and slacks. 'Hope you're enjoying the view. You've picked a good day to come up to join us; the weather doesn't get much clearer than this. When the tablecloth comes down to settle over the top of the mountain you can't see your hand in front of your face.'

We arched our backs and gazed up at the thick and strangely solitary cumulus cloud above us.

'Christian, Will. Will, Christian,' Phil introduced us.

'Pleased to meet you, Will. Welcome to Cape Town.' Christian smiled. 'Where you from?'

'From England. The West Country. Do you know the area I mean? It's the bit that . . .'

'Of course I know it. I was at uni at Exeter. Was there for about four years.'

'Really!'

Happy that he did not appear to have noticed my irrational shock, I asked him where he was from.

'I am a Motswana. That is a person from Botswana. I came from a cattle station outside Francistown. Do you know it?'

'No sorry, actually, I don't.' I was blushing. 'But I have heard about Botswana.'

Oh dear, how uninformed I sounded. Christian did not seem to mind.

'You should visit, you know. I think you would be interested. It is a very successful country. I am hoping to go back soon. I'm just on a secondment here but need to get back to see my family. Excuse me a minute.' He turned away momentarily to answer a call on his mobile phone, and then continued, 'Yes, sorry about that. You should take a trip to Botswana.' He smiled at me kindly. 'You know there is more to modern Africa than just what you will find in the pages of a Wilbur Smith novel.'

2

Hit the Road, Jack!

Springbok is a dusty strip of road with innumerable garages and American-style take-away joints, banks and supermarkets – a functional trading post surrounded by lazy hills. The few hundred yards of 'High Street' were populated by a handful of elderly men sitting in the shade on concrete benches. They studied the big, yellow lorry with a natural, easy indifference and carried on sucking deeply on long, wet, hand-rolled cigarettes. When we drew to a halt outside the emigration building, some wisps of their tobacco smoke floated across the pavement and snaked up through the open window of the bus where I sat trying to rub away the mark of the rough bulkhead from my sleepy, scratchy cheek. The smoke seemed to head directly for my nose, assaulting both nostrils with nauseating effect.

Phil jumped down from the front cab with a light bounce and a tuneless whistle. He turned to look up at me, slipping some wraparound sunglasses from his forehead, and laughingly gave me an enthusiastic thumbs-up when he heard me groan. Emphatically, I gave him the reverse signal and, as he skipped into the office, lifted the lid of the chest freezer that was bolted to the front wall of the bus and stuck my head into the anaesthetising cool. Momentarily, I considered climbing inside, dropping down the lid for ever. Unfortunately, the effect of lowering my head so abruptly combined with the drop in temperature made me suddenly and frighteningly dizzy. My knees sagged, and I ended up leaning heavily against the side of the chest. Sensing some movement behind me, I hurriedly tried to extricate myself from the icy interior. In the process of standing up, I grabbed the first object that came to hand and so it was that I turned round to face a rather startled, middle-aged French lady with a tight auburn perm and winged Bardot sunglasses wielding a long tube of brilliant pink, deeply frozen sausage meat.

'*Ahhh, Williams, vous préparez le diner déjà?*'

'*Ah, oui! Ah, oui c'est ça.*'

'So you are not forgetting that the members of my group they are *Vegetarieren*.' The German sitting across the aisle looked up from his copy of *Reisen in Afrika*, glared at the French woman and then glared at me. 'No way you are going to stick this pink thing in our evening eating!'

'*Ach nein, mein Herr* . . .' I burbled sliding the sausage meat back into the cold box. '*Kein Problem!*'

'*Gut, so.*' He nodded emphatically at the rest of his group who were listening intently to the conversation. They nodded back, one of them through the mosquito net attached to the brim of his very new safari hat.

The French group leader '*Oh là là*'d audibly, shook her head, and returned to painstakingly manicuring her nails.

Bloody Phil.

Agreed, I should have seen what was coming, but that didn't mean it wasn't really mainly Phil's fault. Once the two of us had shambled our way back down from the top of Table Mountain and returned the truck to the hostel car park, he had come up with the brilliant suggestion of having one last night out on the town. First, though, he had had to call a few people including his girlfriend. When he re-appeared from behind the door of the little telephone booth, a frown was crossing his otherwise not-a-care-in-the-world countenance.

'Oh, mate, you'll never guess what. It's a pretty serious one, mate.'

'Oh no, what's up?' I started up guiltily from a glass of iced water that I had hoped to be able to drink while he was making his calls.

'Bloody Janey. She's gone crook back in the UK. Not gonna make it tomorrow. What am I gonna do with all those French and German bastards? She's the one who can speak the lingo and she's got to do all the tucker. Oh, mate!'

'Oh, right, damn, bad luck! Is she OK?'

He nodded brightly enough but was clearly disconsolate.

'Funnily enough I can speak French and German quite well,' I added, unsure why.

He shrugged, deep in thought.

'Let's go to the Buddha Bar. Two for one on the tequila.'

While I was ensconced on the balcony watching a whole lot of street-walking going on down below, Phil camped out at the telephone on the far end of the L-shaped bar.

'Shit, Sabine can't make it either. She's got a tour doing Malawi, Uganda and Kenya starting next Tuesday.' Phil was a little morose on his return. He had worked his way through a tatty address book, trying desperately to find somebody to accompany him on his tour. With admirable stoicism, he downed the waxy contents of the last three tumblers of tequila.

'At this rate, I'll be getting you along to help out. Let's hit the road, Jack!'

'And never come back no more,' I enjoined with surprising vehemence.

Embarking on a binge involving the obligatory bathtub quantities of beer, we sailed through a variety of establishments and an increasingly bleary succession of shots, shooters, chasers, slammers and sharpeners, finally running aground at a poolside bar full of very over-excited twenty-something girls and a large beach ball. Here, for some mildly worrying reason all the drinks were served in chemical test-tubes. I shuddered at the thought of the chain reactions that were taking place inside me, but I quaked even more at the thought of landing back in London. Warm and exciting, Cape Town really was a party town, and I was going to miss it. 'Six degrees and drizzling' would no doubt be the forecast of the airplane pilot as we circled endlessly in grey skies over Heathrow. Well, at least for the time being nothing had been decided – no bookings had been confirmed.

'Did you say you spoke French and German?'

I nodded even though I tried very hard not to. Already, the little sober me, who always lurks in the back of my mind however bad things get, was wringing his hands – he could see what was going to happen. Paths were going to converge in a rather familiar way.

'So, seriously, why don't you come along, Will? Go on, do me a favour. I'm up you know where and I'm ill-equipped.' Phil sighed as he snapped his neck back and the green oily liquid drained from his test-tube. Watching his eyeballs bulge, I wondered how I was going to cope with my own lurid cocktail.

'No, seriously, it'll be great. You get to go all the way through these amazing places and you see the sights. When we get to Vic Falls I'll make sure they get you a flight back to Cape Town. All you've got to do is a bit of cooking. You can do that, can't you? Yeah?'

I wasn't aware of having responded, but he pressed on. 'Yeah? Great, you see?'

'Hang on, wait a minute, do you go through Botswana?'

'Yeah, course we do. Straight across.'

'Do you go to a place called Kasane?'

'Certainly do, mate. Great place. Stopover there.'

Idly, I fingered Professor Botting's card in my pocket.

'Now what was I saying? Nothing to it. Few steaks and stuff. And you can speak the lingo. So there you go – you can do the guiding too.'

'But I've never been to Africa before. I don't know a tiger from a leopard!'

'Well at least you don't have to worry about that – no tigers in Africa.'

'Oh, right!' I blushed and took a brave swig of the green stuff in my test-tube. It was exactly the same shade as something that had once seeped from the bottom of my car and had to taste worse.

'Anyway don't worry about that. I'll tell you what's what, and I've got a book with all the different names in all the different languages. It'll be a breeze, Will.'

'Well, yeah. I see what you mean. No, you're right it does sound like fun – an adventure.' The green depth charge had exploded in the pit of my stomach as I rolled this last word around my mind, and the toxic afterburn shrouded my heavy brain, entirely obscuring my capacity to be realistic, let alone sensible. 'How long you going for? You know I can't really spare too much time.'

This last of course was not strictly true.

'Told you, bit over two weeks. You'll be back by the end of the month. Easy. Honest, it'll be a once in the lifetime opportunity. Don't give it away, mate.'

It was true that in the past, on the couple of occasions that I had taken up curious offers, doors had opened up to experiences that I would never forget. Beyond doubt, if I said no now, then it was almost certain that a similar offer would not come my way again in this lifetime. Also irrefutable was the fact that I was very drunk.

'Oh, okay then, Phil. You've got a deal! Why not?'

Wildly and rather rudely, it being very late in the evening or perhaps rather early in the morning, I telephoned Professor Botting from the call-box. Unfortunately, I have no real recollection of the conversation, but seem to remember him saying something about how he would sort it out and would I now, please, go away.

Slapping Phil on the back I told him for the umpteenth time that we had a deal, feeling euphoric about my new job or rather my two new jobs. Quite out of character, overtaken by a sudden roaring rush of artificially induced enthusiasm, I unbuttoned my shirt and threw myself into the dancing, sparkling water of the swimming pool.

My beautifully executed dive-bomb had hit the surface of the water at about two-thirty am. Phil's fist thumped on my door approximately three and a half hours later. By this stage, of course, the whole scheme seemed to be very much less viable. In fact, in a remarkably short space of time it had transformed itself into what looked, from any angle, like a huge mistake.

Fortunately, due to my enthusiasm the night before, I had already packed my bags after a fashion, which seemed to have involved rolling each item of clothing into a small ball. All I needed to do was to make it down the stairs vertical and on to the yellow bus. As the clear light of early morning slipped around the monolithic corners of Table Mountain, I slid onto the front seat of the Yellow Beast and tried hard to recollect what it was that I had signed up to.

The true weight of my new responsibilities became all too clear half an hour later, as I staggered out of the big, sliding galvanised doors of a meat packer's with an immense cardboard box full of frozen steaks and Catherine wheel-shaped boerwoers – Afrikaner, dense beef-and-pork spiced sausages. Wholesale slaughter was most distinctly not what the doctor ordered for my present condition. The smell of blood still thick in my nose, we stopped twice more to collect other comestibles: rice, pasta, sacks of spuds, tins of vegetables, sauces, fruit and packets of yeast and flour with which to make bread.

Make bread?

As we stacked each item in the large storage trunk bolted to the back of the truck, I snuck furtive glances at the cooking instructions.

'Don't worry, Will,' laughed Phil who seemed, quite unjustly, to be on top form. 'It's all in here!' And with that, he tossed me a battered, creased and dog-eared exercise book. Grasping a water bottle, I flicked it open at the first page.

Day One.
Lunch: PAX purchase.
Dinner: Hobas, Fish River Valley. Steak cooked on fire, Pommes Lyonnaises, tinned peas. Omelette with cheese for vegetarians.

To my relief, it went on to list very precisely what the menu was to be each day for breakfast, lunch and tea. I returned nervously to Day One. *Pommes Lyonnaises.* What on earth was that? I had heard of something called *Pommes Dauphinoises* – although I wasn't entirely sure what it was – but *Pommes Lyonnaises* – no idea at all.

Noticing my furrowed brow, Phil reached over from the steering wheel and flicked to the back of the booklet.

'Look, you see, you got all the recipes at the back. It's an absolute doddle.'

Riffling to 'P', there indeed it all was:

Pommes Lyonnaises for twenty. Use largest tray. Slice twenty medium-sized potatoes, onions, add stock cube, boiling water, peppercorns etc, etc.

Oh, a doddle indeed. I read the instructions carefully several times and felt a great deal better. Or at least as well as a man who thinks that he might at any moment faint can feel.

Unfortunately, unbeknownst to me, the gastronomic challenges of this particular trip were to be as nothing compared to the social ones. These became abundantly evident when we held up two pieces of cardboard in the arrival hall of the airport. Mine read *Voyages De la Rozière*, Phil's *Reisegruppe Von Beinbruch*. After a little while, a figure emerged from the traffic jam of trolleys, umbrella aloft, and marched towards us, followed by a group of about eight or ten people of varying ages. The leader made his way directly to Phil.

'Wolf Dieter Von Beinbruch from Reisegruppe Von Beinbruch. You are Philip?'

I snorted a short laugh – I do not suppose Phil had been 'Philip' since his birth certificate was filled out.

Phil nodded. 'And this is Will. Your tour guide and entertainment manager.'

'What! Oh, yes. Absolutely. Hello. Welcome to Africa!'

This last greeting from me was almost fraudulent.

'Ah, yes. Good you will be doing the entertainment. Good. We will look forward to this, *ja*?' He turned to his inquisitive group who all rapidly agreed, nodding in unison. 'And of course, Will, you did not forget that we are all vegetarian!'

'Oh no, goodness no. No, it's all been planned out. Got it all written down. No problem.'

'Then that is great. Let us go forth on our adventure.' The furled umbrella rose skyward again.

'Er, hang on, Wolf. We are just waiting for the others,' interrupted Phil surprisingly meekly.

'Others? By the way my name is Wolf Dieter, please remember. There are others coming with us on our adventure?' Wolf Dieter's bushy eyebrows rose noticeably. 'You did not mention this in the paperwork!'

'Er no, bit of a late booking, but I'm sure that you will all get on like . . . er, anything. In fact, I think this is them now.' Phil grabbed my cardboard, swapping it for his, leaving me in at least titular charge of Wolf Dieter and his band. Waving the other sign above his head, he finally managed to attract the attention of a rather indolent group as they slowly wheeled their way from behind the screens. A female figure at the front noticed and waved a wisp of handkerchief in our direction.

When, finally, they reached us and stood alongside the other group, the stark contrast in their appearance became wildly, comically clear. Whereas Wolf Dieter's group seemed to have been kitted out at an army surplus store and were complete with thick rugged shorts and sub-flak jackets, floppy hats and large lace-up boots, the new group was made up of figures in crushed cream suits and flimsy summer dresses, tasselled loafers and backless sandals. Two of them, a young couple, shared a bottle of eau de cologne, the contents of which they dabbed on their necks and foreheads.

From the moment Wolf Dieter, hirsute and healthy, shook hands with Madame Marie-France de la Rozière, a *Parisienne* of *grand standing*, sleek in silk and with skin that glistened slickly from moisturiser abuse, it became abundantly clear that these two wildly disparate groups were not going to get along. Battlelines were quickly drawn and the first skirmish took place over the relative merits of their respective national airlines. Despite the fact that I have never been convinced that such a thing as a national character exists, I was quite alarmed by how these two groups played up to the full range of their home countries' stereotypes.

Nevertheless, Phil, who clearly had more experience in these matters than I (who had none) grinned cheerfully at the PAX – I was not sure I would ever get used to this travel operators' terminology – and waved them through the glass doors out to the awaiting truck.

Pax?

Pax Franco-Germanica?

I rather feared not.

Phil helped the Germans heave their rucksacks onto the roof – but not before they had unzipped various essentials in natty pouches – and allowed a couple of boy-scout types to stand up there and hump the bags into neat position. Meanwhile, I accompanied the De la Rozière group to the other side of the truck and gazed in astonishment at the gargantuan pile of luggage that they had deemed necessary for their African trip. Not for them the travail of struggling in and out of unwieldy backpacks. Instead, they had come equipped with smart suitcases with wheels and long handles, sporting combination locks and gold-embossed designer initials. As I attempted to lug the first one up the aluminium ladder that led to the roof I could practically smell laundry starch mingling with fine *parfums*.

Eventually, it was all done, and Phil expertly wrapped and tied a waterproof sheet over the now mountainous stack of belongings as I shepherded the PAX into the truck.

No seating plan was provided – none was needed. One group sat on the left side of the narrow aisle, the other as far over as it could on the right. Phil slid down the ladder fireman-like, his feet either side of the rungs, and joined me up in the front cab.

'Not sure you're going to be able to spend much time up here with me,' he said gloomily as he crunched through the gears and we made our way out onto the freeway. 'You know ninety percent of my punters are great. Statistically, I think that this lot belong to the remaining ten.'

'Oh, I know. I've got a nasty feeling you're right. What are we going to do?'

'We? Listen mate, I'm going to have to drive this crate. You'll just have to keep them entertained!' He looked at me and grinned as he wound down the window and leaned out to check the traffic. 'You shouldn't have too much trouble with that, not after your antics with those girls in the pool the other night.'

'*What?*' I racked my brains for any small recollection.

Still, it looked as if I had a bit of time to play with because, when I peered through the glass into the back, I realised that the long flight from Europe had caught up with most of the passengers, and the vast majority had slumped down in their seats in various postures of slumber. The few who remained awake were re-adjusting inflatable pillows around their necks, changing the batteries in their personal stereos or starting to scribble great thoughts in brand new diaries. Heaven only knew what they had got to say at this stage.

'Arrived at *Kapstadt Luftbahnhof* exactly on time and then had to wait for a long time for these people from France. Already we do not like them . . .'

'*Malheureusement nous ne sommes pas seuls.* I do not dare to write more at this moment lest one of THEM should see. *C'est la guerre, mon cher.*'

Who knew what they would be writing by the time we reached the end of our journey?

Phil, the pro, had a plastic-protected map of sub-Saharan Africa screwed to the dashboard. A thin purple line marked our route, and at intermittent stages were noted our stop-off points and the date. It looked like a very, very long way. How on earth was I going to keep them 'entertained'?

As I rested my head against a fire extinguisher and attempted to stop my brain from bursting through the top of my head, I closed my eyes and tried to imagine how I might diffuse the hostile glares. Jokes and amusing stories weren't going to do the trick, as apart from the group leaders, none of them, to my surprise, seemed to speak much English. Wanting to keep some of my powder dry, I had not yet admitted to being able to speak their respective languages, fearing that if I did so I might disappear under a landslide of complaints. French had always been my preferred language, based simply on an early amorous encounter, and my German, I feared, was now a rather rusty, blunt instrument. Swallowing the wallpaper paste that seemed to have formed in my mouth, I took another swig of warm water and remembered, with a shiver, as much as was possible in this intense heat of the only time that I had ever made a foray into stand-up comedy in a foreign language.

At one stage early in my happy teaching career, someone had seen me coming from a great distance and volunteered me to organise and be master-in-charge of the French exchange. Our twin town was a small and not particularly beautiful collection of post-war bungalows on the fringes of the vast petrochemical fields that surround Le Havre. That particular year, one hundred and fifty twelve-year-olds had volunteered to spend the week with their little *amis français*, which proved, more often than not, to be something of a hopeful description. When our three coaches arrived on the Place de l'Hôtel de Ville, I discovered us to be parked alongside three more from the respective twin town in Germany. They disgorged similar chocolate-smeared, fizzy-pop-belching passengers to our own. In addition, at a little distance was parked a smart Mercedes minibus containing the Burgermeister and half the German town council.

Despite the odds, and the occasional incident involving bangers, flick knives and pornographic playing cards, the week passed off quite smoothly. Indeed, in a rather self-congratulatory fashion, I was beginning to pat myself on the back for a job well done and was almost looking forward to the *Fête du Jumelage*. This was to be a luncheon attended by the worthies of all three towns involved in the town-twinning association. Only a couple of days earlier, I had discovered that our own Mayor was, in fact, one of our coach drivers, and therefore enjoying a busman's holiday of sorts.

At the eleventh hour it was discovered that nobody amongst the guests and functionaries could speak all three languages required for the introductions and translation of the speeches – 'apart from Will,' a kind colleague volun-teered, 'he can speak French and German!' So it was, at the end of a very lengthy and equally weighty lunch, during which I had tried to resist the advances of one of the bibu-lous, German, leather-clad lady bus-drivers who had been intent on ensuring that my wine glass was either full or empty for the best part of three hours, that I had risen a little unsteadily to my feet and addressed the assembled company.

'*Meine Damen und Herren, Mesdames et Messieurs*, Ladies and Gentlemen . . .'

So far so good.

Then it was, in the flash, or flush, of alcohol-induced inspiration, that I decided I would tell a joke. My favourite one! Perhaps you know it? *Vous connaissez peut-être l'histoire?* Well, once upon a time . . .

In its shortened version it is the very funny story of two statues in a park, of a man and a woman, who have gazed from their respective plinths into one another's stony eyes for a hundred years. One day God flies over and grants them twenty-four hours as human beings. They are delighted. But, says God, when I get back I expect you to return to your plinths no questions asked. Fantastic, thanks so much, no problem, whatever you say, you're the best, the Boss, they reply.

So off he goes, but on his return the statues are nowhere to be seen. He is unamused. Just as he is about to lose his temper he hears some rustling in the bushes and fearing some lubricious activity, he clears his throat in order to make the two aware of his presence. As he does so he hears one statue say to the other, 'Right, you hold the pigeon now and I'll crap on his head!'

Brilliant.

The English version went well, apart from some un-appreciative colleague saying rather loudly just as I was warming up, 'Oh no, not this one again. He always tells this one when he's a bit . . . Ssh, ssh!' But at the end I received a nice little round of applause.

Great.

Allez! I launched into French and was pleased to see some beaming faces amongst the umpteen glasses, shining up at me from the banqueting tables. A great cheer and shouts of '*Bravo!*' followed the punchline about '*les pigeons*'. It was all going really very well.

Swigging from my overflowing cup to re-whet my whistle, I noticed that my bus-driving lady friend had fallen asleep. *Tant pis pour elle*, I thought, not very aptly, as I launched into my German version. Now, I saw the delegation from Königsberg sit upright and concentrate hard. The Burgermeister jabbed his colleague in the ribs and whispered, '*Ach, ja, wunderbar, Englisch Humor, sehr gut. So wie Benny Hill!*'

German is a terribly confusing language.

Unfortunately a huge number of words look almost exactly the same, and then there are all those genders to remember.

'*Der Taube*' and '*die Taube*', for example – there's nothing in it.

In any event, when I came out with the punchline, 'Right, now you hold the deaf man down and I'll shit on his head,' the silence was pan-European.

So, no jokes on this roadtrip.

Desperately racking my brains for other entertainments, I did remember a rather clever trick that my uncle used to perform in which he would arrange his hands in such a fashion that it appeared that the end of one of his thumbs had come off. And years before, I had also had a friend who had been rather good at turning napkins into realistic-looking animals – the rabbit was particularly good. Fumbling with my handkerchief for a while only served to produce a beast that looked as if it had lived at the bottom of a swamp before animals had ever walked on dry land.

The cotton creature and I gazed at the straight heat-shimmering road ahead of us and knew we had a long way to go. Still, I attempted to cheer myself up after recognising my severe limitations as an adult entertainer, this was a grand adventure. Now that I was no longer worried about my imminent demise through alcohol poisoning, I could also look forward to arriving at the school and meeting the children in Kasane. And anyway, I thought as I absent-mindedly marched the handkerchief mutant along the dashboard, young people have a much better sense of humour than grown-ups.

3

The Desert Dome 250

Immigration successfully negotiated, we finally passed over the border into Namibia as the whole country was bathed in the saffron-yellow light cast by the fat, buttery evening sun. Until that point neither I nor, I think, many of our PAX, had taken in much of the scenery. In my case, this was mainly because I had become deeply concerned by the possibility that I was going to feel this ill for the remainder of the trip – that somehow I had developed a permanent hangover which I would have to cart with me across southern Africa. The passengers in the back, on the other hand, were either so busy sneaking glares at the opposition across the aisle, fiddling with cameras and binoculars, or trying to refold enormous maps, that they had scarcely a moment to gaze out of the window.

In truth, there was not a great deal to see in the midst of the rocky plateau of Namaqualand. Phil, saving me on this occasion from my first foray into tour guiding, explained that had we been driving through the plain in the spring-time we would have witnessed one of the great natural wonders of the world. The winter rains would have transformed this barren strip into a multi-coloured floral carpet of daisies, gladioli, aloes, violets and mesembryanthemums (whatever they were). So yes, while in spring it was absolutely beautiful, *très beau*, *sehr schön*, now it was just a few rocks and boulders. Er, sorry about that, everybody.

As we crossed the Orange River, which forms a natural frontier with South Africa for about three hundred miles from the Atlantic coast, I gazed down into its tranquil, powerfully winding stream. It looked extraordinarily enticing, and I almost considered asking Phil to stop so that I might throw myself off the steep scrubby bank into its cool, fresh, limpid water to absorb it through every pore of my body – a magic panacea for my dilapidated state. Our driver, though, had his itinerary, and we were going to make it to Hobas before nightfall.

On we went, following a sinuous road that led up into the hills and out onto the ridge of one of the most spectacular geological features that I have ever seen. Over countless millennia titanic forces in the bowels of the earth and the rushing waters of the Fish River have combined to create the second largest canyon in the world. Fearing I might become bogged down in a complicated explanation of the faulting of the earth's crust and lower reaches, river erosion and oxbow lakes, I retreated to the back of the bus and flicked as nonchalantly as I could through a guidebook that I had plucked out of the book box. Unfortunately, the book turned out to be written in Spanish, but I need not have worried because the warring factions had called a ceasefire, and the most aggressive noises to be heard were the incessant clicking of cameras and mutters of '*Ach, ja wunderbar*', and '*Ah, oui, ça c'est trop beau*'.

So content with the experience did they appear to be, that I began to relax and take in the immensity of the scenery, the eye-popping grandeur of the canyon walls on the other side of the river; they seemed enormous, majestic, towering above us even though they stood, according to Phil, some fifteen miles away. Now, in the late afternoon, was clearly the best time to admire this natural wonder as the colours of the rocks and the skies and cloud-shadows shifted infinitesimally, kaleidoscopically. Of course, despite my inward excitement at this glorious sight, my new-found job required a certain degree of dissemblance. Although I was as overwhelmed as the others were by the scenery, I felt I had to adopt a certain insouciance, a certain languor, a certain seen-it-all-before, not-another-bloody-canyon indifference. That said, my semi-stifled yawns were actually very genuine – I was exhausted, although quite the most demanding part of the day was yet to come.

Fortunately, the small clearing and the two long-drop latrines that made up the campsite of Hobas were only a few minutes' drive from the viewing point at the edge of the canyon.

'Will, mate, go and tell them that they're putting up their own tents. Show them how. Then tell them to get on with it.'

'How?' I whispered, as we pulled to a halt in a mist of fine sandy dust that I was beginning to connect inextricably with life in Africa.

'How what?' Phil whispered back under the cover of a gale of Gallic coughing as we slipped down in our seats to better hold our covert conversation.

'Well, how do you put a tent up?'

'You're joking, right?'

'No! I haven't been in a tent since I was in the cub scouts, and I was thrown out before we were old enough to put up our own ones. Can't you do it?'

'No, I've got to set up the cooking stuff – I don't want you to do it, you'll blow the bloody truck up!' he muttered as he reached for the door handle.

Sensing a certain lack of confidence in my abilities, I made my normal, fatal mistake of trying to bluff it out.

'Oh, OK, no problem. It can't be too complicated. I'll sort it out. Let's go!' We sat back up in our seats and slid non-chalantly out of the cab.

With varying degrees of enthusiasm, my travelling companions brought down their bags from the roof whilst I pulled out the smooth green tube-shaped bags containing the lightweight tents and distributed them, suggesting that everyone found themselves a suitable site. As soon as they had found their preferred spot, some of them set about opening up the bags and pulling out the contents, whilst others (mainly, it has to be said, from Madame de la Rozière's group) looked round dazedly, feebly holding onto their bags in a way that suggested that they were in sore need of a good Samaritan. Once a teacher, always a teacher, I could not help stepping in when I considered that progress could not be made without my strict supervision.

'OK, stop! *Arrêtez! Halt!*' Ignoring my total lack of experience in tent erection, I pulled open my own bag in what I hoped was a confident, constructive fashion and pulled out the contents. Panicking slightly upon viewing them, I feared that most of the vital parts must be missing. All that I found was a large domed pocket of canvas and two poles in sections that appeared to snap together like a blind man's cane. Hoping to attract Phil's attention, I began to whistle tunelessly as I snapped the poles together, but he was engaged in screwing or unscrewing something underneath the truck.

'OK, off you go then!' A useful teaching trick of old I had remembered was to offer to give a demonstration, thereby asserting my credentials as the expert, and then ensure that nobody was able to see what I was doing. Now that I had my poles assembled, I searched over the tent canvas for something to attach them to, but it seemed entirely smooth – no tags, no toggles. Sweating, I glanced over my shoulder to discover that some of the others had already put their poles together and were glancing over at me for further assistance. I grinned back a little grimly. Pulling up the door flap and what looked like mosquito netting, I stuck my head inside the floppy envelope and saw that loops were stitched into the inside in a cross shape. I reached outside and grabbed a couple of the poles, which I proceeded to stuff through the holes. To my dismay, I discovered that they were a good six inches too long and resultantly, once they were in place, the whole frame was as wobbly as a blancmange. I retreated backward, and turning on all fours, I found myself facing a pair of new but dusty lace-up boots, above which were the hairy knees and protuberant stomach of Wolf Dieter, who was staring down at me.

'So I think my tent is now ready for your inspection.' He gestured over to his effort, which stood, perfect as a brochure picture, under one of the bushy trees on the far side of the camp. 'I think that your tent – you are trying to build it inside out? It must be the other way.'

Unhappily, I stared at my own structure, which was slumping lazily over on its side.

'What? Inside out? I don't think so! Oh yes, yes, you may be right. It must be the, the uh . . . oh of course this must be the new model. How silly of me! *Dummkopf!* Normally I'm used to the older one. Great to be using the new ones, don't you think?'

'The new one, why is this the new one?'

'This is the er . . .' I glanced at the shiny, green holdall and managed to read the label stitched on the outside. 'The new one, the Desert Dome 250. I'm more used to the 150!'

Shameless.

'But are you sure? I don't think that you are meaning the 150, maybe 175?'

'Yes, well that's as may be. You know what it's like, put up as many tents as I do, you forget after a while.' Still on all fours, I scurried back into the tent and hastily removed my poles, dragging the tent inside out as I retreated again. By the time I had followed the correct steps, an embarrassingly easy procedure, anybody who was going to put their own tent up for themselves already had. The remainder smiled wanly at their companions who, either because they wished to show their camping prowess or because it would have been *too* rude to refuse to help, gave them a hand. Relieved, I left them to it. Perhaps it might result in some sorely needed bonding.

Phil had pulled down an impressive-looking set of gas rings from the side of the truck and put up some trestle tables alongside, on which I hurriedly piled plastic plates, knives and forks, potatoes, the steaks and tins of peas. In a pit a few yards away a fire lit by Phil was blazing cheerfully, and slowly our group drew close, blankets, jackets or shawls draped around their shoulders. Sitting low on stools, they gazed, in that primordial way that affects us all, into the flames. After checking that I was happy with my culinary preparations, which surprisingly I was, Phil hurried round taking orders for drinks – beers and Klipdrift South African rum (the thought of which made my very being shudder) – which he proceeded to supply from his makeshift bar.

Although I had never really cooked for more than four – the size of my old kitchen table precluding any more guests from being invited – I was surprisingly confident about being able to cope. One of Wolf Dieter's charges, a nervous but super-keen youngster in his early twenties with a moustache that had never been shaved off and certainly should have been, volunteered to open the tins of peas. This gesture was born less out of a desire to help than from a desire to get out his brand new, shiny Swiss Army knife, which was almost the size of the ones that you see automated in shop windows. He clearly hoped to put it to good use. I left him to it.

Peeling spuds like a convict on a low stool, I had soon stripped off the skin of twenty potatoes and my left index and ring fingers. With a couple of rather dangerous flourishes that I had learned from the television, I sliced the spuds up. Sucking my digits and lugging the enormous kettle from the fire, I filled an *Astérix*-sized cauldron with boiling water and poured in the white oval discs. I fried the onions and, once the potatoes were cooked, mixed them all together in a baking tray with a meaty broth and peppercorns, covered it in foil and placed it directly on the edge of the fire.

Due to an injury sustained some years earlier whilst attempting what would have been a pretty impressive feat of sporting derring-do, I had no little difficulty standing back up from where I had squatted to make minor adjustments to the cooking temperature with a bit of stick. After the clicking and snapping of cartilage and ligament had subsided, I noticed that one of the younger Germans, a spindly sort of man called Otto with big ears and a shock of blond hair that waved like wheat in a field, had appeared from his tent. He was dressed in full Bayern Munich soccer kit and had a shiny, white football under his arm. After a few leg-bending flexes and stretches that made me wince, he hopped off high-kneed to a clearing some twenty yards from our encampment. Having bounced the ball a few times experimentally on the sandy ground, he was quickly engaged in balancing it on various parts of his anatomy before flicking it up in the air and catching it on his toe.

Soon, various of his male compatriots appeared from their separate tents similarly attired and a fully fledged practice session was quickly underway. The tranquil atmosphere of the campsite, until then almost silent but for the crackling of burning wood, was shortly filled with shouts of *'Hier bin ich!'* and *'Schön, Willi!'* which almost immediately caught the attention of their French counterparts, who stood around under the trees and muttered conspiratorially. When Otto failed to connect with a lofting ball struck sweetly by Willi from behind a Desert Dome 250, a linen-suited, open-toe-sandalled Frenchman called Marcel took control and performed a number of deft acrobatics that culminated with a blinding shot hammered between the rucksack posts of the German goal. Battlelines were drawn and soon an impromptu international was underway. All the women, many of whom had previously been busy repairing the damage caused to their appearance by a day in a bus, were drawn to the 'touchlines' and were soon voluble in their support.

Also spectating, to my mild consternation, were a troop of baboons, who had scampered in a line of descending size from some cover on the roadside and had now arranged themselves on a low ledge some distance from the moving dust cloud that contained the competing players. Alert, their deep-set inscrutable eyes followed the action and occasionally they bared their mighty incisors, longer than a lion's, in admiration at the players' skill. Pointing them out to Phil, I was somewhat reassured by the way he just shrugged and returned to a task that involved a spanner which I doubted I would have been able to lift let alone manipulate.

'Just as long as no bugger tries to approach them, they'll be right. Baboons can be right bastards if you go for them.'

I didn't doubt him for a minute, particularly when the

largest of them raised himself onto his hind legs and took a slashing swipe at one of his companions who had for some unapparent reason annoyed him. Suddenly, to the monkeys' surprise, the ball squirted out of a particularly fraught mêlée and, bouncing high, bobbled up to them. For a moment they looked at it and at each other in confusion. Then, like a gang of naughty schoolboys, they collectively grinned, the eldest male picked it up and they all took off at high speed in the direction of the road.

For a few moments, the players, unable to find the ball, regarded each other with deep mistrust, suspecting someone of a malign conjuring trick. Marcel was just about to rearrange his jacket over his shoulders and stomp off to his tent when he spotted the tearaway monkeys and alerted the others. Momentarily united by a mutual adversary, he and Otto set off in pursuit of the thieves. Otto, who was more suitably attired than Marcel, appeared initially to be gaining on them but, their taut muscled bodies pumping their powerful thighs, the monkeys were soon far beyond his reach. Undaunted, he carried on, slipping and scrabbling across the rough terrain. Low, wiry thorn bushes snatched at his knee-length socks, pulling out the threads to produce feathery wisps and badly gouging his calves.

As if to taunt him, the baboons lounged along the edge of the tarmac, retreating only slightly when he lurched closer. Considering his new prize closely, the dog baboon finally held it high above his head like a championship trophy and in so doing dropped it behind him. Turning and snarling as if the ball was purposefully trying to evade him, he bit down hard on the shiny plastic, which exploded with an impressive report that caused the baboon to spit it out in surprise and the former owner to howl in annoyance. Leaning low to his left, Otto picked up a stone and winged it at his tormentor. Although it missed by some margin, this was clearly considered an act of aggression and suddenly the tables were turned.

What had been initially a rather amusing, cartoonish scene soon took on a rather more dangerous allure as one of the monkeys gave chase. Angry baboons were clearly extremely aggressive animals. This fact had not escaped Otto who, with scant regard to the remains of his socks, was now beating a hasty, not to say panicky retreat. As he neared the campsite, the baboon closing on him, Phil, who had become aware of the situation not least from the cries of '*Hilfe!*', seized a burning stick from the fire in the most dynamic fashion, and waved it furiously in front of him. Shrieking, Otto jumped behind him as the baboon, equally alarmed, stopped dead, and with great agility turned and headed back to his friends. Once at a safe distance, he slowed to an amble, attempting to give the impression that he had just become bored with the whole episode. He had clearly succeeded as the rest of the group followed him admiringly as they disappeared off into the bush.

The excitement over, I looked about and discovered that the rest of the PAX had taken cover behind their tents, and only very slowly did they reappear. To my secret irritation, our passengers, particularly the women, I noticed, spent most of the next hour or so congratulating Phil on his bravery. Even more tiresome was how modestly he accepted their thanks. I would have expected a ticker-tape parade.

Fortunately, as soon as cooking smells started to waft across the campsite, a number of the French contingent suddenly became deeply interested in what was happening in the kitchen. As I grappled with a plastic bowl that I could hardly get my arm around and whisked furiously at the two dozen eggs, various pieces of advice were proffered. A little *crème fraiche* was the key to a really succulent omelette. Had I thought to whisk half the egg whites first? Where were my chives?

Trying to combine the various dishes and serve them all at the same time was tricky but, as it turned out, it all went surprisingly well despite all the meat-eaters wanting their steaks cooked slightly differently. *'Moi, par contre, je le préfère comme ils le mangent les Australiens – bien cuit'*, *'Ah, non, ah ça jamais! Je le mange que bleu.'* And so it went on until Phil equipped each of them with a fork and told them they could bloody cook them themselves. So, fired, occasionally literally, with gastronomic zeal, they knelt down over the steel grill in the embers, and with a certain amount of singeing but a good deal of enjoyment, they poked, prodded, flicked and squeezed until their piece was just *comme il faut*.

Feeling a certain degree of satisfaction, or at least relief, that my total lack of tour-guiding experience had not yet been rumbled, I watched as everybody happily chewed away in near silence. Winking at Phil, I tackled a piece of meat in my fingers. I almost felt like a beer.

Despite my tiredness, I thought it a wise precaution to read up on the various places that we would pass through the following day, so once zipped up in my tent, I flicked on my torch like a secretive schoolboy and opened up the only English guidebook that I had discovered. Soon, though, I could no longer focus on the page, and rolling back I snapped off the flashlamp and closed my eyes. Out there in the bush there sounded a whole range of weird, animal noises, although none of them was nearly as weird or as animal as the ones emanating from the next-door French tent.

Luckily, Phil had the good sense to give the side of my tent a friendly boot the next morning before the rest of the happy campers awoke, and we settled on our haunches to poke and stoke the embers of the fire. The steely dawn was already warming, and I could see plum-coloured sprays of light on the crests of the canyon hills in the distance. Only now, after the teething problems of the day before, did I have time to take stock of my new-found situation in life. As I plonked the heavy kettle back on the fire, I became fully aware that I was out in the African bush and, despite my moderately mundane domestic duties, I felt a thrill, a flash of innocent expectation.

Namibia, I had learned the night before, had an average population of two people per square kilometre. When I was living in urban India, I had heard that each person had but two square metres of living space. Here, now, as the sun rose, the wide open spaces seemed to open their arms to us and the horizons were inviting us to travel endlessly and freely. Unrestrained by urban planning, road signs, traffic lights and highway codes, I had a feeling of being amongst the first to walk the earth, drifting through an untrammelled garden of Eden.

Paradise was slightly unsettled, however, when a furious argument broke out about whether the only metal jug should be used to brew up coffee for the De la Rozière group or some ghastly smelling herbal tea for the Von Beinbruch brigade. Finally, Phil settled the argument by announcing, as he hurled the hospitality text book over his shoulder, that unless everyone was capable of taking turns then he would scoop up all their supplies and throw them on the fire. Later, I noticed the two group leaders drawing up a 'tea and coffee rota'.

As I had not yet dared to test out my bread-making skills, we made do with some tasteless dry biscuits for breakfast, but there was a sense of eagerness to get back on the road and differences were quickly forgotten as all the considerable paraphernalia were reloaded on and into the bus. Finally, Wolf Dieter, who had reappeared in an extraordinarily small pair of shorts made, it seemed, from chamois leather, and which embarrassingly displayed his not insubstantial assets, raised his umbrella aloft, and he and his group climbed crocodile-style onto the bus, followed rather more shambolically by the rest. After spraying water on the grey remnants of our fire, which sighed like a vanquished, tired vampire at dawn, I clambered on board. Phil, up front in his cab, wielded steering wheel, clutch and handbrake and we set off in the direction of the Namib Desert.

Moonscape or Mars-scape, landscape of fantasy or dream, the Namib surrounds you, loses you so entirely, that you believe after a short space of time that you have always inhabited such a world of tawny mountains and red, red dunes dotted unexpectedly by vivid, lush oases. Between the Kuiseb and Swakop rivers stretch sparsely vegetated gravel plains occasionally interrupted by island mountains, isolated remnants of a different ancient world.

In the shimmering midday heat, mirages create visions of massive lakes on the horizon, a lone gemsbok or desert hare takes on a grotesque shape, and the plains seem to be otherwise totally devoid of life. It is a wild landscape of badlands crisscrossed by a maze of dry river courses which eventually make their way to the Kuiseb river. Although the river is often dry for several years, after heavy rains in the highlands it is transformed into a bubbling, bursting mass of water which rushes like a snake across sand through the barren landscape. Floods wash away the debris that has been blown into the arid riverbeds and the waters flow from a few days to more than one hundred days. The pools in the middle of the desert, many many miles away from any centre of human existence, supply water for the drifting herds of antelope, Hartmann's mountain zebra, klipspringer, and even three troops of baboons which scratch an existence there.

Madame de la Rozière was struggling badly. Her group, utterly ill-equipped for the conditions, complained sorely about their blisters, flea-bites, chapped lips and the general uncomfortableness of their accommodation. The only thing, thank the Lord, that they had not yet made a fuss about was the food. This did not, on the other hand, stop her from throwing a terrible, varnished-finger-nail-waving wobbler in the middle of a large sand dune moments after we had blown the second tyre of the day. The first episode had involved a great deal of shoving and pushing and cranking, plenty of German muscle and a pleasing we're-all-in-this-together attitude. Extra encouragement had been provided, at a little distance, by the French group, who occasionally wiped imaginary specks of oil from their suits and hopped from toe to toe in the hot sand.

When it all went *Pfff* again a few hundred miles later, the entire group looked rebellious. Yet again, I winced at my attempts to bring everyone back to good humour. 'Well of course this always happens out in the desert. You know that's the kind of excitement you get on a trip like this.'

Phil unscrewing the last spare wheel was muttering 'What a bunch of lazy wankers!' so loudly that I feared that Wolf Dieter and Marie-France might well not only hear him but understand his sentiments.

I pushed on.

'So here we are! Out in the bush. Us against the elements! Now come on let's all give Phil a hand? What do you think?'

Sadly the only response was silence, and a bit of listless and possibly antagonistic movement in the back row.

'Anyone remember the joke about the two statues in the park?'

I attempted it in two languages.

Fortunately, halfway through the German version – *die Taube, der Taube*? – Wolf Dieter became aware that his troops were on the verge of desertion and raised a hopeful umbrella. Grumpily, they realised that they could either lend a hand or stand and sweat. Soon we were back on the road with that unforgettably wonderful red dust spuming out again behind us. We were on our way. All twenty-two.

Swakopmund is a very strange sort of place. It looks like a little German town – it is a little German town. It's just that it sits in southern Africa on the Atlantic Coast and is surrounded by huge dunes and deserted mines. Yet when you roll into the place you are struck by its attractiveness. Lots of smartly constructed buildings with wooden-beamed fronts and steep-pitched, gothic roofs stand along the golden beach. Behind them are to be found all amenities, hospitals, schools, supermarkets and offices – and plenty of *Bierkellers*. No wonder the settlers had come and made this 'Sudwest Afrika' – the Germans' little colony by the sea. It is lovely, apart from the occasional and quite astonishing framed pictures of Hitler and other Nazi grandees in some of the shop windows that reflect the Atlantic rollers sweeping along the swathe of sand, whose passage is interrupted only by old, wooden, tooth-like stumps, once the supporting pillars of long-washed-away fishing jetties.

Africans speaking impeccable English, often as their second or third language, cause no surprise in a city like London, and I had enjoyed the sing-song variant of French spoken by Malian and Congolese friends when I had lived in Marseille, yet it was a genuine surprise when a rather elderly, genial waiter came over to take our order in German, once we had sat ourselves at pine tables and chairs on a creosoted café terrace overlooking the slate-grey sea.

'*Guten Morgen, meine Damen und Herren,*' he greeted us with a nod of a bow.

Our German companions were immediately delighted and could not prevent themselves from adopting a rather

condescending air towards the mystified French. Wolf
Dieter took considerable satisfaction from translating the
menu with my assistance, and recommending various
undoubtedly delicious but nevertheless incongruous
Bavarian teatime specialities.

High above the little town we spent an uncomplicated
night at a permanently erected campsite, having dined on
enormous dishes of steaming, aromatic Sauerkraut in a
basement restaurant that instantly took me back fifteen
years to an evening I had once spent in Berlin. On that occasion I had lost a tooth in an enormous piece of pork, and
had had to take flight when I discovered that the charming Fräulein who had approached me at the bar was not a
Fräulein at all. Fortunately, that night in Swakopmund I
encountered no such problems.

Early the next morning, we wearily embussed in near
silence and groaned up the straight road out of town as the
first golden tips of light brushed the crest of Dune Seven
– the highest sand dune in the world. Soon the country flattened out into a powdery grey plain almost entirely bereft
of vegetation or any signs of life. Travel through scenery
like this, I soon discovered, developed an almost hallu-
cinogenic quality. Views through the dusty windows were
akin to looking through the smeary camera lens of a 1970s
science-fiction film. Quickly, we all descended into a quasi-
trance state – a dream from which we were only to awake
when we dropped down a sharply winding incline into the
Namibian capital, Windhoek, some nine or ten hours later.

As many of the suburbs are hidden behind the surrounding hills, the city, although possessing a population of some
200,000, appears to be remarkably small – a toytown. Set
out on a grid, which seems to be little more than three
blocks by four, the two or three high-rise buildings are
interspersed by two-storey colonial buildings with large

display windows looking out onto tin-roofed walkways. All the trappings of a modern city are there – the international hotels, the banks, hire-car centres and shopping arcades all appeared surreally out of place when we remembered how desolate the surrounding countryside had been.

Barely one hundred years old, Windhoek had been settled by Germans attracted by the stories of fabled seams of semi-precious stones that soon they would be enthusiastically mining – gems that would make many colonisers fabulously wealthy. Stone Age tools some five thousand years old, and fossilised elephant bones discovered in the tranquil Zoo Park in the centre of town, were proof that both man and beast had been attracted for millennia to the abundant springs that rose out of this most barren part of the world.

The colonisers had quickly stamped their architectural influences on the place, and from behind the street market of handicrafts, wooden toys and rag dolls which was now being folded up and wrapped away, peeked buildings that would not have looked out of place on the set of *The Sound of Music*. More astonishingly, perched on one of the hills that separated the main town from the outlying villages stood three fairytale castles. With their turrets and leaded windows, their dark stone walls and grim demeanours, they appeared to be on permanent loan from the Hammer House of Horror.

We would do well to make the most of the facilities, opined Phil, as it was the last outpost of civilisation that we would see for some time yet. What sensible advice this turned out to be.

4

Coming to Kasane

Happily, relations improved amongst our Franco-German party and, as we drifted towards the Botswanan border, I began to feel a little more in control of the situation. Phil was not only extremely competent in all areas technical but also seemed to have nerves made of fine, natural rubber. Between us we cajoled, mollified and generally cheered up everyone that needed it. As the days passed, we all seemed to adapt to the rigours of our travels and, as I have found so often to be true, the Western world, the only world for most of us for so long, seemed to recede in the vast open landscapes, the rocks and the dust, the strange, spiky plants and trees, into the recesses of our minds.

Soon, nothing seemed more normal than to pull up on the side of the dust road with views in all directions to the shimmering horizon and not be able to see a single sign of other human habitation. There was no longer any surprise when we were directed to erect our tents, forage for enough wood to last us the night and build a large communal fire to sit around together either in broken conversation or harmonious silence. Finally, nobody, or nearly nobody, complained about having to do the washing-up, or the packing up, or the pushing or the shoving. In fact, as we trekked further across Namibia and into Botswana and the fringes of the great Kalahari Desert, I sensed that a number of us would have extended this journey indefi-nitely. Such was the feeling of freedom, adventure and camaraderie that returning to work – whatever, in my case, that might be – seemed to be an increasingly impossible proposition. I did however become rather tired of the thigh-slapping folksongs.

The Kalahari Desert is of course just that – a desert. However, it cannot claim to possess the charm of the Sahara – *la mer de sable*, the sea of sand – or the majesty of the Namib Desert through which we had just travelled. Instead it was impressive for its vastness, its awe-inspiring scale. Here there were no shifting dunes, no changing landscapes, just mile upon mile of flat land covered uniformly with low grey-brown bush. It appealed to those attracted to covering great distances in a day. Some of us kept log books chronicling our daily journeys but, due to the barren nature of the land, descriptions were sometimes reduced to recording the number of hills or even shallow inclines that we had encountered in ten hours of driving. On one day spent entirely on the road, this had amounted to two. Still, it was true that the sheer scale of the continent was breath-taking. As my eye followed the thin purple line on the map in the front cab, I was amazed by how little progress we made in a day.

Occasionally, very occasionally, we would travel through some minor outpost. More often than not, this amounted to little more than a garage, perhaps with rooms, perhaps even a restaurant. Although Phil was keen to press on, we all pleaded for a chance to stop and stretch our necks, arms and legs. Such interest did we display in the

meagre confectionery, the postcards and the terrible
mementos, such delight did we take in buying ice creams
and cold drinks, that you would have thought that this
was indeed our first brush with civilisation. Yet such was
the sense of purpose and of direction that our energetic
group leader instilled in us that there was rarely a moan
or complaint when we climbed back on board.

There were long days – days that seemed to slip one
into another seamlessly. However, when it seemed that this
desolate landscape did indeed go on for ever, that somehow we were irredeemably lost or had in fact disappeared
through some temporal portal into a different world, I was
reminded that unfortunately there was indeed a limit to
this universe of ours. One day, after I had finished serving up a particularly successful breakfast and was enjoying the various muttered comments: '*Ja, schmeckt gut!*', '*Oui,
tout à fait comme elle le prépare ma Tante Claire*' etc., I noticed
over the shoulder of an enthusiastically scribbling diarist
that we had traversed the full width of northern Botswana
and would soon be arriving at the Zimbabwean border.

With something of a sinking feeling, I realised that this
adventure was shortly to come to an end. To make matters
worse, I also knew that once I had returned to Cape Town
and flown back to London – and this was an experience
that I had encountered more than once over the last few
years – I had no very clear idea of what I would do when
I got there. Slopping water out of a green-metal jerrycan
into the large washing-up bowl, I half-wished that I had
never embarked on this trip. Experiences here would make
taking up the reins of 'real' life again much more difficult.
Perhaps it had all been a big mistake setting off across the
world, content as I had been with the teaching career that
I had taken up shortly after leaving university. Now it
seemed that every time I discovered what lay over one

horizon, I could not help wanting to discover what lay over the next. To my dismay, I had discovered that the desire to see more of this planet had become like a drug to me, and I feared that it would only be old age and infirmity that would allow me to break the habit. Wouldn't it have been so much easier just to have become a deputy headmaster as someone had once suggested, and to eventually retire to a peaceful existence in the West Country? Going back now would be hard, getting back into the 'swing' of things nigh on impossible.

Rather efficiently, practice making perfect, we packed everything up, each item finding its own particular place, and headed on eastwards. By mid-morning the landscape began to change quite dramatically. No longer did we find ourselves in dry arid terrain. Where once all had been brown and grey, now amongst the trees and bushes little splinters of green and bright colours appeared. Thriving grasses and exotic flowers had, seemingly impossibly, burst out of the dust. With increasing fascination, we watched as the countryside around us grew verdant and blooming. Emerging from a narrow valley, we simultaneously gasped in astonishment as we found ourselves in an enormous river delta. A wide sheet of silver water spread out below us, weaving in and out between large islands on which grew impossibly tall palm trees that leaned softly over pastures and wetlands.

At a natural vantage point, we pulled up and clambered excitedly out into the hot sunshine.

Phil grinned.

'Welcome to the Chobe River! You know every time I bring guys here, I get the same reaction. It's amazing, isn't it?'

His question received no reply as like children we skipped around trying to take in this enormous view. At first, it was the freshness, the greenery, the lushness of the valley that struck me most. In fact, it must have taken me some minutes to realise quite how extraordinary the scene was. Not only was it naturally beautiful but it was also vibrantly alive. Wherever we looked below us there seemed to be animals of every description. Buffalo, perhaps a couple of hundred of them, stood knee-deep in the chocolate-brown water at the river's edge; in a small pool between two islands wallowed a family of hippos; scattered across the far shore grazed immense numbers of different species of antelope and there, just below us, most extraordinarily of all, swimming and wading in our direction, were fifteen elephants – I counted each and every one – trunk to tail, making their way across the river.

Laughing, giving up any pretence of being a seen-it-all-before travel expert, I slapped Phil on the back.

'Quite incredible! Really incredible! Almost impossible to believe that it's real.' And it was. My childhood vision of wild Africa, born from the printed page, was blown into dull, unimaginative fragments, and in its place appeared a fresh, vibrant world of astonishing, electric magnificence. Again, Africa had taken on an utterly unreal atmosphere. The documentaries and natural history programmes I'd seen, however well shot, had suggested that there was some kind of law and order to the animal world. Yet here it was, in utterly random interaction, and it was much too much to absorb.

'You ain't seen nothing yet!' replied Phil, without a great deal of originality. 'Come on, everyone, jump back in. We're going down there!'

Our collective breaths held, we did as instructed, and the bus, whining in low gear, started to roll down the steep incline towards the river-bed. The lower we got, the more of the river in either direction we could see, and everywhere, everywhere, there roamed animals, too many to comprehend at once. Not only animals but birds too, and there seemed to be no colour that was not included in their plumage. Some I recognised – a pelican, some kind of kingfisher, and a bird that looked suspiciously like a vulture circling over our heads – but others I had never seen, nor even dreamt of, so exotic was their appearance.

Despite our worldliness, our education, all that we had been exposed to on the television screen, our Western sensibility and our sophistication was stripped clean away. We became as children, speechless, motionless but for the rocking of the bus on the rough road, awe-inspired by the majesty of our surroundings. We felt an excitement, a pleasure that could not be hidden. Naturally, with no sense of awkwardness, these near strangers were putting their hands around each other's shoulders, grabbing hold of arms to attract their neighbour's attention to some astonishing sight. Quiet laughs and smiles were exchanged; we were sharing this fabulous experience together.

Slowly we rolled to a halt on the side of the river and all of us became instantly still – well, all of us but one. Phil, who was sitting alongside me at the wheel, was decidedly animated. Tapping on the round circles of glass on his instrument panel, he fiddled nervously with a small lever just below the steering wheel. Initially, I hardly noticed, but when I turned to him to point out a toothy crocodile lying motionless on a bunch of reeds forty or so yards away, I saw that his normally unfurrowed brow was creased with anxiety. We had not come to a halt on purpose.

'Don't get it. That's so weird. Never had anything like this before.' He swore briefly before returning to his checks. 'Hmm, what time is it, mate?'

'Oh, around about twelve, I think.' Suddenly, my mind was rather more focused on what was happening in the truck than on the staggering view outside. 'Some sort of problem? You want a hand with anything?'

Although I have spent a quite considerable amount of time trying to tell myself not to be such a wimp when difficult situations arise, I am willing to admit that it has been to little effect. Instinctively, I knew that something was badly wrong. My increasingly sweaty palms told me so. Difficulty swallowing was another distinct pointer to rapidly mounting panic.

'Well, mate, worse-case scenario, it could be the Big One, but normally you'd expect some sort of bang and I didn't hear anything, did you?'

Not entirely sure what the Big One was, I agreed that, no indeed, I had not heard anything suspicious.

'Bit of luck it could be the fuel supply. Probably just have to change the filter. Pretty sure I got one here.'

He reached behind the seats and pulled out a large, red, metal box with snap-down latches. Opening it up, he rummaged around amongst numerous alien, plastic objects until he found what he was looking for.

'This is the one.' He pulled out a paper canister. 'Seem to remember this old baby has got the filter just below the seat which is handy.'

Very, very, I thought as I looked back up and out of the window, sensing a mood change in the group behind me. While a moment ago they had been almost entirely quiet, now there was some hushed but insistent chattering. When I realised what the object of their interest was, I was not at all surprised.

Lumbering in a slow but decidedly unstoppable fashion, the line of elephants was clearing the river, brown mud slipping and slithering down their pillar-like legs and spraying like spilled paint across the cracked river bank. We seemed to be in their way.

'Yes, oh, but listen,' I muttered, looking down at an almost upside-down Phil and trying desperately to remain cool. 'Yeah, just thought I would let you know, just so you know, but we've got elephants at . . . er . . .'

I tried to work it out.

'We seem to have elephants at about seven o'clock. Well more like seven-thirty, quarter to eight.' I had heard people use this kind of description in war films when an enemy aircraft was on someone's tail. This didn't seem to me to be an entirely inappropriate comparison to our own situation.

What also struck me quite suddenly was how very quickly a life that had seemed relatively normal had now been completely tipped on its head. Only a couple of weeks ago, I had been much enjoying Cape Town hospitality and viticulture. A mere fourteen days later, I was about to be squashed into a European mush by a herd of elephants. Through the open windows I could now hear the animals breathing. I could even smell them. To our general relief, they seemed to be taking stock some thirty yards away.

'The old filter seems okay. Mind you, you can never tell with these things. Anyway, we'll give her a go.' Phil turned himself the right way up. 'See whether she likes it.'

She didn't.

Now the whole cab smelt very strongly of diesel and I thought I could spot fumes rising up from below the driver's seat. Turning to look through the screen, I tried to see whether any of the chain-smoking French women had cigarettes burning. Fortunately, they were much too absorbed by the array of pachyderms that were stamping the ground not very far from us.

'No, no, it's no good. Nothing for it, mate. Just going to have to pop the lid.'

Lid?

As I was considering the practical implications of what Phil was suggesting was necessary to make the running repairs, a shadow passed across the lorry. Forcing my eyeballs to swivel left, I glanced nervously out of the window. In strokable distance, an enormous elephant was now standing sideways on to me. He, or possibly she, was not only certainly quite as long as our vehicle but also just as tall. There was also about this animal a robustness that seemed to outweigh the truck and its now quietly squeaking inhabitants. Shifting slightly, elegantly, it turned its back to us. Audible sighs had to be quickly sucked back in as the massive head, sporting tusks my height and weight, swung back in our direction.

'Okay, you just hold on there. Better have a quick peek,' said Phil brightly.

Really, I didn't need his advice because as I looked down I discovered that my hands were gripping a foam and metal handrail like scaffolding clamps. I turned around and watched incredulous as my friend opened the driver's door. The rest of the herd had now ambled around the back of the truck and were giving the strongest impression of attempting to surround us.

'Okay, no problem. You sure that there is nothing that I could . . .' My voice that had started in a quavering falsetto tailed off into an embarrassing husky whisper.

'You'll be right. Just going to pop the lid a minute. You keep an eye on the punters.'

I turned and looked through the screen, raising a weak smile and one of my disengaged hands in a weedy wave. Madame de la Rozière glared back at me balefully and wafted a small bottle of something powerful under her nose before administering it to the sickly-looking young man sitting next to her.

In a flash, Phil had bounded to the front of the truck,

'popped the lid' and was busily rootling about, his efforts admired by a baby elephant who, as he rubbed himself up against his mother's side, reminded me strongly of little Babar. Had circumstances been different, I might have felt almost affectionate towards it. As it was, I just wished it would go away, a long way away, and take all its family and friends with it. This sentiment was reinforced when I heard a voice from under the lid pronouncing the words that I most dreaded.

'Mate? You couldn't just lend us a hand, could you?'

'Yes, sure. Although I thought I was supposed to be looking after the passengers . . .'

'Oh, fuck them,' came the assertive reply.

Glancing backwards, it seemed that nobody behind me had heard this somewhat unprofessional utterance. Of course, being surrounded by fifteen enormous animals, who in one or two cases were certainly behaving in a manner that could only be described as frisky, was quite enough to distract them from what was being said up front.

'So what do you need me to do? Switch something on or off?'

'Just come here a minute, mate. I need you to hold something.'

Oh, I knew it.

I opened the door.

Very slowly.

Whistling quietly and trying to imagine that I was not being watched, as I sometimes do when caught admiring myself in a high-street window or when realising my flies are undone, I moved to the front of the vehicle. There was something quite comforting about being next to a professional. Safety in numbers – or something like that.

'Okay, mate, just grab hold of this.'

From the guts of the engine he produced a hot rubber

tube, which I grabbed like a lifeline. Sweat from my brow dripped onto the engine and fizzled like spit on an iron.

'So, er . . . well, what would your analysis be then?'

I leaned one hip against the chrome grille as I noticed Phil had done.

'I mean your diagnostic? That's what it's called, isn't it? Yes, that's it. Diagnostic.'

Rather pleased to be using the right terminology, I smiled at the nearest elephant. The way that it flapped its ears and curled its trunk up above its head was most authentic.

'So, do you still want me to hold onto this pipe, or should I just go back and check that everything is all right in the truck? Maybe I could see if everybody's got enough to drink?'

'Just hold on to the bloody pipe while I try to see where all the water has gone. Jesus, it's as dry as a bloody Kalahari swimming pool down here.'

Detecting a note of irritation in his voice as well as a sharp decline in the standard of his vocabulary, I held onto the pipe. One of the medium-sized elephants was in the process of pulling a large-sized tree out of the ground.

'So, you really want to know what my "diagnostic" is?'

'Yes, sure. If you want to tell me, that would be great.'

'Well to be blunt, mate, she's completely and utterly fucked.'

'Meaning?'

The normally even-minded, level-headed Australian groaned. 'Well, either we get everyone out and push, or we walk, or we hang around until someone turns up and tows us out of here. Which do you fancy?'

Not entirely sure whether this was a trick question, I felt somewhat confused. Whilst I was giving it some thought, I climbed into my seat. Neither pushing nor walking seemed remotely attractive options.

'Do you think anybody is likely to turn up?' I asked, trying to avoid a falsetto again as Phil got back into the truck.

'Well, we're just on the fringe of the Chobe National Park, so the chances are we'll see some other overlanders, or with more luck, some of the game wardens. They're normally really well kitted out. Trouble is we might see them today, but then we might not.'

'So, what exactly do we do if nobody turns up?'

'Well, we don't have much choice, do we? Come dusk, the elephants will clear off back into the bush, but I'm not going to take the risk of camping. Just too many lions round here.'

'Oh, good one – lions! Lions! Ha, ha!'

Laughing, I looked through the thin screen again. This time the passengers did seem to have heard what was being said. I could tell by their pallor. Attempting to suppress a broad grin, I turned back to Phil.

'They all believe you! Certainly not lost in translation! You should see their faces.'

Phil glanced in the mirror before looking back at me.

'Why, don't you believe me? There was a pride of eleven in almost exactly this spot the last time I was here a few months back.'

Glancing down out of the window, I couldn't make out any paw prints on the ground. Real lions? No way.

What was I doing here?

'So, how far away is the nearest village?'

Maybe we should after all make a run for it.

'Not that far. Maybe five or six kilometres. We could just take light packs and try to make it back up onto the main road. I'd have to get the rifle down and dig out the thunder flashes. You ever used those before?'

'No, no, no.' This was turning into something far too much like a real adventure. Not since I had once been adrift in the Pacific Ocean had I felt quite so unsuited to the environment in which I found myself. At least I wasn't on my own. Mind you, as I looked back at the passengers in the back I wasn't entirely certain that they were going to be any great support. Wolf Dieter was smearing on Factor 45 suntan lotion, no doubt in the wild hope that it would provide him with some sort of protection from the elements. And the wispily moustached youth had for some reason opened the blade of his Swiss Army knife. Here, he was going to be presented with a rather greater challenge than he had been as the tinned-pea sous-chef.

Fortunately, the elephants did not seem to be in combative mood and began to wander away into the tree line. Magnificent creatures, really magnificent. After pointing out their departure with a finger that now trembled a little less than before, I gave the thumbs up to my travelling companions.

'So, do you really think that there's a chance that we'll have to stay here a very long time? I mean, like all night?'

Before Phil had a chance to point out to me that he was not Nostradamus, my question was answered. From the narrow track that ran down to the bank between dusty bushes appeared a khaki-green Land Rover with two uniformed Africans in the front seats and two more behind.

'No way, we couldn't have struck luckier than this. It's the BDF. Perfect.' Phil grinned broadly and opened his door much too widely.

'BDF?'

'Botswana Defence Force. It's the army, mate.'

Stepping out of their vehicle, two of them came strolling, yes strolling, over to us, pulling on smart green berets as they came. Rather worryingly, I noticed that the two who were still sitting in the back of the truck both seemed to be carrying highly polished machine guns. Out of the frying pan and into the fire?

When they reached the driver's door, the two soldiers came to a halt and saluted smartly before leaning backwards slightly to inspect the increasingly nervous passengers.

'*Dumela*, Rre!' called Phil, slightly to my surprise but, it would appear, not to theirs, for they both responded promptly.

'*Dumela*, Phil. *Le kae?*'

'*Re teng*,' continued the pleasantries. I waved a little wildly when they smiled at me and saluted again.

A few more rather impressive sentences from Phil were enough to explain our predicament to our two new best friends. Both men smiled broadly and marched back to their Land Rover. As the man in the passenger seat reached for his radio, his driver threw the vehicle into reverse and with a rather impressive spin of the wheels disappeared back up the path.

'So, what exactly, you know, did you all decide?'

Neither of us managed to quite ignore a distinct sob coming from the back.

'Don't worry. Told you that these guys are the best. There's no way they could tow us with the Landy so they've gone off to get one of their eight-tonners – the big ones. Reckoned they would be about half an hour. Probably will be, they're normally pretty good like that. Particularly if they're on your side.'

Remembering the machine guns, I briefly wondered what would happen if they weren't.

'Right, I suppose we better explain to these guys what's going on. We're never going to hear the end of this one.

Just imagine the stories that they'll be telling when they get back home.'

Surprisingly, Phil was rather good at calming them down, particularly with a little translating help from me. I didn't know what the French or German was for 'don't be a bunch of bloody whingeing whussies', so I opted instead for words like *courageux* and *très brave*, *furchtbar* and *wunderbare Gruppe*. It all seemed to have the correct placatory effect.

'Just admire the view and stop bloody complaining about everything,' said Phil.

'*Quel beau paysage, n'est-ce pas? Vous êtes un groupe vraiment charmant. Surtout vous, Madame de la Rozière. Ah oui!*'

As good as their word, the same four soldiers returned, this time in a large lorry with an open back on which was mounted, to our collective alarm, what appeared to be the modern equivalent of a cannon but also, rather more reassuringly, an industrial-strength winch. Within a matter of minutes we were chugging slowly on down the riverbank watched by a group of only mildly curious giraffes.

'What's this place called, then?' I asked Phil as we eventually hit some semblance of a road on the outskirts of a village.

'Kasane,' he replied.

'Kasane? This is Kasane already? This is my destination! So what kind of a place is it?' It struck me then that in the last two weeks or so we had hardly encountered any form of habitation at all and thoughts of my proposed teaching job had rather receded into the background. Now, with a fillip of excitement, I realised that here a new chapter was opening. 'Do they have any shops or anything? Or a telephone? Hadn't really thought about what kind of place it is.'

Phil's sigh led me to understand that I was just going

to have to wait to find out. Yet it was true that really I had no idea at all what to expect. It dawned on me again that most of my images of Africa had either been plucked from the television screen or from those fantastic 'Adventure' books by Willard Price chronicling the exploits of two brothers, Hal and Roger – a series which I had consumed avidly from first to last as a boy at school. Unhappily, as an adult I had read too much and seen too much about civil war, disease, famine and drought, corruption and repression. Now, as we rolled into this sizeable village, I realised I had no real or true understanding of how people here lived. What was modern-day Africa really like?

Of all the things that I had imagined that I would perhaps see first, an enormous white supermarket with fluttering flags, trolleys, wide aisles and high shelves was not one of them. Many of the people going in and out of the Spar supermarket that early afternoon must have been somewhat surprised to see the Botswana Defence Force towing a large yellow truck down the main street of the town, each of its windows filled with gawping, amazed and slightly pallid faces. Near the supermarket was a tidy parade of shops, a bank, a tourist office, a builders' merchant, a butcher's and a baker's. Signs advertising the presence of the police station, several hotels, boarding houses, travel agents and bus companies were displayed on the street corner where people were standing waiting as a number of smart, wide, four-wheel-drive vehicles pulled into the main street and headed off out of town.

Quite suddenly, I felt overcome by embarrassment; for I now realised that I had wanted Africa to reveal itself as some representation of the romantic notion that I had. Not that what I found now wasn't an entirely fascinating world. While the army truck slowed down to turn north, I watched a man loading his shopping into the back of his pick-up as a family of warthogs – father, mother and three little children – their short little legs clipping briskly along and their bristly thin tails sticking straight up like mini-car aerials, trotted past and rounded the corner in the direction of the video shop.

Eventually Phil and I, accompanied by our rather bewildered passengers, were towed to the doors of a smartly equipped garage, and our truck was reversed into the garage with a lot of *'eins, zwei, drei'* and a half-hearted *'allons-y'* from the French party. Our arrival was greeted with a smart salute by Maurio, an Italian, who was pleasant-looking and oily in the nicest possible way, and the owner of the establishment. He and Phil were clearly good friends as evidenced by the noisy and rather painful-looking back-slapping and hugging that took place. Rather flamboyantly, Maurio requested that we 'poppa ze lid', and as the PAX spilled out of the bus into the forecourt and engaged in stretching exercises, mutual massages and more general physical jerks, the maestro inspected our problem.

To cut a long story short, his pronouncement was that our trusty steed was going to require the mechanical equivalent of a heart transplant. That new heart would have to be put on a lorry and driven over from South Africa. It was unlikely to arrive for another week. Phil looked glum.

'Well, I'll just have to bus them to Victoria Falls and they can stay a few days at the campsite there before I get shot of them. What do you want to do, Will? You can come with us to Vic Falls and then head back here afterwards. But it's fully catered at the place we're going to stay at, so it wouldn't be any problem if you just wanted to stop here now seeing as it's where you're going to be living.'

To my surprise, Phil appeared to be considerably more confident and certain about my future than I was.

'The reason I say that is because this place is amazing.

You've got so much to see and do, and it's really unspoiled. There's a little place you can stay just up the hill here if you want – pretty nice and cheap, and it's run by some friends of mine. It's up to you.'

Guiltily, I had been thinking how nice it would be to have a break from the pressures and pains of all this group living. To have some time to myself without being badgered or questioned mercilessly would be great. Was he sure he didn't mind?

Shaking his head, Phil smiled. 'Just hope you enjoyed coming for the ride. Actually, Will, there is one other thing – one last favour – that you could do for me which would be really useful. While I'm explaining to these guys what the plan is – which should be fun – could you please go into town to the bus company and ask them to send a bus up here, big enough for twenty people and their kit. They'll know what kind of thing we need – just say it's going to Vic Falls. That would be great if you could.'

Of course I could. But I wondered how I was going to get down into the town, which must have been two or three miles away. No problem. Maurio would lend me one of his old bangers. Phil gave me careful, concise directions and I went out into the sunshine to find my ride.

As it turned out, the old banger was in fact what I considered to be rather a cool Jeep. I slid on my sunglasses and kangarooed out of the yard waving nonchalantly. Once I had mastered the gears, all was relatively straightforward. Botswana like most of southern Africa drives on the same side of the road as its former colonial master and there were relatively few other road-users. This, in light of my past motoring history, could only be a good thing.

Once I was back on the main street, I felt fairly confident that I knew where to find the bus company. Two hundred yards ahead of me I could see the sign. Mirror, signal, manoeuvre. That's what they tell you when you're doing your driving test, I thought to myself as I turned slowly and sensibly to my right and someone or something smashed hard into the back of my car.

5
Having a Smashing Time

Whd an excitement!
From every direction people came running, enthusiastic spectators. Little boys dressed only in pairs of raggedy shorts came to stand close to me, small hands shading their eyes in order to better squint up at my face in the fierce sunshine. They appeared a little disappointed not to see any blood. More than one of them held a fishing rod, their catch, small, dull and opaque-eyed, still hanging from the hook. Little girls, less interested in possible death and destruction, carried on skipping intricate steps over lengths of stretched elastic while clapping and chanting. At any other time this might have been rather charming.

Working women, dressed in a wide but invariably bright variety of Western and African outfits, stopped to inspect the scene as well, but not wanting to give the impression of gawping, they chatted quietly to one another. Shopping remained piled on their heads, and newly born infants continued to sleep peacefully in slings strapped tightly but comfortably across their mothers' bosoms. On the other hand, many of the men who congregated were not at all shy about becoming involved in what, it soon became clear, was something of an *événement* in Kasane.

Once the two cars had come to rest, mine halfway into the driveway of the bus station and the other slewed halfway across the oncoming lane, and after my heart had finished sinking to my boots, I switched off the engine and slowly, very slowly, climbed out of the car. As I did so, in simultaneous slow motion, two men climbed out of the dark-green, lightweight pick-up truck that had hit me. Smashed plastic rear-lights crunched under my feet like bones.

Arms swinging loosely by their sides, faces hidden under the brims of broad leather hats, they approached me. Finally, they stopped in front of me, the crowd behind them blurring as I concentrated on their every move. The driver lifted his hands to his hips, his friend folded his arms.

Pause.

Deep breath.

'Hello, my name is Clever,' said the driver, his voice rich and in no way confrontational. He had lifted one hand from his waist and stuck it out towards me. It seemed to be weapon-free. 'What is your name, Mister?'

'My name is Will.'

'Okay, Willy. What shall we do with this terrible problem? Why didn't you use your indicator? You must always use your indicator, you know.'

'But I did! I definitely did. You know, manoeuvre, mirror, signal, accelerator, brake, turn. Er . . . I think. You know, that's how I always do it, it's what you've got to do, isn't it?'

We both looked rather baffled. So did everybody else.

'Well, I am sure I did not see an indicator!' replied Clever after a moment of suitably earnest thought.

Forlornly, I remembered the numerous other occasions

in the past when the conversation under such circumstances had been reduced to a simple 'Yes I did–no you didn't' ping-pong match. Smiling, for want of anything better to do, I wondered what the outcome here would be.

Help arrived, however, in a speedy and most unexpected manner. Clever's travelling companion, who had been amusing himself and others around him by putting his entire fist through a hole that had been punched in the side panel of my car had clearly overheard our conversation. Slowly he came over and, placing his hand on Clever's shoulder, he smiled broadly.

'No, it's true!'

Clever nodded enthusiastically.

'No really, it's true. I did see an indicator. He wanted to turn right so he was slowing down and putting on his indicator. Then Clever is a bloody fool. I don't know what he's thinking when he tries to overtake. *Vroom, vroom!*' Clever's friend performed a rather realistic steering-wheel and gear-stick mime for everyone's benefit before continuing. 'He is always the same. He doesn't have any of this commonsense so that's why he always makes these blunders, and that's why I'm telling you. So there you are, you see. So we can't say it is your mistake, can we?'

Clever's nodding had slowed to a shocked halt over the course of this discourse, and by the end of it he was staring in slack-jawed astonishment at his friend. He took a few moments to pull himself together. Once he had managed to do so, he took my hand in his and led me a little way away from the crowd. Pushing the brim of his hat up until it was sitting on the back of his head, he smiled cheerfully.

'Well, Willy, what do you think is the best idea? Maybe you can repair your car and maybe I can repair my car. What do you think? Good idea?'

'Well, it's quite a good idea, but there is only one thing I was thinking.'

'Yes?'

'Well, it's just that, you know, I don't want to be difficult, but it's just that you ran in to me.'

'Exactly! That is why I'm going to repair my car! No *matata*. "No problem" like we say in Botswana.' Clever was warmly shaking my hand.

'Umm . . .'

Then just as I felt that we were about to encounter a negotiating impasse, a tall figure emerged from the thickening crowd and strode purposefully towards us.

'Good afternoon, gentlemen.' This clearly required a response.

'Good afternoon,' Clever and I replied simultaneously, like children immediately respectful in what appeared to be the face of authority.

'First, let me introduce myself. My name is Detective Constable Motswagole from the Kasane Police Station. In fact, I am now out of duty and going for my lunch-time. But I have taken the opportunity to inspect the scene of the accident and I recommend that the police come to investigate.'

As Clever and I opened our mouths and lifted up our hands in ill-concealed remonstration, DC Motswagole pulled a slimline mobile phone from his jeans pocket, pressed a number and listened to it dial before turning away from us and quietly reeling off some instructions.

'So, they should be coming in about ten, fifteen minutes,' he explained matter-of-factly once he had turned back to us. 'We mustn't move the vehicles before they arrive. May I suggest you sit under the tree where you will find it more shady? Shouldn't be too long now.' And with that, the policeman headed off in the direction of the shops.

Clever and I smiled weakly at one another and sat down at the foot of a grey, brittle-leaved tree and watched the crowd milling with continued interest around the accident scene. All the cars that passed slowed down to walking speed, and the drivers leaned out of their windows as far as they could without actually getting out. A few minutes after DC Motswagole had left, a large open-sided Land Rover with padded benches bolted into the back pulled up beside us, unable to make its way through the throng. In the back, shaded by a large canvas sheet, sat a dozen or so European tourists dressed not dissimilarly to our own group – neatly creased shorts against bright, white skin, unblemished boots, and things on straps strung around sweaty necks. When they came to a stop, tension and concern suddenly etched themselves on their faces. Shifting about uncomfortably, it appeared that they were physically trying to urge the driver on, hoping he would press forward through the crowd. On seeing the two crashed vehicles, they reacted as if both contained a bomb, and shrank and cowered in their seats. Much more used to seeing tourists than the tourists were to seeing them, the crowd bustled about in an increasingly festive manner.

As I had noticed on other travels so many times, the vast majority of people who visited foreign countries on holiday were happy to observe, even occasionally to sample, the day to day life of the local population, but it was a shame-fully small minority who actually wanted to participate in it. To watch, record, but not actually engage in the culture was unfortunately the norm. There seemed to be an invisible wall of mistrust that kept the two sides apart so that the visitor remained in a comfort zone. Of course, it is perfectly understandable that people should have a fear of the unknown, but that is hardly the fault of the unknown.

One of the tourists noticed me sitting under the tree and

excitedly nudged his neighbour, who in turn appeared to prevaricate between taking a photograph of me and suggesting that they organise a hostage rescue. Before any such decision could be made, a gap in the road opened up and the group continued on their way. As they approached the next corner, I noticed one of their number rising surreptitiously above the back row, his or her binoculars trained firmly on me.

DC Motswagole's prognostication had been almost perfectly correct. With little fanfare, or indeed wailing of sirens, a brand new and highly polished light-blue and white police car rolled up at the scene. Out of it stepped two smartly dressed police officers with peaked caps, blue uniforms and white belts, highly polished shoes and clipboards. They made some inquiries of the crowd who nodded in our direction. Whilst one of the policemen reached into the boot of his car, the other approached us. He saluted:

'Good afternoon, gentlemen. *Dumela*, Clever!'

Clever replied quietly.

'Where are you from, sir?'

'England,' I replied, suddenly feeling a nervousness not experienced since an unfortunate incident years earlier involving a police officer, a student me, a moped, no shoes, helmet or relevant paperwork.

'England. Good, I see. My name is Inspector Ramotswe. No relation!' he announced, before smiling broadly. Now, let me first apologise for my lateness. We have been somewhat busy at the station today. Do you speak Setswana?'

Shaking my head, I mumbled something rather ineffectually.

'Very well, we will conduct this investigation in English from now on. You are happy with this, Sir?' he asked Clever.

'Oh, no problem at all, absolutely no problem at all, Sir.'

Clever, I noticed, was less buoyant than he had been before and, when we were duly asked about what had taken place, he mumbled that he thought that he probably hadn't seen an indicator.

Whilst we were talking to Inspector Ramotswe, the other policeman had removed a measuring wheel on a stick, and was in the process of pacing along the thick, black, snaking skidmark left by Clever's pick-up truck. This done, he sat down on the edge of the pavement and started, rather artistically I thought, to sketch out a scene of the crime. Occasionally, he would lift a thumb and hold it out in front of him to measure an angle or a distance or some such. Soon a group of admirers stood behind his shoulder and commented on his efforts, much as people observe the work of caricaturists in Montmartre. On the whole, from the nods of approval, they appeared to think that he was producing a pretty worthy representation of what had happened.

'Thank you, Gentlemen,' the inspector said, snapping closed a most authentic-looking notebook. 'Now, if you're ready we will go to the station so you may give me your written statements. I don't think it will take a very long time. Maybe one hour.'

Due to this whole rather unsettling experience, I had completely forgotten about Phil and the group, who were still waiting at the garage for their transport. Nervously, I explained to the inspector what my mission had been and, pointing over to the bus depot, asked if I might be allowed to pass my message on. No problem, he replied – as long as I moved my vehicle completely off the highway first. Clever followed suit. Once the bus had been dispatched, we climbed into the back of the inspector's car, and minutes later we pulled up into the car park of a three-storey, modern, red-brick building with a shiny glass frontage. We stepped into air-conditioned cool and were led down bright, light corridors to a waiting area with soft chairs and a cold-water dispenser.

'Please sit here while I prepare my dossier,' requested the inspector.

After only a little while, he returned and asked Clever to follow him. As he stood up, Clever smiled at me briefly, and momentarily I thought about wishing him good luck as I remembered doing to people going in to a job interview before me. The two men disappeared behind a thick wooden door, and shortly afterwards I was summoned to another room where the inspector's colleague noted down in great detail my version of events. Finally, he read it back to me in a clear, calm, well-modulated voice and, once I had agreed that this was indeed how I remembered the event, he asked me to sign it in triplicate.

Guiltily, I realised how impressed, no, surprised, I was, not only by the efficiency and competence of these men but also by their level-headed politeness. Certainly, there was no ostensible reason why this should have struck me as being unexpected, but the wheels of Botswanan bureaucracy turned impressively smoothly even here in this remote and dusty backwater. When Clever and I found ourselves again on the other side of a boardroom desk from the inspector, he leant back in his chair, placed his fingertips together and gazed neutrally at the ceiling. There was silence for a few moments while we listened to the air-conditioning hum, and then the inspector began his summing up.

'In this day and age there are so many more motor cars than before. This is why all drivers must concentrate very carefully when they are driving, always ensuring that they look out for any surprises, always ready for the unexpected.'

Clever and I, our hands folded in our laps, leaned

forward and nodded sagely in unison as we listened.

'It has been quite clear in investigating this matter that one driver was careful and considerate, and the other driver was driving like a bloody fool.'

Clever and I nodded all the harder.

'Sorry, yes, I am very sorry, but I have to say that that driver who was driving so badly,' the inspector continued to gaze at the ceiling, 'that driver is sitting on the left side in front of me.'

On his left side? Or on our left side? The two of us looked at one another in some confusion – confusion that was only cleared up when the inspector slid a sheet of paper across the table to Clever and, indicating with his pen, requested him to sign.

'I am afraid that I will have to fine you four hundred Pula.'

Clever's eyes widened slightly but he nodded. 'No *matata*.'

Having been in his predicament more times than I cared to remember, I instantly felt sorry for him.

Our business concluded, the inspector turned his mind to more important matters.

'So who is better, Manchester or Chelsea? I think Manchester.'

'No way, Rra, Chelsea is a much better team. Didn't you see them playing in Europe the other week? I think it was against some Italian club? They are much stronger side, Rra,' concluded the newly recovered Clever.

'What do you think, Mr Randall? Who is your favourite team?'

Now, I had for a while coached the school football team back in another life as a teacher in Somerset. My leadership had been inspirational rather than technical or tactical, and had involved a great deal of shouting, occasional cheering and getting very muddy feet. On a couple of occasions, as an end of season treat, I had taken my team to watch Silverford Town and eat a few hot dogs – nothing much, but the outings had seemingly been enjoyed by all.

'Well, I don't know if you have ever heard of the team called Silverford. They play in a league which is a bit like the premiership but is called something like Dr Marten's League . . . although I think the name has changed now. In fact, it's now called something to do with Builders' World, I think . . .'

I seemed to have lost them. As per usual I blathered on.

'No, of course you're right. Manchester and Chelsea are the best and then there is . . . er . . . who else? Oh yes, Arsenal? Do you know them?'

Oh yes, they certainly did. The Chief Constable's favourite team, in fact.

We made our way to the entrance hall, chatting away quite amicably about all manner of things. Not least, why The Zebras, the Botswana national team, were so useless. Oh no, I said. I was sure they were not. Oh yes, they were, my new friends insisted. Very lazy. Really very bad.

The inspector shook our hands on the doorstep and wished us a steady journey home. Clever and I walked to the front gate.

'So, Willy. Very nice to meet you. How long are you staying in Kasane?' He seemed to have recovered from the initial sting of his fine and had put the incident firmly behind him. The bearing of grudges seemed to be refreshingly absent amongst the Batswana. 'Maybe you will be able to come to my house? My wife will cook us some nice food from Botswana and you can meet my children. Then we can swap some nice stories.'

When I told him that I was not sure what I was doing

in Kasane yet, he looked a little crestfallen, but cheered up when I announced how flattered I was by his kind offer.

'Maybe see you, then?' He flashed me a cheerful smile and giving his hat a tug over his eyes, he sashayed his way down the main street, leaving me more than a little bemused.

Just as it was dawning on me that although we might have solved the problem of who was responsible for the accident, we certainly did not seem to have decided who was going to pay for the damage to Maurio's car, a white charabanc pulled up. Touched, I realised it was Phil and the gang. They were all very genuinely concerned, as they had heard from the bus driver that the last time I had been sighted was as I disappeared into the back of a police car. Once more, I recounted the story of my motoring disaster to the accompaniment of a great deal of ooh-la-laaing. When I suggested to Phil that I ought to return the damaged car to Maurio, he told me that I would have to wait until the following day, as he had already shut up shop and gone home.

Finally, it was time for them to get going so, as they handed me down my pack, I wished them *'Bon voyage'* and *'Gute Reise'*, and thanked our leader most genuinely and sincerely for what had been, for the main part, a really fun adventure. Was I sure that I was going to be all right? No, but then I very rarely am, I laughed in a kind of devil-may-care fashion waving them off until they were out of sight. And a little while after that, it occurred to me that I still didn't know what PAX meant. And I don't now either. Sometimes, when I think wistfully of travelling through southern Africa, I still occasionally wonder.

Although not technically lost, for I knew precisely which part, however remote, of the planet I was on, I sensed once again that strange paralysis that overcomes me when I begin to wonder what on earth I am going to do next. At some stage, I was going to have to find this Graham person, although I had next to no idea how. My recollection of my conversation with Professor Neville Botting and my departure from Cape Town being somewhat hazy, I was a little unsure how things had been left. Anyway, it was getting a bit late to mount a search party. As it was now nearing four o'clock in the afternoon, accommodation for the night was certainly edging its way up my list of priorities. Shouldering my backpack – the equivalent of holding up a large placard reading 'I am a lost tourist' – I made my less than certain way back down onto the road.

Schoolchildren in white shirts and dark shorts or skirts, grey socks, black shoes, and with neat satchels on their backs were making their way home with a relief shared the world over. I stumbled on in the opposite direction.

'Hey, Mr Football Man, where are you heading?'

Looking down, I noticed with a slight twitch of alarm that one of the light-blue and white police cars had pulled up alongside me. The window had been wound down, and Inspector Ramotswe was leaning out and smiling at me. I stopped, and the car stopped.

'Well, I was thinking of staying a few days in Kasane. I am going to have to get the car repaired before I can do anything else.'

'Where are you staying?'

'Er . . . well I am not too sure at the moment. Probably just try and find a guesthouse of some sort. Do you know anywhere around here . . . not too expensive?'

'Well, there is the Garden Lodge. They say that is a nice place. You could try there. But listen, don't worry, why don't you come with us to the prison?'

'What?'

'Yes, we have a very good prison in Kasane. It is the

biggest in the whole district. And,' he added with some pride, 'we have the best football team.'

'No, I wasn't really thinking of going to . . . er . . . to prison. Thanks anyway. Maybe I will try the Garden Lodge. Thanks.'

Inspector Ramotswe laughed.

'No, we are going to play a match down there. Police against the prisoners – it is always a great match. You would really like it.'

Only then did I notice that the inspector and his driver were both dressed in football kit, shorts and socks, boots, the lot.

Well . . .

'Come on, let's go. You can find a place on our way back. No problem.'

So it was, with an ancient sense of fate taking the upper hand, that I opened the back door of the police car and threw in my bag and then myself. We must have been running a little late, because as we reached the outskirts of the village the driver casually flicked a switch and the sirens wailed into action as we shot forward. Within a few minutes we were out in the open bush – goats and donkeys, men, women and children scattering in all directions in an attempt to get out of our way in time.

'By the way,' I attempted to ask over the screeching noise, 'I am looking for someone. His name is Graham . . . umm . . . yes, Graham.' It dawned on me then that I did not know his surname. 'He is a South African man, I think. Do you know him at all?'

Half-hoping that the inspector would not be able to hear my question, I suddenly felt ridiculous.

'Graham, yes of course I know him. Lucky for you, you will find him here at the prison.'

Not daring to reply to this, I wondered what on earth I

had become embroiled in. My only contact in the village was at present doing porridge, possibly breaking rocks, almost certainly ball and chained. Fancifully, I wondered in which direction the arrows on his uniform would be pointing and whether he would throw himself upon my mercy, begging me to help him secure his release.

My gloomy thoughts were interrupted by the inspector who announced that we had arrived. There on our left were the barbed-wire fences, security lookouts, gate houses and searchlights of a modern penitentiary. We sailed in with a quick salute from the guard at the gate.

Pulling up in a huge cloud of thick brown dust, the policemen hopped out of the car and ran onto the perfectly flat, perfectly grassless pitch to join their team-mates. At the far end, a gaggle of players dressed, as far as I could see, in orange knee-length boiler suits were limbering up enthusiastically. In the centre circle, formed by small white pebbles, a white man in a black outfit blew his whistle and gestured rather professionally with one arm. A sizeable number of spectators, comprising the rest of the population of the jail, started up a noisy and enthusiastic barrage of shouts of encouragement and sighs of disappointment. It was not really difficult to work out which side it was that they were supporting, although their allegiance seemed to be entirely good-natured.

Before long, both teams were pouring with sweat and were covered thickly, comically actually, with dust. I did not laugh. Both sides were powerful and energetic, clattering into tackles that made me blanch, before bouncing up and carrying on. At half-time both teams mingled happily, sharing a joke or two before getting back to the action. When full time was up, the police were down by two goals and at least one player.

My new friends came breathlessly back to the car to grab

towels and soap. Just a quick shower and some nice drinks, and then we will take you back into town, they told me. No problem, I smiled. The first person to return abluted and changed was the referee. He came up to me, hand outstretched.

'Hi, I'm Graham. You're Will, right? The inspector was telling me. We have been expecting you to turn up. Nev said you were on your way.' The South African accent was unmistakable.

'Yes, hello.'

'So, I hear you had a spot of bother today. Have you recovered?' He smiled. 'Doesn't sound like the perfect beginning to your stay in Kasane.'

'No you're absolutely right. It was a complete disaster. Although I'm not actually sure that I will be staying in Kasane for long.' Again I was assailed by terrible doubts about whether being there at all was in any way a good idea. 'You know, I might have to be heading back soon, you know.'

'You're a Brit, right? Yes, I spent a bit of time over there myself. Had a lot of fun. You enjoying Africa?' Graham seemed to have completely ignored what I had just said.

'Well, apart from today's disaster, it has been fantastic.'

'Is it?'

'Is what?'

But Graham seemed to ignore me once again. It was to take me some time to understand that the South African 'Is it?' was a much over-used expression employed to signal interest in what had just been said.

'So what do you do back home?'

'Oh,' I replied distractedly, as I watched the prisoners running off in single file towards one of the rather grim-looking buildings at the back of the compound accompanied by jogging prison warders. 'Oh, I'm just a teacher, but I've been taking a bit of time off.'

'Oh, you're a teacher? Is it? Wasn't quite sure what Nev said. Didn't know whether you were actually a teacher or just a volunteer. That's great.' He seemed to be mightily pleased to hear this news, and this in turn suddenly reignited some sensation of enthusiasm within me that had been nigh-on extinguished by my somewhat turbulent arrival. 'You could be a great help to us, you know. Nev probably told you, I'm actually here as the headmaster of a little school. We came up from South Africa on a two-year contract. My wife teaches here too, and my girls are in the pre-school and Standard Five. Maybe you would like to come and have a look at our set-up?' he asked innocently.

'Oh, yes, sounds interesting,' I replied brightly, before the reality of my present situation dawned on me. 'Thing is, I have to try and find somewhere to stay tonight.'

'Is it? Well that's easy enough. You can come and stay with us. We've got plenty of room.'

'Really? That's incredibly kind of you. Are you sure it won't put you out?'

'No way! And then you'll be able to come and have a look at the school.'

'Oh yes, great. That would be brilliant.'

Fatal.

Bidding farewell to the cheerful, if slightly over-heated, inspector and his grimacing, ankle-clutching sergeant, I humped my bag over to Graham's smart Japanese station wagon and climbed aboard.

As we headed back along the main road towards town, Graham asked me a few questions about my teaching experience in the UK. I sketched out the reason for my sudden, accidental appearance in Kasane, which seemed to amuse him no end. Before long, our conversation took on a familiar character – the conversation between two teachers, two pedagogues, passionate about passing as much information to others as possible.

'So what you know about Botswana, Will?'

'Well, fairly little to be honest . . .' Despite rummaging around, I had not found any publications in the little library on the bus that dealt with this corner of the continent.

However, Graham, as I was coming to recognise, was a man who seized on all new experiences fervently, sucking them dry with relish, and his knowledge of Botswana was practically encyclopaedic. Sadly, having no ammunition of my own, this was to be a one-sided conversation. I braced myself.

'So, let's have a look at the history. Go right back.'

An adept story-teller, before long Graham had me entranced, opening wide for me a door of understanding into this new world.

'You've heard of the Bushmen, of course? The harmless people.' He didn't wait for a response and missed my rotating, non-committal head movement. 'Some people call them the San, "people who can't farm", because they were historically, and still are, hunter-gatherers. They are often known as the Baswara by people here, although that is thought to be a bit pejorative – it means "people from nowhere". Some that I know like to be called the Ncoakhoe – the "red people", from the colour of the earth. You're bound to find out more about them while you're staying here. Anyway they're believed to have inhabited Botswana for at least thirty thousand years. They were apparently the indigenous people of southern Africa. They were followed by the pastoral KhoiKhoi – what the whites used to call "the Hottentots" – and later on by tribes of the Bantu, who migrated from the north-western and eastern regions of Africa sometime during the first or second century AD. They settled all along here, all along the Chobe River.' Here he finally drew breath,

swept up, as he gazed absent-mindedly and rather disconcertingly out of the window of the car at the huge panorama
of history laid out in front of us. Some donkeys displaying
poor road sense were narrowly avoided before he pressed
on in a surge of billowing dust.

These different groups, including the predominant
Tswana, he soon went on, had lived relatively amicably in
small groupings across the Kalahari throughout the
eighteenth century. Disputes were solved through frag-
mentation: any disgruntled factions simply upped sticks,
gathered together their few belongings and animals, and
trooped off to set up another home somewhere more
conducive to good neighbourly relations.

Unfortunately, by the beginning of the nineteenth
century, all suitable grazing lands around the fringes of the
Kalahari had been settled by pastoralists, and peaceful frag-
mentation was no longer a practical solution to disagree-
ments. Much more distractingly, Europeans had arrived in
the Cape and were expanding northward with 'the sticks
that spit fire', a progression that was to result in the near
decimation of the Bushmen. Further aggression from the
south and west, after the 1818 amalgamation of the Zulu
tribes, made the scattered Tswana villages highly vulner-
able to attack. In response, the Tswana regrouped, and for
the first time they began to form highly structured societies. Each Tswana tribe was soon ruled by a hereditary
monarch, and the king's subjects lived in centralised towns
and satellite villages.

The orderliness and structure of the town-based
Batswana society impressed the Christian missionaries who
began to arrive in the early 1800s. None of them, including the great Livingstone, seemed to impress nor managed
to convert great numbers of Batswana, though they did
manage to advise the locals, sometimes wrongly, in their

dealings with the encroaching Europeans. Meanwhile, the Boers began their Great Trek over the Vaal, crossing into Batswana and Zulu territory and attempting to impose white rule on the inhabitants. Many Batswana went into service on Boer farms, normally not of their own free will, and the association was rarely happy and often marred by rebellion against random violence and persecution. By 1877, animosity had escalated to such a level that the British finally stepped in to annex the Transvaal and declared the first Boer War. The Boers hung back for a little while paying lip-service to the Pretoria Convention of 1881, but once again moved back into Batswana territories in 1882, prompting the Batswana to again ask for British protection. When little response of a helpful nature came from London, a missionary, John Mackenzie – a friend of the Bangwato Chief Khama III of Shoshong, one of the few Christian converts – went to campaign on behalf of the Batswana. Mackenzie soon became deputy commissioner of the region and things were settled for a little while, and most importantly the Boers were kept at bay.

Sadly, no one had catered for the appearance of Cecil Rhodes. Intent on achieving his expansionist plan of British domination of Africa from Cape to Cairo, he managed in distinctly underhand circumstances to take over from Mackenzie. Before long, the African chiefs had realised that Rhodes's intentions were distinctly more financial than honourable. Alarmed at the way he seemed to be increasing his control over the territory, Khama III, in the company of the chiefs Bathoen and Sebele, sailed for England and an audience with Queen Victoria. Despite the welcome given them at the palace, Joseph Chamberlain, the colonial minister, had more important things to preoccupy him. He went on holiday.

Fortunately, aid came to the beleaguered, and no doubt

rather cold, chieftains in the form of the London Missionary Society. Terrified that Rhodes and company would
allow alcohol to be sold in Bechuanaland (as the modern
day Botswana was at that stage known) the LMS applied
pressure on the government to administer the affairs of the
country and Rhodes's ambitions, in this part of Africa at
least, were thwarted.

'You Brits had control of Bechuanaland for a bit then,
and it was all pretty uneventful until 1966 when Botswana
got its independence. Yeah, so it's really a pretty young
country.' I was rather pleased to hear this last description
of Graham's. The republic of Botswana and I were, it had
now come to light, exactly the same age.

'Seretse Khama was elected the president. You know
about him I expect? Married an English girl. You don't? Oh,
OK, I'll tell you about that a bit later.'

Thanking him, I felt sure that he would.

Botswana had been economically transformed from one
of the ten poorest countries in the world to the strongest
sub-Saharan economy after South Africa by diamond
mining. The mysterious discovery in 1967, a matter of
months after independence, of an enormous 'tube' or vein
of 'ice' near Orapa, right out in the Central District, led to
suspicions amongst the Brits that the Batswana had known
of its presence well before then but had successfully
managed to conceal it until they had ensured the departure of the colonisers. The announcement of this discovery
must have caused a few self-inflicted kickings in Whitehall,
I mused with a chuckle as we ran into town. While most
of the population still subsisted, for the time being, in the
low-income bracket, this mineral discovery had transformed the desert nation into the biggest producer of
gemstones in the world with enormous foreign currency

reserves. Soon the Pula had climbed to its position as Africa's strongest currency.

Compared to the rest of the African nations, Botswana still had tremendous wealth and stability and, uniquely, had the good fortune to have a sensible, proud government that was regarded as pragmatic and altruistic. Despite suffering from devastating floods in 2000 that left 70,000 people homeless, and despite droughts in recent years that had caused considerable hardship, especially in the western part of the country, Botswana remained a peaceful nation with, it appeared, an ever-improving future.

As we turned down a short driveway, Graham concluded his history lesson, and soon we came to a halt at a wire gate overhung by hibiscus and frangipani.

6

On the Banks of the Chobe River

'So, do you think you've got everything that you need?' Graham asked as he stowed the last of a dozen or so suitcases into the back of his large family car. His wife, Janey, was making sure that their two young daughters, Becky and Samantha, were both snugly strapped into their seats.

'Yes, this is absolutely fine.'

'You know, Will? I think this is really going to work out well. You just help yourself to anything in the house. All you have to worry about is feeding the dogs. Easy!'

I sneaked a look at the two great big, growling Rhodesian Ridgebacks that were prowling the fence looking for something to savage and slavering at the mouth. Saliva drooled down their fronts.

'Enjoy!'

And with that, the family reversed their car up the drive, swung out onto the road and headed for Johannesburg. When they were out of sight, I beat a hasty retreat back into the house. Just in time, I managed to slam the front door shut before the two hounds could follow me in. Propping my bag against it, I considered my new state of fortune.

Graham had turned out to be the most engaging host. As soon as we had got back from the football match to his sizeable and comfortable Western-style house in the middle of the village – a perk of his job – he had introduced me to his family, opened the fridge, pulled out the beers and lit the *braai* – the ubiquitous South African barbecue.

Once the flames had taken hold and we had sunk contemplatively into folding canvas chairs, he launched into his second lecture on Africa. As his family slunk back into the house – apparently 'to get things ready', but I suspect because they had heard it all before – Graham told me, with glowing admiration, of Seretse Khama of the Bangwato tribe.

Seretse Khama, founding President of Botswana, was a man whose name still loomed large throughout the country. He had inherited an impoverished and internationally obscure state from British rule, and had left behind an increasingly democratic and prosperous country with a significant role in southern Africa.

Seretse was born on 1 July 1921 at Serowe in the southwest of the British protectorate of Bechuanaland. He was of royal lineage as the son of Sekgoma Khama, and the grandson of the internationally famous Kgosi Khama III, who was ruler of the Bangwato people of central Botswana. It was he as chief who had visited Buckingham Palace for tea and eventually broken the hold of the British South Africa Company and Cecil Rhodes over his country.

The boy was named Seretse – meaning 'the clay that binds together' – because of the recent reconciliation between his father and grandfather. Seretse's mother, Tebogo Kebailele, had been chosen by Khama to be the new wife of the ageing Sekgoma. When Sekgoma died in 1925, the four-year-old Seretse was proclaimed Kgosi – 'the chief'.

His uncle Tshekedi Khama became regent and sole guardian for him until he reached his majority.

Lonely and often sickly as a child, he was sent to boarding schools in South Africa, but despite the unhappiness of his early years he developed into a healthy, sporty and gregarious adolescent. He attended Fort Hare University College, graduating with a general BA degree in 1944, and in August of the following year he was sent to England for a legal education. After a year at Balliol College, Oxford, he enrolled for barrister studies at the Inner Temple, London, living in uncomfortable lodgings on the other side of town. Without the financial security of many of his contemporaries, Seretse must have been one of the few heirs to a throne to have had to walk to work.

In 1947, he met an English woman of his age, Ruth Williams, daughter of a retired army officer. Despite efforts in both the United Kingdom and Africa to thwart this union, including a last-minute delegation who appeared on the steps of the church the very morning of the wedding, the two were married in September 1948. Uncle Tshekedi ordered Seretse home to berate him and demand a divorce, but after a series of public meetings in Serowe, Seretse turned his people against Tshekedi, and was popularly recognised as Kgosi together with his wife. Tshekedi gave way and went into voluntary exile.

The ratification of a black chief with a white wife, in a territory of strategic importance between South Africa and the Rhodesias, caused outcry among white settler politicians. South Africa had come under the control of white Afrikaner nationalists in 1948, and the British were told that there was no chance of the pro-British opposition party winning the next all-white election in that country if Seretse was allowed to be chief of the Bangwato. Enthusiastic segregationists would never be able to stomach a mixed marriage, especially a royal one, only a stone's throw over the border.

Pragmatic rather than romantic, the Labour government in Britain, which desperately needed South African gold and uranium, agreed to bar Seretse from chieftainship. The Commonwealth relations minister denied that the government was bowing to racism, and lied about this before the House of Commons. A judicial inquiry was subsequently set up to prove Seretse's personal unfitness to rule. However, a certain more open-minded judge, Justice Harragin, concluded that Seretse was eminently fit to take up his duties; astonishingly, his report was suppressed by the British government for thirty years. Seretse and his wife were exiled to England in 1951, and in 1952 the new Conservative government declared the exile permanent.

The treatment of Seretse and Ruth Khama by British governments received international press coverage, and outrage was expressed by a wide range of people including human-rights activists, Scottish, West African, Indian and West Indian nationalists, British communists, conservatives who supported the principle of aristocratic inheritance and a groundswell of ordinary people who just could not get enough of a good love story. Eventually, in 1956, a new Commonwealth relations minister finally realised that Britain must distance itself from institutionalised racism in South Africa, and decided to allow Seretse and Ruth home as commoners and private citizens.

Once returned to his homeland, Seretse discovered that he was still respected as a man of principle and integrity, but was generally seen as being out of touch – yesterday's man. He was a none-too-successful cattle rancher, having had little practice in suburban London, and although he dabbled in local politics, he proved unfamiliar with local customs and ancient traditions. To make matters worse, he seemed to endlessly decline in health until incipient diabetes was diagnosed in 1960. Then, much to everyone's surprise, in 1961 he suddenly became energised as a nationalist politician.

The Bechuanaland Democratic Party (BDP) with Seretse at its head drew overwhelming support from rural progressives and conservatives alike. The liberal-democratic BDP swept aside its pan-Africanist and socialist rivals in the small railway towns that ran from the capital Gaborone to the second city Francistown to win the first universal franchise elections of 1965. Seretse became prime minister and then, on 30 September 1966, president of the Republic of Botswana. Unfortunately, President Khama and the new republic began with an international image problem. It was widely assumed that his country had no option but to sell out to its all-powerful white neighbours, South Africa, which still included South West Africa, today's Namibia, and Southern Rhodesia, now Zimbabwe.

Botswana was rightly believed to be the poorest country in Africa. All of the thirty poorest countries of the planet, with the exception of Bangladesh, are in Africa. A poor nation, of course, does not breed admiration and respect from other wealthier countries. In fact, it is rarely taken seriously. Presidents, particularly American ones, occasionally wafted through, deigning to spend a few hours there. In the 'developed' world, the opinion, one that has by no means disappeared today, seemed to be that Africa was a huge contradiction – on the one hand a dream – a white man's playground and a place of endless fascination and beauty, and on the other a nightmare – financially corrupt and decrepit. Underlying this was the rarely voiced but deeply ingrained prejudice that Africans were simply not equals to Westerners. In the early days, the new Botswanan government could not cover the costs of administration from taxes, and was continually and painfully indebted to Britain.

The first task of President Khama was to lay the ground-work for a self-supporting economy, based on beef-processing and copper and diamond mining. He then turned his personal attention to foreign policy, seeking out allies such as President Kaunda of Zambia to free Botswana from its image as a docile 'hostage' state. Using his unique authority to develop local democracy and quash the powers of traditional chiefs, he promoted the rule of law in the operations of the state.

Although for a time Botswana came to be described as a 'paternalist democracy' under the dominance of one political party, it succeeded in establishing itself as both prosperous and peaceful. Between 1966 and 1980, Botswana had, astonishingly, the fastest growing economy in the world. A magnificent epitaph for their first Premier. It also came to be seen as a remarkable state with high principles – upholding liberal democracy and racial harmony in the midst of a region embroiled in civil war, racial enmity and corruption. State mineral revenues were invested in infra-structural development, education, health and subsidies to cattle production. The result was a great increase in general prosperity in rural as well as urban areas.

Seretse was known for his intelligence and integrity, and a wicked sense of humour that punctured the pomposity of those who had too high an opinion of themselves. He also went through cycles of ill-health and depression, exacerbated by diabetes. His wife, Ruth Khama, remained the guardian of his health and homelife, and was an indomitable and much admired figure.

In his last years, Seretse looked increasingly outwards and onwards. He was one of the 'Front-Line Presidents' who negotiated the future of Zimbabwe and Namibia. He developed a vision of southern Africa after colonialism and apartheid that was peaceful, democratic and prosperous.

He was thus the key founder of what has since become the Southern African Development Community. The rigours of constant air travel for international negotiations leading to the independence of Zimbabwe finally exhausted Seretse, but he had the satisfaction of witnessing both that event in March 1980, and the launching of the Southern African Development Coordination Conference in April, before his death on 13 July 1980. He was buried in the Khama family graveyard, a simple plot on the hill at Serowe overlooking his birthplace.

Genuinely interested by Seretse's story, I quizzed Graham further but, like all good teachers, he had decided that enough was enough for one day.

'Let's have a chat about what's going on here then. I think you'll be interested,' he assured me, as he flipped some large steaks on the grill and I disappeared into another cloud of aromatic smoke.

Graham, as he had told me earlier, was the headmaster of a small church-run primary school. Although for the moment they had only seventy children on their books, over the last few years it had been rapidly expanding. When he had taken charge of the school eighteen months earlier it had been based in a former garage at the back of one of the stately, luxurious safari lodges. Although it had been brightly and comfortably decorated and the children appeared to have been provided with no end of resources, the premises were only on temporary loan and anyway were rapidly becoming too small.

The local government, pleased with the way that the school was being run, was happy to provide them with a new site in the residential area of town a little way up the hill – known either as the plateau, or 'platoo', as it was pronounced by the locals, or as Chinatown, for the simple reason that it had originally been built by Chinese workers. This plot was clearly of no inconsiderable value. Flat, and shaded by big trees, there was plenty of room for expansion. Already some second-hand prefabricated classrooms had been erected – single storey, with a tin roof and a little shabby, they were in distinct need of refurbishment. At some distance from the main buildings was a large wooden hut 'especially for the babies' – the Standard Ones, Janey's class. All the place needed was a lick of paint, Graham had said when he had taken me up to have a look the morning after the football match. It was not until later that evening that I fully realised what he had in mind.

Over a beer in a small but friendly bar-cum-restaurant, called The Old House, a few doors down from the supermarket, Graham outlined the plan that he had dreamt up for me. If I was interested in staying a little while in Kasane, they would be more than happy to have me along as a voluntary teacher of English and sport, and anything else that came to mind. He was very sorry but he didn't think that they would be able to pay me; however, they would let me have somewhere to stay and give me Maurio's Jeep to use for the duration of my stay. All this, of course, was based on the assumption that I wanted to get involved – something that until then I had not actually confirmed. But as I grew to realise, this was not a factor that would unduly worry a man like Graham. Some people have the gift to inspire, and he was such a man. Before I knew it, he had pulled me in to his great design, because, and this only struck my reserved English sensibility much later, he was willing to take a risk in life. On this occasion I was that risk, but as he kindly remarked, 'You have a nice sort of face, Will. You can tell a lot by a face.' I think he was probably right – at least about the last bit.

The school term was to finish in a couple of days' time and Graham and his family intended to spend the next three weeks staying with his parents in Johannesburg. On the understanding that he would receive references for me by fax, helpfully sent in by my former long-suffering employers, he invited me to make use of his house whilst he was away so I could explore the area. In exchange, I would be expected to help with the refurbishment of the school buildings into which they hoped to move at the beginning of the new term. He didn't imagine that it would involve too much, just collecting the paint and other materials, and making sure that the painters and decorators had food for lunch etc. Unbeknownst to him, this of course appealed to my new-found interest in all things culinary.

Anyway, he said, maybe I would like to sleep on it and give him an answer in the morning. He thought it might well work out to the benefit of everybody. I could stay for free in Africa and gain a better understanding of the place, something he, Graham, thought important for people the world over, and everyone at the school, I now realised, would be more than grateful for the extra pair of hands. Certainly, I did not feel any conscious or, however hard I dug, sub-conscious desire to return to England, let alone London, where I knew if I returned to teaching I would soon disappear through the crusty surface of the Slough of Despond. All that awaited me there was a murky world of drudgery in the company of my moaning colleagues. Ignored by the rest of society who were so busy that they did not have time to notice the perilous, parlous state of their schools, we would live out our days complaining about the playground supervision rota and failing to finish the crossword in the *Times Educational Supplement*. Fortunately, everyone decided to turn in before I was able to get up a full head of steam about the state of the UK education system, leaving me to fulminate alone and be soothed by the white light of the full moon that hung impassive and timeless over the Namibian plains.

The following morning, before I was asked to voice my decision, I was invited by Janey and Graham's two little girls to go to the end of term assembly and prize-giving. Please would I come? They were going to have a party afterwards and there would be lots of fizzy drinks, cake and sweets.

Fizzy drinks, I replied, sweets? Who could possibly refuse an invitation like that? Grimacing, I hunted around in the dark, somewhat malodorous depths of my bag for anything that resembled clean clothes.

When we arrived at what was now being referred to as the 'old school', the boys and girls were already arriving with their parents. All of them had dressed up in the smartest party outfits. Within minutes, of course, boys' shirts became untucked and even the odd hole appeared in the knee of a new pair of trousers, much to the parents' chagrin. The girls, however, made an altogether better attempt to keep themselves presentable before we went into the hangar that currently served as the schoolroom. Seated in neat rows on the floor, the children looked up expectantly at the teachers who were seated in chairs in front of them. My presence amongst their number did not seem to trouble any of them at all, preoccupied as they were with the excitements of the morning.

Somewhat to my surprise, I noticed that a wide range of ethnic groups were represented. Although most children were African, there were a number of white children from South Africa and Zimbabwe, two Chinese children and a little boy from the Indian subcontinent.

Assembly began with the singing of the school song *'Nokya ya Botselo'*; it was also the name of the school – 'The River of Life'. Sung partly in Setswana and partly in English, and with accompaniment on the piano by a large and enthu-siastic lady, it was surprisingly tuneful and extremely well sung. More than one parent, seated along the side of the room, became distinctly watery-eyed. Next on our pro-gramme was the national anthem, this time sung by the children standing smartly to attention, their eyes to the front, and hands placed proudly and firmly over hearts. *'Fatsho lena la rona'* – Blessed be this noble land. The musical effect was slightly spoiled by the patriotic efforts of the piano player, who sang so loudly as to drown out the combined efforts of everyone else. Despite this, I felt so drawn to the experience that I too found myself standing straight-backed and solemn. It was all conducted with a simple dignity and a pride that did not involve chest-beating expressions of self-satisfaction such as I had occa-sionally glimpsed in younger countries in both hemispheres. In one corner of the room stood the national flag: its two strips of blue denoting the sky and water and two thin strips of white and one thick strip of black representing the happy mix of peoples of differing skin colour.

The musical interlude over, a number of children stood up to report in English – for this was what was classed as an English medium school, and all lessons and activities were conducted in English – on the term's events, which seemed to have been impressively numerous. Football tournaments, netball games, swimming competitions, maths prizes, school camps, trips in every direction, choir practices, academic achievements and sporting triumphs all seemed to have played their part in the course of the term. Bearing in mind the isolated location of the school, I was deeply impressed that the efforts of the staff had provided all this for the children. To my surprise, I heard one little boy mention that his football team had been to a town called Ghanzi to play a match. On the road with Phil and company, we had passed through Ghanzi – a very remote outpost and a cattle station on the fringes of the Kalahari. I estimated that it must have been roughly 600 miles away.

Prizes were duly awarded, and I think each and every child had the chance to stand up and shake the hand of the pastor of the local church and receive his small neatly wrapped parcel. Eventually it was time for Graham to wish everyone a happy holiday and tell them how much he was looking forward to seeing them the following term.

'Oh, before we say our final prayer, let me introduce Mr Randall. He has come all the way from England to be with us today, and we very much hope that he will be joining us next term.'

All eyes were upon me.

'Don't you think it would be nice, children, if Mr Randall could join us next term and help us with our school?'

Loudly the children burst into a blackmailing round of applause as Graham turned to me, smiled and shrugged. Closing the lid of her piano, the music teacher turned and gave me an encouraging biff on the shoulder.

Well, I thought, as we went out under the shade of the trees and I gazed across the school grounds to the mirrored valley of the Chobe, here I go again. But this time there was almost no hesitation.

By the time that I had made it to the trestle table, no less than four parents had introduced themselves and their child or children to me, and had told me how pleased they were that I would be joining the school.

'*Dumela* Rra, *o tsoga jang!*' a smiling woman with extra-ordinarily intricately braided hair greeted me in the traditional manner: 'How did you rise this morning?' I was not sure I could remember. She was wearing a plain but elegant blouse and skirt, and copper African jewellery at her throat and on her wrist alongside a small but modern, digital wristwatch. 'This is my son, Arthur. I hope he will be a good boy.'

Standing in front of the woman, her hands round his neck, was her son smiling up at me shyly.

'He likes to work hard at school, don't you, Arthur? He likes to draw and paint. But if you have any trouble or any problem you can contact me anytime. I work at Builders' World. You know this place?'

Smiling, I shook my head and offered Arthur a virulently pink bun that someone had forced on me. He took it in the Batswana manner, placing his left hand on his right forearm as a sign of politeness and murmured, 'Thank you, Rra'.

'Never mind,' continued his mother. 'Here is my card with all my details. Email, cellphone. Just give me a ring anytime. Oh, here is my husband and Arthur's brother and sisters. This is Mr Rando. He will be a teacher here.'

A slight man had just wandered over with three or four very small children, the youngest barely toddling. When he shook my hand, we looked one another in the eye, and I realised in that first minute that something was badly wrong with him. From the immense fatigue written on his face, the pallor around his jaw and the slackness and dullness of his skin, I surmised that he was seriously ill. He attempted a brave front however, and bid me welcome to Kasane.

'We are very pleased to have you here with us and teaching at Nokya Ya Botselo.'

'Oh, yes, well, I am very pleased too,' I replied, frowning slightly as events hurtled ahead of me again. As I watched the boys kicking a football at some whitewashed posts, and the girls skipping and singing whilst the teachers chatted amiably with the other parents, I was reminded of happy days teaching back at home. When conditions are right, teaching is the most satisfying, occasionally, even, the most thrilling, of professions. Of course, I also knew from fairly bitter experience that when conditions are wrong it can also be the most depressing and debilitating of jobs. Here, though, I instinctively knew that all was well. You could tell simply from the expressions on the children's faces.

Hell, why not stay for a while? This was certainly the first time I had been to a speech day and prize-giving that was attended by a tribe of mongeese, a family of warthogs, a couple of circling eagles and a distant but attentive buffalo. It would be a pleasure, a privilege, to spend some time here at Nokya Ya Botselo.

Graham chuckled as he handed me a cup of squash that appeared to contain Agent Orange. 'Knew you would go for it. Always get a gut feeling for a good teacher. I'm very pleased you showed up.'

Laughing, I agreed. When a little boy, whose name it transpired was Blessings, came up to me, took my hand, asked me to be Manchester and then dragged me onto the football pitch, suddenly I felt very lucky.

Three weeks of holiday gave me ample time to get my bearings in and around Kasane. Invariably described as a village, it was really more like a small town with a population of some ten thousand people. The main street followed the course of the river running from east to west, and as well as the shops and offices that lined it on either side there were a number of grand safari lodges, their lawns and rooms looking out on to the banks of the river. Invariably populated by white, Western clients, they were in lavish contrast to the local accommodation that ran back up the hill to the plateau. Running along the ridge of the hill was an attractive housing development, comprising small, squarish wooden and brick bungalows each surrounded by its own small garden and metal-link fence. Each house had access to all the normal local amenities, electricity, running water and mains sewerage. Although the majority of people did not own a car there was a system of small white minibuses that ferried workers from the offices and hotels back up the hill to home. Like so many places that I encountered in Botswana, once you left the perimeter of the town there was little habitation in any direction for some hundred miles. Surrounded on all sides by the bush, Kasane was to all intents and purposes built in the middle of a wildlife park.

The town itself was in a unique position, sitting at the meeting point of four different countries – Botswana, Zambia, Namibia and Zimbabwe – and at the confluence of two major rivers – the Chobe and the Zambezi. As the administrative capital of the Chobe District, the gateway to Chobe National Park and a stopover for travellers on the way to Victoria Falls, Kasane, once nothing more than an outpost for hunters, herdsmen and missionaries, was slowly and quite deliberately developing.

As a result, despite its isolated position, it was easier than I expected to purchase the materials required to decorate the new school. Builders' World, a large warehouse selling building materials of all varieties, stood opposite the marketplace. Owned by an Indian, who turned out to be the father of the little boy I had seen at the school, it was also the place of work of Mma Kebalakile, Arthur's mum and the chief accountant. Coincidentally, the name of the store was the same as that of the sponsors of Silverford Town's football league, but I never did discover whether there was a connection. The warehouse received regular deliveries from the more substantial towns of Francistown and Maun several times a week. In theory, at least, this would make our job easier.

I had gleaned all this information from the foreman of the painting and decorating team, who turned out, to my considerable surprise, to be none other than Clever, my new friend from the road accident. He was no less surprised to see me, and considerably more embarrassed. No mention at all was made of motoring matters at our first meeting, except that he admitted that the car he had been driving had in fact belonged to his cousin who not unexpectedly was no longer very keen to lend it to him. This indirectly meant that my role in the proceedings became increasingly important because I still had possession of Maurio's now somewhat battered Jeep. (Much later, Clever did disclose that most of his earnings over the next few weeks would go directly to the garage to pay for the eventual repairs.) Without my vehicle, any equipment and supplies would have to be carried from the town to the school – a two-mile uphill slog.

Embarrassingly, it transpired that in the minds of the workforce – who numbered anything between three and seven depending on the day and on their other commitments – I, by simple possession of the car keys, de facto became the boss. This, needless to say, was a role that I was in no way qualified to take. What also became increasingly clear to my great discomfort, a discomfort that would remain with me throughout my stay in Africa, was that my fellow workers found it only too easy to accept me in this new position because I was white. At that moment, I realised how profoundly and indelibly the colonial history of the last two centuries had subjugated African people. Somehow, without even realising that it was happening, individuals, particularly poorly educated ones, allowed Westerners to call the shots, despite efforts by certain governments to adjust the balance. I wished then, as now, that this was not so.

As everybody seemed to be keen to go for a ride on that first day, we all headed down the hill to the builders' merchant. Clever had made what turned out to be a very accurate calculation as to the amount of paint that we would require and had already decided on the colour scheme – green for the roof and doors, a pale, sandy brown for the outside walls and cool, clean white for the classrooms – all in keeping with the natural environment. Rollers, brushes, sandpaper, paint trays and thinners were all loaded into the Jeep.

'And now, let's get the important things,' announced Clever, smacking his lips, and with that we all marched off to the supermarket. 'What would you like to cook us then?'

Graham had left me a small amount of Pula – which means 'rain' in Setswana, rather neatly denoting its impor-tance – money that had been provided by the church found-ation that had created the school and funded its day-to-day running. His intention was that we might be able to purchase supplies for lunch rather than waste too much time going home and coming back. Unfortunately, I had next to no idea of what to buy.

'What do you all like to eat then?'

'*Bogobe!*'

Once it had been explained to me what that was, we purchased a 25kg sack of sorghum flour.

'Meat!'

A tall ceiling-to-floor refrigerator was filled with a variety of cuts of a variety of animals – as well as those that I recog-nised, there were others that I could not imagine in life let alone in death: impala, kudu, and four or five other types of antelope. The team chose some very scrappy, fatty cuts of beef which I noticed were no less expensive than top-quality steaks.

'Vegetables!'

Carrots, cabbage, greens and turnips all seemed to be readily available.

'And cakes!' requested Gabamukuni, a teenager with a sweet tooth that seemed to be shared by everybody else.

'Yes, for our tea-break!' I agreed, and we stocked up on iced buns at the 'Hot Bread' bakery.

Once I had worked out, with careful guidance, how to prepare *'bogobe'*, a type of porridge made from sorghum flour, cooked in a big saucepan on an open fire and served with a meat and vegetable stew, work began in earnest on the redecoration of the school. It was a hot, dirty, messy undertaking. Little by little, however, the buildings began to look more presentable. Fortunately, running water was available from the two shower blocks at the back of the building, and soon after everyone arrived I would start to build my fire, stirring my porridge and laying the table under the trees that surrounded the buildings. At about 12 o'clock everyone knocked off. It reminded me of eating in France, although the food was finished off in record time and there was a singular lack of red wine.

No sooner had the meal been consumed than everyone would find their comfortable little corner for a snooze – for what would lunch be without a siesta? My pampered bones were quite incapable of finding comfort in the positions assumed by the others, and more often than not I would have to resort to the back seat of the Jeep.

Naturally, the longer that we worked together, the better we knew one another, but what was so pleasing initially was that I was never treated with any suspicion. These men were so good-natured that they were willing to take me at face value, and as long as I was considerate of them, so were they of me. Before long they were asking me all manner of questions about my life in England. How old was I? How long had I been a teacher? Was I married?

When I replied no to the latter, there ensued a lengthy if somewhat earthy conversation about who would best suit me. They all seemed to know someone who would be just perfect.

In turn, I learnt a great deal about their own home lives. Most seemed to be deeply religious. Christians all, they appeared to belong to completely different denominations. Rivalry between churches seemed to be like rivalry between football teams. In order to join in, I purported to support the Church of England as I do, let us say, Aston Villa. Despite professing their belief in a Christian God, many of these men were also deeply superstitious – each offering their own different solutions to problems. When one day Clever complained of a headache, due mainly to having to breathe the intoxicating fumes of the paint in the hot class-rooms all day, a variety of suggestions were put forward about how he might best cure himself, which involved amongst other things standing on his head, eating some disgusting concoction – the main ingredient of which seemed to be some kind of rotting fish – or, and this was the remedy that he chose, to drive out to a salt pan and drink deeply of the brackish water there. The resulting vomiting would apparently cure him in a trice. As we drove back to the school that afternoon, he professed himself very happy with the results.

Sadly, it became clear that young Gabamukuni's ill health was not going to be cured by such a simple treatment. Gabamukuni, a young, trendy man with a penchant for American tracksuits, trainers and rather outlandish bandanas that he tied around his head and low over his eyes, was in fact the school groundsman, who would be moving to this site with the children at the beginning of the new term. As well as helping Clever, he had already created attractive areas of lawn and pricked out perennial plants in square flowerbeds – the orderly neatness of the arrangements made all the more striking by the surrounding wilderness. Gabamukuni was a friendly soul, always helpful, but quiet, and this I had initially put down to shyness. Soon, however, I began to suspect that perhaps he was suffering from something much more serious. Although he was barely out of his teens, he seemed to tire remarkably easily and often dozed after a lunch that he barely picked over. When one day I found him convulsed with a coughing fit which had stained the bandana that he held to his mouth with thick, dark blood, Clever and I took him to a clinic some few hundred yards down the road in a small shopping complex. When he returned some days later, he flashed a bottle of tablets at me but seemed unready to discuss the matter further. His colleagues displayed a not unkind indifference, and it was only to be some little while later that I fully understood the matter.

Occasionally, in the evenings, the gang would invite me to go and drink in their local bar, The Cool Joint, which was tucked just round the corner from the builders' merchant. When they said drink, that was precisely what they meant. Sadly, the London Missionary Society's aims were not to be upheld. Never have I seen so much beer carried in through the back door in bottles and out through the front in stomachs. Fortunately, I only needed to totter across the road to Graham's house afterwards and avoid being savaged by the two dogs, who were most inappropriately called Bambi and Lady.

My relationship with these two did not improve over my short stay with them, but when they realised that I was the purveyor of their evening meal, they tolerated me and did not try to kill and eat me. Sometimes, in order to put a little safe distance between me and them, I would take myself to The Old House where I had been on my first evening with Graham. The building itself had been rescued from an old mine and had been rebuilt stone by stone in its present location on the side of the river. There was a pleasant shady garden and a tasty menu.

Being in close proximity to the safari lodges, the pub had rather more western customers than local ones. One common denominator shared by all the expatriates amongst them was their alarming oddness. Afrikaner, British South African, Zimbabwean (or Rhodesian as some of them still rather ludicrously chose to call themselves more than twenty years after independence), British, French, German, Dutch, Chinese and Indian drinkers all congregated here to outdo one another with extraordinary tales of their adventures in Africa – the bullshit quotient was high and many a passing tourist left feeling giddy, amazed by tales of derring-do that were based more on fantasy than fact. Many could trace their family's presence in southern Africa back many generations but, almost without exception, they appeared to float on the surface of modern Botswanan society like small, tentative insects on a great pond, eager to discover what of value lay below the surface of the water, but at the same time terrified that they might be sucked under and subsumed. Most arrived with their own and left at the end of the evening in the same company. Although the native Batswana carried on enjoying themselves regardless, there was a clear intention on the part of the white minority that never the twain should meet. On the occasions that there was some interaction between a local person and an expatriate, more often than not, at the end of the conversation, blue eyes would be raised heavenward and then knowingly make contact with a compatriot's as if to say, 'Yes, I know we're right, you and me.' This rejection, this animosity, this petty and graceless insularity marred some of my days in Africa and I will never forget it nor come to accept it.

The bar itself was run by a couple, Oliver, an amiable German very fond of his *Wurst*, and his Chinese wife, Boan, who managed to keep some sort of order even in the early hours of the morning.

Many expatriates came in droves to relate daring exploits of hunting from four-wheel-drive vehicles armed with ultra-high-powered rifles. I was introduced to a number of them, but when I didn't express any great enthusiasm for big-game hunting they quickly gave up on me and turned in on themselves.

'It was the greatest shot I've ever seen when I took out that giraffe. Do you remember? Must have been about thirty yards with a .272. Went for the heart shot, and it nearly exploded. That's hunting, my *bru*.' Colossal and drunk, the heavy-lidded, bearded man wiped his beery mouth with the palm of his hand and reached it out towards me. 'What's your name, my *bru*?' he asked for the third time.

'Will,' I squirmed as he slapped his wet paw around my nervously proffered hand.

'Yes, and it's made the most *beeeautiful* rug, it's so soft and lovely. I won't even let our maid walk on it; it is *soo* precious to me. Dirk shot it just for me, didn't you, my darling?' The man's blindingly blonde wife caressed his beard and stomach, and kissed him on one hairy ear.

'Yes, just for you, Karen,' he replied stroking one of her red-nail-varnished talons. Her dewlaps waggled with delight.

'But Will, you'll never guess what.'

'What?' I asked, repulsed.

Karen leant towards me confidentially. 'My maid is *soooo* lazy. You know she never even washes the floors before I get up.' And with that revelation she continued to massage various of her husband's spongy extremities.

The more I saw of Dirk and his wife Karen, the more appalled I was by them but, I am sorry to admit it, the more fascinated I became too. There was something of the *grand guignol* about them. Their sons, Edwin and Erwin, were if anything worse. Bloodthirsty chain-smokers in their early twenties, they were most likely to be seen with a beer can in one hand and a pump-action shotgun in the other. Although Botswana had strict legislation concerning wildlife and game which included comprehensive hunting seasons and lists of protected species, it did not seem to be of great concern to this arrogant pair, who, most people were sure, treated the country as their own adventure park.

'Hey, Pa, come and look what we got in the *bakkie*. You'll never guess what. We just clipped it and it broke its neck. It's a big kudu.' Edwin, the older but slighter of the two, who both looked like mongrel lurchers with lank, longish hair, engine-grease-stained jeans and offensive t-shirts, walked into The Old House one evening, his arm bloody to the elbow.

Despite his bulk, Dirk shifted surprisingly swiftly off his stool and lumbered through the door into the night. Before long he was back and in earnest conversation with a number of his friends, who swiftly struck a financial deal with him. As they left Edwin and Erwin dispensed selected cuts of dripping meat which were thrown onto sacks in the backs of pick-up trucks before picking up a fine coating of African dust as they were driven home.

At the end of the night, father and sons were burbling drunk. Karen had had to be taken home some hours earlier by a neighbour as she was barely continent. As I made to leave and was paying Boan for my food, I overheard the boys imploring their father to recount for the third time that evening the story of how he, Dirk, had shot a 'kaffir', a Namibian, who had been rowing across the Chobe. He had been certain that the 'moona' had been on his way to steal from him – 'they always steal, it's their way' – and so had reached for his rifle – 'Mauser .272. Beautiful weapon' – aimed and pulled the trigger. He had been pretty sure that he had hit his target. 'Trouble is, it was dark, and you can't see them at night unless they're smiling at you.'

I was to endure another encounter with Dirk when I was working on the school renovation. Clever and I had been in a bit of a rush to get the classrooms finished off before the beginning of term, but once we were satisfied with the redecoration we were able to pay off the team. Then we had been faced with the quite serious task of moving fixtures, fittings, furniture and books from the old place up to the new. Although there was nothing particularly complicated about the job it turned into an experience considerably more disagreeable then I had imagined. An experience that, sadly, I was to encounter only too regularly while I lived in Africa.

Clearly, if we used only my Jeep to ferry everything from A to B we would never be finished in time. Kindly, and I suspect partly because we had put a great deal of business his way, Mr Hussein, the owner of Builders' World, was willing to lend us a flatbed lorry which, if loaded properly, would get the job done in two or three trips. Unfortunately, due to its size, it required a driver in possession of an HGV licence and he would not be able to spare any of his men. He was very sorry but he could not help us.

One evening, in The Old House, I inquired of Oliver, the manager, whether he knew anybody who had the kind of truck we needed and, more to the point, a licence.

'Well, you could try Dirk. I know he used to have a licence. Buy him a couple of beers and I'm sure he'll help you out with a good price. Oh, look, here he comes now. Dirk! Come here, my *bru*. This young chap needs a hand tomorrow. You still got your old truck and your lorry licence, isn't it? Will, this is Dirk.'

'Yes, I know, I remember,' I replied, with what I hoped was not too obvious a sigh.

Dirk looked down at me slightly aggressively, breathing heavily through his nose before sucking hard on a tar-black cigar.

'What is it you want from me?'

Rather tentatively, I explained my dilemma. We didn't have too much money, I explained, but I could help out moving stuff and get a few guys to help out. He named a price and I agreed. It seemed fair.

'All right, meet me here at seven tomorrow morning, right?'

'Good, that's great. Thank you. See you tomorrow.'

I bolted.

Early the next day – the only time to do anything physical because of the heat – we turned up outside The Old House.

'Ah, good morning! Glad to see you've got some boys to help out.' He climbed into the front of the truck as he spat black cigar tar over the wheel hub.

Gabamukuni, who although still on the mend had insisted on coming along, was certainly young, but I wasn't sure that Clever and Barolong, his brother, necessarily fitted into the category of 'boys', both being at least my age. Between them they were fathers to half a dozen children.

Dirk invited me to sit in the front seat of the lorry and directed the three 'boys' to climb into the open back. In near silence, we bounced out onto the main road as I looked at the empty seat between us.

When we reached the Old School, Dirk poured himself a cup of tea from a thermos that he had brought with him and positioned himself in the shade from where he directed operations. This was fine. I had not asked him to get involved in furniture-removing, only in driving the truck.

As I had half-expected, Gabamukuni became quickly exhausted and, in his normal quiet tone, asked me whether I would mind if he sat down and rested for a while.

'What is his problem? Why is he being so lazy. Get back and work. Hurry!'

Gabamukuni looked in dismay at Dirk who was waving his arms at him.

'It's OK, er . . . Dirk. He isn't feeling too good right now.' I winked at Gabamukuni who retreated.

Dirk grunted and slurped noisily at his tea.

Once the three of us had emptied the contents of one classroom, Dirk suggested that Clever and Barolong start to load up the tables, chairs and cupboards. Meanwhile I set about taking down the various decorations from the walls. Suddenly through the open window I heard the most terrible commotion. Somebody had dropped a table and it landed in the dust on the other side of the truck.

Dirk exploded.

'Ach, man! Why didn't you listen to what I said? Didn't you hear what I said? Why don't you listen? Is it because you are stupid? Are you a bit stupid? Yes, stupid. I'm asking you. Don't you even understand English? You blacks, you're all the same. You don't listen when some-body gives you instructions. That's why you're always fuck-ing it up. And not only are you thick but you're also lazy. Now get your black butt down off the truck and pick up the table, and put it where I said you should put it. Jesus. Fucking unbelievable. Come on. Move it. I don't want you to hold me up because you are stupid and lazy . . .'

And he went on and on and on. Drawn by the noise to the open window, as I looked out I quite by chance caught Barolong's eye. His face was etched with what seemed like not just a lifetime's but generations of resignation. There was scarcely a trace of anger, only weariness. Aghast, I stepped back into the room, unable to look him in the face, but worse, far worse, incapable of doing anything to make the situation better. Blushing profoundly, I busied myself pulling out drawing pins and posters with bleeding nails whilst work resumed outside in near silence.

Dirk's anger and the resulting antagonism were palpable when eventually our first load was ready. In some sign of silent solidarity, I climbed onto the back of the truck with the others. Somehow we managed to complete the deliveries without any further outbursts from him, yet still I felt sick about my cowardice in not having said anything when he had treated the two men so shabbily. I felt sicker still when, at the end of the day, I had to shake his hand and thank him for his help.

'Dirk, um, thanks for everything,' I started as I handed over the zebra-patterned Pula notes, my hands shaking with disgust.

'Don't give me any of your shit.' He breathed in a gust of choking smoke from the wet, frayed butt of cigar. 'You're not even an African.'

He turned his huge back on me and grunted as he strode off.

Some of the sting that remained after this unpleasant episode was salved later by the clear pleasure that the children took from their new surroundings when the new term started. And once I had learnt how to skirt around the ropes, such disagreeable interludes were kept, by my design, to a minimum. Soon, as had happened on my trip from Cape Town, life in Kasane became quite normal – or at least the surprises that everyday life threw up became quite normal. More often than not, it was the natural world that proved itself to be the most unpredictable and capable of completely disrupting what otherwise might have settled into a regular pattern. That was certainly part of the reason why I came to love Africa so quickly and so deeply, although there were occasions when I would have been happy to have flopped back into the comfort zone of routine.

Before I knew it, the first morning of the new term came around and with a measure of 'new boy' nervousness, I set about deciding what would be the most suitable attire for my first day at school. I all but dropped my best shorts when Lady and Bambi set off the most appalling racket. Naively, I opened the door only to discover a King Kong-sized baboon bearing down on me followed by the two horrible hounds. Just in the nick of time I managed to slam the door shut, upon which it received three resounding, crashing thuds. There ensued a horrible silence.

Several minutes later, I slowly opened the door. Veering somewhat unsteadily one way and then the other, the baboon was lolloping back up the driveway holding its bumped head, whilst Lady and Bambi whimpered quietly in need of urgent sympathy. I locked the front door behind me and made my way to my Jeep, quite unable to wipe away the smile of satisfaction that had spread across my face.

7

First Days at School

Marvelling at the new school, with its airy bright classrooms and wide open grounds, the children scampered around in high excitement that first morning of the new term. Many of them, unused to so much space, confined as they had been to the garage premises of the old school, contented themselves by stretching out their arms like airplane wings and flying around the newly marked-out football pitch and netball court making the most authentic Spitfire engine noises.

Finally, when I rang a large brass bell in impressive town-crier fashion and Graham clapped his hands, the children lined up in ordered rows in front of their classroom doors according to their age. When finally they had stopped fidgeting, dusting themselves down, wiping the sweat from their brows and doing up buttons that had come undone in the excitement, all became calm.

'Good morning, children!'

'Good morning, teachers!'

'How are you all today?'

'I'm fine and how are you?'

This sing-song exchange, a daily one, was to become

almost the signature tune to my stay in Africa. It rushed me back to my own time at primary school, when children, for the main part untroubled by outside concerns, had all arrived with one common purpose. Everyone was here today wanting to join in, wanting to be a part of the whole community that is a successful school. Here, I found an organisation that was almost perfect in terms of size, scale and location – children that a teacher could give individual attention to, in an environment that promoted learning.

After Graham had welcomed all the children back for the new term, he explained a few minor changes to the rules and regulations, which had mainly to do with school uniform, the complexities of which I failed to grasp – something to do with black shoes with shorts but not tracksuits, and white socks with plimsolls, and grey socks with sandals. That done, he reintroduced me to the school.

I had momentarily forgotten the genuine open-heartedness and friendliness of children, particularly these children. For when Graham announced that I would be helping out for the foreseeable future, they broke into spontaneous applause, one or two of the smaller ones jumping up and down with excitement. Half embarrassed, half delighted, I grinned until it hurt. My pleasure was only increased when the children entered their classrooms and squealed with excitement when they noticed that their pictures, paintings, models and toys had all been displayed on the freshly painted walls and newly installed shelving. There was a fairly unholy uproar as everyone vied for the best seat in the house. Eventually calm was restored using strict alphabetical order.

That first morning was spent on minor administrative matters. Graham showed me how to operate the photo-copying machine, the computer and how to get an outside line on the telephone. He had brought with him the sporting equipment, which we stored in an empty classroom: bats, balls, gloves, stumps and a selection of brightly coloured hula-hoops. Whilst we were discussing the curriculum that they used in the school, I practised with a bright green one to demonstrate that I had not lost that old magic.

At mid-morning break, the headmaster introduced me to the rest of the staff. This did not take long. Janey I already knew, of course, although I had not noticed, because I don't very often, that she was quite considerably pregnant. She was the Standard One teacher, responsible for a class of six-year-olds. This not negligible task was shared by the charming and maternal Elizabeth, three of whose own children attended the school, and who more often than not was to be found patching up an article of clothing or wiping down a small child, sweeping up pencil shavings or making cups of tea.

Kibonye, a tall striking woman, taught Standard Two, and was also responsible for the teaching of Setswana. Standard Three was taught by the elderly and rather deaf Mrs Sichilongo, and I now recognised her as also being the teacher responsible for the somewhat strident singing and piano playing at the end of the last term. Seemingly contra-dictorily, she was at the same time great friends and in furious competition with a white Zimbabwean lady called Mrs Krantz, who was of a similar age and manner. She was the Standard Four teacher – a class that she told me at our first meeting, with a meaningful glance at Mrs Sichilongo, was full of 'very able students – some of the best in the school'.

Professional to the tips of their sticks of chalk, all my new colleagues were happily unencumbered by legislation and form-filling and therefore free to teach. As I was soon to discover, they also did not have to contend with the fall-out of the schisms in the nuclear family that so often ruined the chances of schools and their pupils succeeding back at home. Behavioural problems, so prevalent among pupils in the UK, were refreshingly absent. Of course, some youngsters were good at some things, some more able at others, some were just plain brilliant at everything, and then there was the minority – always my favourites – who found everything a bit of a struggle.

My colleagues were surprisingly similar to those I had known at home. Most of our conversations together in the staffroom-cum-sports store revolved around our pupils, their progress or lack of it, their character, their families and other school matters. When our discussions strayed away from school, I was of course reminded that we were living in a remote and often fairly wild environment. Kibonye and her English husband, Simon, ran a small guest-house further along the plateau, and fairly often she appeared at school in a state of exhaustion. Hardly had they and their young son Lele gone to bed than a herd of elephants that roamed the forest nearby would arrive at their garden gate and, rather than disturb them, would just knock it down and head enthusiastically for Kibonye's flowerbed. So often had this happened that Simon was becoming almost obsessive in his attempts to dissuade them from entering. He had built a solid wall some five feet high around his entire compound, and the elephants had stayed away for the five days that it had taken him to build it. Simon had a small party to celebrate this construction on the evening he finished it. By the following morning it had been reduced to rubble. Cheaper by far were the saucepan and ladle that they kept under the bed to scare away the intruders, but after a couple of weeks they were not only redundant, as the elephants had become used to them, but were causing the family tinnitus until midday the follow-ing day. Over a considerable number of break times, we heard about Simon's new career as a sapper, as he was now placing large explosives at strategic points about his garden. I think this was finally abandoned when he accidentally blew the postman off his bike.

Mrs Sichilongo liked to reminisce about her late husband who had died a few years earlier from the bite of a black mamba. Her story, which she repeated almost verbatim about twice a week while she knitted endless woollen clothes, always finished with the line, 'And you know why it is called the black mamba? Because it is black? No, for it is green. No, because it has a black inside to its mouth! Never forget.' I have not.

Often we talked of local politics or African matters – particularly the economic crisis in Zimbabwe, where there was no longer any bread or petrol, and where gin cost twenty-five pence a bottle on the burgeoning black market. Victoria Falls was now, as I would soon discover, a ghost town, and Mrs Krantz would often drive over the border to take cakes and scones, that she had baked that morning before school, to her maiden aunt who still lived there.

Graham, as well as being responsible for the day-to-day running of the school and its administration, was the classroom teacher for Standards Five and Six, who were taught together in the same room, and it was to their first lesson after break on the first morning of the new term that he took me for a feverish question and answer session.

How did I like Botswana? How had I travelled there? What was the best thing that I had seen during my visit? How long was I staying? (Here I had no answer.) Inevitably, *what was my favourite football team?* And when I had answered all these questions, at least several dozen more and the bell had rung, *would I like to go out and play with them?* Exhausted by the lesson, having forgotten the demands of classroom teaching, I gently declined, and plonked myself down in one of their chairs.

'So,' asked Graham with interest. 'How did you find them, my youngsters?'

'Eager! Really on the ball, aren't they? I think I shall enjoy teaching them. You know what's refreshing? In comparison to kids I have taught at home they seem so genuinely enthusiastic about their lives. So curious to know more, to find out about things. And you know how much easier that makes our lives! Perhaps they're a little more naive than other kids their age, but that's certainly no criticism. No, I shall certainly much enjoy teaching them. What do they do now?'

For the rest of the afternoon, the older children were to have a choir practice with Mrs Sichilongo, and the younger ones an art class with Kibonye.

'Now might be a good time to make ourselves scarce,' grinned Graham. 'I suspect that it won't be a quiet afternoon. Anyway, there are a few things that we still need to get sorted out for you.'

He climbed into my car, leaving his own for his wife and daughters to use later, and I followed his directions as we headed out of town in the direction of Kazungula and the ferry to Zambia.

'So where are we off to?'

'Well, I thought we ought to see if we couldn't find you your own house to stay. I mean you're more than welcome to stay with us, but it might be nice for you to have your own space. Also, I think you're going to like this place. In fact, I'm not sure that I'm not rather jealous! Here, here, turn left just here!'

Skidding in a secretly rather pleasing way, I brought the Jeep off the road and onto a small track that bisected an orchard of mango trees. Rutted and overgrown with wiry weeds, it did not look as if it was in regular use. On all sides the trees were heavy with pendulous green fruit just beginning to blush yellow and red, and zooming in and out of them as if in an enormous maze were thousands of birds. Clearing the orchard we turned right onto an even more overgrown path, as we did so startling a young water-buck, whose white rear end shone in the dappled light like a target, its legs kicking with fright as it leaped away over a small hedge.

Flickering away to my right through the blur of trees was the silver water of the Chobe River. In places it splashed and frothed over flat rocks as if approaching some rapids. There was now no longer any view of the road and although we were not far from it, it felt like we had slipped into a secret natural world. A few hundred metres further down the path we came across a rectangular, man-made clearing, its fringes planted with ornamental bushes and tall trees. In the middle of the plot was what appeared to be a very large mobile home standing up on blocks two or three feet above the ground. At Graham's direction we pulled into a small carport to one side of the building and walked up the two or three wooden steps to a wire mesh door.

'What do you think? Nice spot, isn't it?'

'It most certainly is.' Looking around me, I realised that a great deal of work had gone into the creation of this garden – it really was a tiny paradise. Birds flitted in and out of a small pond that appeared to be fed by some under-ground spring.

'So, who does it belong to? Isn't there anybody here?'

I noticed that Graham appeared to be in possession of the keys. He fiddled around until the door finally came open.

'Well,' he appeared a little hesitant. 'It belongs to a good friend of ours from Johannesburg. In fact it's because of him that we ever ended up here in the first place. He heard about the job and we applied for it. He's been here for quite a while. He was the guy who sorted this garden out. When he got here it was just bush. Built this place too.'

'Oh, I see,' I replied, wondering what the outcome of this tale would be as we walked into a comfortable if slightly creaky living room.

'Yeah, so last month, must have been just before you arrived, he got into his car and a black mamba had climbed through the window and was wrapped around the steering column. Poor bloke didn't see it until it got him in the neck.'

'Oh my God! Was it big? I mean was he OK? What happened after that? Where did this happen?' I remembered the fate of poor Mrs Sichilongo's husband.

Graham laughed, I thought rather inappropriately.

'Well, it happened about where your car is right now! They had to airlift him to Gaborone, you know, the capital. He's more comfortable now but for a while he was paralysed down one side of his body. And then he got some pretty nasty abscesses. He's going to be laid up for a while, but all he's worried about is somebody breaking into his house. You look through there.'

We looked out across the Chobe.

'That's Namibia there. So it's a bit exposed here. Mind you, I think he's just a little paranoid. Loads of these expats are . . . Beautiful, isn't it?' he continued in his nonchalant way.

Gazing over his shoulder, I agreed it was stunning, although I was somewhat taken aback by the half dozen or so large, dozing crocodiles on the slick, grey mudbanks. 'You'll love it here. Can you imagine what a great spot this would be to live? Come on, where are you going? Have a look around at the rest of the place.'

The dangers presented by both animals and possibly humans drew me back to the car and thereby back to the road and the village and the comfort of the houses and the shops. But as I glanced down the river-bank, keeping a watchful eye out for canoe-borne marauders, I realised what a unique opportunity this was. To live on the shores of one of Africa's great rivers in the midst of a huge wildlife sanctuary was a matchless chance to experience all that this corner of the world had to offer.

As well as the pretty living room with its creaky wooden veranda that looked out across the lawn, the river and further on to the plains of Namibia, there was a bright, airy bedroom with mosquito nets at all the windows and a teak airplane-propeller fan hanging from the ceiling. Down two shallow steps, a low doorway opened into a smart, clean bathroom, and through an arch at the far side of the living room was a spacious, if slightly old-fashioned kitchen containing a large heavy dining table and six plain chairs.

Outside on the lawn was a set of incongruously English garden furniture, even including a shaded, swinging bench seat, and built into a framework of bricks was the inevitable *braai*. While Graham busied himself poking around in cupboards, checking to see what I would need to bring with me, I stood on the veranda and listened. The noise of the natural world seemed to surround this little hideaway, completely enclosing it. Although my ears were at this early stage quite unattuned to the individual sounds that I was hearing, I sensed the vibrancy of the jungle, the living, breathing world into which, it appeared, I was about to move. Sensual and real, certainly, but also just a little bit scary.

'Well, you might as well move in straight away!' laughed Graham. 'The only thing you'll have to get is a good torch and some candles. Apparently, they're forever having power cuts down here even though it's on the mains. The elephants are always knocking down the power lines when they come down to the river and drink.'

'Drink here?'

What was I getting into?

'Yeah, sure. They love it down here. Look over there; you can see where they've been.'

Forty or fifty yards away, a patch of blackish earth had been reduced to a small swamp, and all around it the trees had been stripped of their bark. Irregular straw-coloured lumps of dung about the size and shape of deflated foot-balls littered the ground.

'Yeah, you'll see them all the time but they never seem to do too much damage, at least, not to people. Unfortunately, they do seem to make a bit of a mess of the trees. Now listen, let's get going, I've got another small surprise for you. Well, actually, it's quite a big one.'

Mystified, I drove us back into Kasane and followed Graham's directions until we arrived in front of the white weather-boarded Baptist church. Getting out, we wandered around to the back of the building, which comprised the small vicarage and an ancient lean-to garage. Graham hammered on the door of the vicarage, and in a little while a small girl, her hair teased into two huge bunches over her ears which made her look like a junior member of the cast of an American sci-fi series, opened it and looked shyly out.

Automatically realising the reason for our visit, she darted inside and called for her mother who, shuffling out into the yard in a pair of busted slippers, greeted us cheerily in the sing-song manner that had become so familiar.

'*Dumela*, Rra!'

'*Dumela*, Mma!'

'How are you?'

'I'm fine, and you?'

With a huge bunch of keys in one hand, she grabbed the padlock on the garage door and began to work her way through all the possible options. Typically, it was the last of these fifty or so keys that proved to be correct. Her job done, not waiting for us to open the doors, she plodded back into the house, from where I could hear the noise of a raucous television quiz.

'So what do you think of her?' Graham asked, after he had swung, with no inconsiderable effort, the recalcitrant garage doors open. 'Isn't she a beauty?'

'She' was indeed. Probably some twenty years old and – as I had once been described myself by an old and valued friend – 'high mileage', a bit bashed and bruised, covered in the droppings of pretty much the full range of African birdlife, and thick with dust and hay that had tumbled down from the loft above, she was still magnificent. Indeed, she fitted into the local landscape almost as naturally as any of the innumerable creatures out there. This 2.8-litre diesel Toyota Land Cruiser had been designed with the African bush in mind. The flatbed at the back had been converted into seating, and was covered with a corrugated tin hard-top with three large sliding windows down either side. This was the kind of vehicle that adventures were designed for and which should never see a city street. It was born for the great outdoors.

Soon to be nicknamed 'the Old Queen Mum', being white, fairly elderly, rather slow, much admired and drinking like a fish, the car became almost as central to my African experiences as all my other friends and acquaintances. She, unbeknownst to her at that given moment, was to travel further afield in the next few months than she had in the previous ten years. Her hibernation in this shed had lasted for nearly four years. To our great delight, once

Graham had reconnected the battery, and I had flicked the key, she started up. Admittedly, she puffed and groaned and wheezed and whined, but she started up, ejecting thick, sooty clouds of fumes like an elderly smoker having her first fag of the day. Owned by an American missionary who had returned to Detroit some years before, and who was keeping her in storage on the off chance he might come back, she had been sorely under-used.

Not only was there room to seat at least ten people, but piled high on the roof under a rotting green canvas similarly spattered with guano, was everything that you might ever require for a safari in the African bush: tents, beds, tables, chairs, covers, knives and forks, water tanks, cookers, cooking utensils – there was even a half-empty packet of now sadly stale Popsicles.

With this discovery, I was suddenly engulfed by a worryingly dangerous sense of excitement. As we washed her down with the help of buckets of soapy water and the enthusiastic assistance of the small *Star Trek* girl, and as we pumped up one tired-looking tyre and checked the levels of water, oil and other assorted fluids, I had a distinct sense that the Old Queen Mum would be my passport to adventure.

8

Standard One

Now with my own accommodation and in possession of a regal set of wheels, I concentrated on my day-to-day activities at the school. Pleasingly, the children took little time in allowing me to settle in. Occasionally, one of the younger ones would look at me shyly, clearly wondering what on earth it was that I would get up to next. Initially, I was really an odd-jobber, teaching a lesson here, a lesson there, and organising a nature ramble or a reading class in order to allow my colleagues to complete their marking, prepare new lessons or simply have some time off.

'What I would really like is for you to try and open the older ones' horizons a little. This is of course a fantastic place to grow up, but I would expect a number of them to be able to achieve grades here in Bots that will allow them eventually to head off and study abroad or down south (the recognised slang for South Africa). Maybe a few of them will end up going to the States or even the UK. That's why it's important for them to start getting to know now what their options are.'

Nodding, I agreed wholeheartedly. Wherever I had taught, either at home or abroad, it had been clear to me that the greater the understanding that my pupils had of the wider world, the greater chance they had to make important decisions for their futures – their options becoming that much broader. Those who, because of the constraints of their background or character, refused to look further than the end of the street, tended to remain there. Sometimes they were perfectly happy with their lot, but more often they were not. Frustration was born from the limited world that they inhabited and its stifling effects. Only through learning were they given the chance to dream. Too often they were not encouraged to do so.

The children here had the distinct advantage of having parents who were convinced of the importance of education. Once upon a time cattle-herding tribesmen had had little need for any formal instruction, and due to the isolated nature of their stations would have found it difficult to attend school on a regular basis anyway. Since independence, a sizeable percentage of the population had now drifted towards the capital, Gaborone, and the other towns of Francistown, Maun and Kasane, and were increasingly employed in jobs that required technical skills. Most of the parents of the children at the school were employed in white-collar jobs as bank officials, post-office administrators, businessmen and women. Some others were also employed in the other primary schools in town. Many had attended higher education either at the University of Botswana in Gaborone or further afield. As I had observed in other developing countries, their children recognised both how little their grandparents had had in the past and what prizes might be available for them in the future, so were determined to work hard, to succeed. What a difference that made to me.

'So, why don't you just come up with a programme for my class?' asked Graham, who was forever bursting with enthusiasm for fresh ideas. 'You know, you can do anything that you like. I'm afraid there's no money to spend on it, but we've got quite a good little library, so hunt around and see what you come up with.' With that, Graham trotted out onto the football pitch, immaculate as ever in polo shirt, khaki shorts, white socks and trainers. A whistle swung round his neck as he barked some instructions at a small dusty whirlwind that, it soon became apparent, was composed of three or four fighting boys.

The corner of the assembly hall that had been converted into the library was attractively decorated with posters displaying famous scenes from different countries. In the centre of the wall was a large map of the world. Avoiding falling into a reverie of plotting places visited in the past and possible future destinations, I wondered to myself how I might bring all these far-flung corners of the globe to life for my pupils.

Several children were sitting cross-legged in silence on cushions, books open on their knees. One little boy from Standard One, Bothle, had taken the opportunity in this quiet corner of the school to have a snooze. His small hands, folded over his round tummy, rose and fell rhythmically. Stepping over him, I carried on down the shelves. To my pleasure, here were stocked many of the books that were landmarks of my childhood: *Treasure Island*, all the Narnia adventures, *The Go-between*, *Rebecca*, *Five Children and It*. None of these, however, had the global appeal that I was looking for.

Around the World in Eighty Days was, on the other hand, ideal; the edition that I found on the lowest shelf had been simplified by the removal of some of the more opaque Victorian verbiage. So it was, through a number of long, hot African afternoons, that we accompanied Phileas Fogg and Mr Passepartout on their wonderful journey about the planet.

Charting their progress on the map on the wall, the children marvelled at all the structures, inventions and institutions that had previously been beyond their ken. Trains were built from cardboard using plans drawn only from vivid imaginations and some rather poor designs chalked by me on the blackboard. Although the school had internet access, images on the screen did not seem to light the same creative touch paper as simply getting their hands dirty fashioning these items out of various materials.

Paper ocean liners were launched in plastic buckets of water often with *Titanic* results. Operas and museums, casinos and dance halls, were all considered most seriously before being built out of putty and pipe cleaners. Different flags, religions and political structures, hitherto unimagined, were absorbed and neatly recorded in neat, buff exercise books.

In many ways, I enjoyed entering back into the structured world of the school week after several years spent foot-loose and fancy free wandering the globe. Now, I was happy to be able to lean back on that complete certainty that is the school timetable. Mornings started, by my standards, appallingly early – the first lesson beginning at seven o'clock – and the day finished in the early afternoon when the heat blasting across the plains made even thinking, let alone learning, almost impossible. Break time involved biscuits and squash, and a huge amount of running around, shouting and laughing as balls of all sizes flew through the hot air. As there was no canteen in the school, children brought their own carefully wrapped sandwiches or even small bowls of pap and seschwa, a traditional ground beef stew.

Graham was tiringly enthusiastic about physical fitness – perhaps too enthusiastic – and we all seemed to find ourselves perpetually pursuing an object, or even just one another, in draining games of tag. Nature rambles resembled paper-chases as we set off at speed over the high, dry hills. These, however, came to an abrupt end one day when Graham, the jogging children and I encountered a terrified male kudu charging down a path towards us, its huge twisting horns heaving up and down in its attempt to escape some unseen predator. When, emanating from some hundred yards behind, came a deep, terrible roar, the children, still gripping the leaves and feathers that they had collected along the way, turned back towards school at high speed. Although Graham had previously been steering the group from the front, it was noticed by his colleagues that he was comfortably the first home. Still, I suppose there is nothing like leading by example.

Although in so many ways the school day was ordered much as it is elsewhere in the world, and indeed the school was set in what might be termed a 'normal' little town by western standards, it was undoubtedly its natural surroundings that really made it unique. Many were the mornings when I arrived at school first in the Old Queen Mum. Rounding the corner of the buildings, I would startle a herd of impala who had been grazing on the sparse blades of grass of the football pitch. Trembling-legged and bleating, the fine and delicate, soft young calves would scamper after their parents, attempting to imitate their noble, graceful bounds as they disappeared into the thickets of thorn-bushes. Regularly, too, as the sun was rising inexorably, the oven-hot breeze that wafted through the classrooms fluttering the thin paper of the wall displays would carry with it the strong, sometimes overpowering scent of rotting flesh. Somewhere, not far away, an animal had been killed – all part and parcel of the continuous cycle of birth and death that seemed so much more real, so much more visceral, in Africa. Above us circled a pair of lappet-faced vultures, the bird world's equivalent of Burke and Hare.

Nevertheless, before long, life took up a regular pattern. It was particularly easy in this small school to get to know all the children not just by name, but by character too, and soon I met their parents out shopping or at the bar of The Old House. For the main part I was welcomed with open arms – children and parents alike interested to know more about me and the world from which I came. Some parents were, of course, well travelled. Many had spent time working in other African countries, particularly South Africa, but others had travelled much further afield. The Chief of Immigration, the father of Blessings, had even been to my university, although some years before me. Discussing favourite Brighton watering holes whilst watching huge flocks of pelicans land in the rush beds of the Chobe was an incongruous experience.

One notable exception to this amicable state of affairs was the rather too regular appearance of Mma Mokwena, the school inspector. Graham was terrified of her, and it was true that her appearance was somewhat forbidding. Her being at least an inch and a half taller than me meant that in her stockinged feet (and they always were – thickly – despite the heat), she must have measured a good six foot three. Extremely thin, she dressed in a dark blue suit and blouse, wore thin glasses that gave her an inquisitive air, and her hair was styled in spikes. Roald Dahl would have delighted in creating her as a character for one of his less kind children's books. Wherever she went she carried a thin black briefcase which she wielded as if it contained instruments of torture. On the occasion of our first meeting, she had slid it onto the teacher's desk – she had taken my chair – and had quietly unclicked the two brass catches. From within she had withdrawn a slim blue folder with my name, for once correctly spelled, written in a neat hand on a white sticker in the top right-hand corner.

Within the first week of living in Kasane, I had, on the instruction of Graham, taken myself to the immigration office, which was happily only two or three doors down from his house, where I was to apply for a temporary resident's permit. As I was a volunteer, this did not seem to present any particular problems. I had left the small wooden office some thirty minutes later with a smart stamp in my passport and the assurance that if I wished to stay longer then I had only to return and I would be given another. Mma Mokwena clearly did not consider this to be sufficient proof of my right to stay, and quizzed me intensively for at least one hot hour about my teaching experience and my general qualifications to remain a member of the human race. It seemed to me, when she finally put away her folder and clicked the brass briefcase catches closed again, that she remained unconvinced.

'Remember please, Randall, that I will have to monitor your progress closely. Please have your mark book and your corrected exercise books ready for my inspection.'

'Your inspection? Oh, I see . . . So, when did you plan to arrange that, Mma?'

'Well, we will just have to wait and see, won't we?' she replied inscrutably, as she carefully folded her glasses and slid them into a smart leather case. 'Goodbye, Randall.'

'Goodbye, Mma.'

'What is her problem?' I asked in a pseudo-American adolescent accent, when eventually I had waved off Mma Mokwena in her dark-blue matching car, and had limped my way back to our little staffroom.

'Don't ask!' replied Graham as he reappeared from behind the photocopying machine. 'She's a complete nightmare, and I mean that really. She actually does give me nightmares! Put it like this, for a number of reasons, she seems to have it in for this school.'

'Well what sort of reasons?' I jiggled my shirt in an effort to waft some cool air around my sweating self.

'Well, for a start her husband is the pastor of one of the different churches in Kasane, and he doesn't, or rather they don't, seem to approve too much of our foundation,' explained Mrs Sichilongo as she knitted away with clicks and clacks to produce yet another indeterminate item of clothing.

'That man is a real rogue, I'm telling you,' announced Kibonye, never shy of speaking her mind, as she ticked and crossed a pile of exercise books on her knee. 'You know how he is a friend of that terrible man Dirk?'

'Dirk, really? Dirk?' I could hardly imagine Dirk having an ecclesiastical friend.

'So, what do you think they have in mind then?'

'Who knows? Dirk is up to his neck in all sorts of murky stuff – and as for his two kids . . . What are they called? Edwin and Erwin. Terrible children. I don't think you could describe them as squeaky clean. In fact, quite the opposite,' added Mrs Krantz, who was the type of person who would certainly have a good idea what was going on. I had seen her in conversational mode in the supermarket.

'Well, who knows? It might be that she just wants to find herself in my shoes one day. Maybe even turn it into a private school. There's quite a lot of demand for them in Bots right now. The only thing that's certain is that she has to provide a report on the school at the end of the year, and who knows what she is capable of coming up with,' Graham muttered, fanning himself with one of Kibonye's exercise books and making a face.

Grumbling generally, we all sipped the cups of tea that Mrs Krantz had made. It was her turn to supply elevenses this week, and she had made sure that her biscuits were the best anybody had ever eaten.

'In fact, my class cooked these. Of course, it is my recipe, but the children cooked them. As you know, Headmaster, my class, Standard Four, are very able. Some of the best students in the school.'

Mrs Sichilongo clicked her knitting needles and cleared her throat.

'I wonder if I mentioned to you, Headmaster, which reading level my class have achieved only this week? Eleven. Yes, eleven. As you know, Headmaster, that is considerably beyond the standard you would normally expect.'

Click, clack.

'We have been so involved in improving our reading we have not really had time for . . . umm . . . baking,' she added, with a knowing nod towards Graham.

Before an argument about the merits of the respective classes could develop much further, we were saved by the bell and the rest of the day passed off without incident. Just as we were leaving, Graham asked me into his classroom and invited me to meet him later for a drink at the bar of the Safari Lodge – one of the grander establishments in the town – at about five. This somewhat surprised me as I had never seen him there before, but I cheerfully agreed.

Between five and six in the evening (the yardarm seems to be rather lower in Africa than elsewhere) locals and expatriates would meet at one of the fairly numerous riverside bars. The Sedudu Bar at Safari was a particularly popular destination; the views across the Chobe were beautiful enough to even still my desire to chitter-chatter. Here, too, imprisoned in these luxurious surroundings through fear of the uncharted and the unscheduled, congregated the resident tourists, changed into clean white cotton clothes and wreathed in insect repellent for the evening.

Now, as I waited for Graham, I took a rather superior sort of pleasure from listening to them talk.

'We had a great game drive just now. You know, we just saw everything. You wanna hear my list? I just had to write it down, you know? OK, here goes. You ready? OK, straight up. Genet, that's a kind of a cat – looks like a big cat. Giraffe, like, loads of them. They are so cool. Then antelopes, like impala; I guess that's kinda normal, huh? Then we saw water-buck, bush-buck – that's the one with a big white ring on its butt. Sorry, Gloria, I know you don't like to hear gross stuff. Yeah, then we saw a leopard. That was pretty cool, I guess. Then, what else, umm . . . Oh jeez, yeah, hippos. But they are just so obese, you know. Someone should do something about that. It sure can't be good for them to get that fat. Oh sorry, Gloria. Yeah, but yours is like a hormone thing, right? Yeah, so it's not your fault, right? Umm . . . yeah then a crocodile and elephants. Oh, yeah, just when we were coming back we saw all these African kids. Yeah, loads of them. They were just walking by the road. They were coming back from school. You could tell 'cos they were wearing kind of school uniform and they were carrying books and stuff. You know we waved at them when we drove by. Hey? Actually no, they didn't. Maybe they don't do that here. You know it probably isn't just the same as back home. You gotta remember this is like a different country . . .'

Silence ensued . . . for a while.

'You know what I think is a real shame?'

'Shoot.'

'Well, I think it's such a pity more of these African guys don't wear, like, traditional dress. You know?'

'Yeah, I guess. That would be way cooler. But I did see one guy and he was wearing like a Lakers shirt and that was pretty cool, y'know.'

Just as I was about to explode in one manner or another, I received a tap on the arm from young Arthur, who had been sitting with his mother and smaller brother at a table nearby. I waved over at Mma Kebalakile, who waved back and smiled gently.

'My mum wants to know why you don't visit her at Builders' World any more. She wants you to meet her cousin's sister; her name is Pinkie. She says you will think she is very beautiful.'

Laughing, I explained to Arthur that now the school was open I did not need to go to the builders' merchant so often, but that I would definitely pop in to see her sometime soon. Then she could introduce me to Pinkie.

'So where is your dad, Arthur?'

'Oh, he's just resting today. Sorry. We are going now. Bye.' The boy tried to remain bright, but I inwardly kicked myself for asking a question that had quite clearly caused him pain. I resolved that I really would get down to see Mma Kebalakile as soon as possible. Arthur wandered back to his table and a little later the family stood up. With the youngest child tied in a broad cloth to his mother's back, they wandered out into the dusk. Feeling rather glum, I watched a family of vervet monkeys dance lightly along the handrail of the veranda and bounce down towards the water's edge to drink, looking out nervously all the while for the bug eyes of a submerged crocodile.

'Hey, Will. How is it?'

'It is fine, thanks, Graham.' I didn't think I would ever get used to this bizarre South African turn of phrase and I was not entirely sure I would ever want to.

Grinning, my headmaster thrust a beer under my nose, and slipped down into one of the low wicker chairs that overlooked the river-bank.

As Graham and I sipped our 'sundowners' – the African

equivalent of 'chota pegs' – the sun, fatter, more massive, than any I had ever seen elsewhere, had just come briefly to rest on the horizon. Silhouetted against it, as if lit by a giant Victorian magic lantern, a herd of buffalo made its way through the muddy marshland and up into the bush for the night. Giraffes moved with their strangely slow leaning gentle gait amongst the palm trees on Sedudu Island. The afterglow of the sun was finally extinguished and on cue the mosquitoes and bats came out to play. I pulled my legs up onto one of the wooden rails of the Sedudu Bar and watched moths the size of a child's hand smash themselves enthusiastically into the frosted glass of the oil lamps that hung from the rafters.

Talking rather too fast and rather too earnestly about how pleased he was with the help that I had been providing him, Graham appeared to be a little nervous.

'Hope you have been enjoying it too, Will? You know, we have been so pleased to have you with us.' He paused to allow the compliment to sink in. 'Actually we're moving on in the New Year. Got a new job at the high school in Mafeking. Well, what I was going to say was that, as you know, Janey is about to have a baby and we were thinking that the best thing would be for her to go to Cape Town to my mother's place. What I don't really want is her to travel when she is too far gone, if you know what I mean?'

'Right, right . . .' My knowledge of obstetrics was not really what it might be.

'So what we were thinking, if it's okay with you, was that she might go a bit sooner than we thought.'

'Okay, so when were you thinking of?'

'Maybe next week.'

'Right, so what would happen to her class? You know, the Standard Ones?'

'Another beer?' He rose. 'No, no. My round.'

Although it wasn't, he was at the bar before I could argue. He soon came back with two frosty bottles of 'Zambezi' – a Zambian brew.

'Well, what I was going to ask. You know, just say if you're not interested. Well, we were wondering if you would be interested in taking on her class. Maybe, just till the end of term.'

By this stage in my life, I was quite used to finding myself in situations which I did not appear to have in any way engineered. More often than not, I didn't seem to mind. On this particular occasion, I was actually quite pleased and surprised.

'Well, yes. I suppose I would.'

They were a lovely bunch of little children, fiendishly enthusiastic about everything that Janey proposed for them to do, be it art, music, sport or even the more mundane matters of reading, writing and mathematics. Fourteen or so in number and pretty tame, they would be a reasonably manageable group.

'You'll have Elizabeth to help in the classroom as well. Don't feel you've got to stay stuck indoors all the time. You can take them all out on trips, visit other schools. They could be your football team! They're only little so they would all easily fit in your truck and away you go!'

Certainly, at a squeeze, the Old Queen Mum could accommodate them all, and in a world sensibly and refreshingly free of rules and regulations, it would be possible for us all to be more adventurous than would have ever been the case in England.

Graham looked distinctly relieved when he heard my reply, and I realised then that he was relying on me quite heavily. Possibly he had even contemplated this turn of events when I had first turned up at the prison football match. There was something rather haphazard about the organisation of the school, something unregulated that allowed us to adapt to and solve the problems that we were presented with. How marvellous it was not to be snared by bureaucracy. After two or three more Zambezis, and with a pleasantly warm breeze blowing through the open sides of the bar, I really didn't mind at all. In fact, it was really going to be an enjoyable challenge.

'I know the youngsters know you quite well already, but why don't you join Janey for her last few days? Might make the handover that bit easier. You'll be able to get a pretty good idea of what kind of things they get up to, and find out where everything is kept.'

'Sounds great. No problem. I think it sounds like fun. Talking of Standard One, I just saw Arthur and Mma Kebalakile. His dad isn't very well apparently.'

'No, you could say that.' Graham suddenly looked dispirited.

'He's HIV then?'

I had known that at some stage I was going to have to face this depressing aspect of Africa that was in such contrast to the otherwise broadly sunny way of life I had experienced in Botswana.

'Well, his HIV has just developed into AIDS and, as so often happens, he's picked up TB pretty quickly. Unfortunately, I don't think there will be too much they can do for him. It's tragic. He was working down south mining, had an accident with some cutting tools and got a blood transfusion. It was infected. That was that. Fortunately, most of the kids had been born by the time he found out and the little ones seem to have avoided infection. Trouble was that he left it much too long before he got any treatment – you know, anti-retrovirals.'

We drank our beers in silence for a while. The huge

challenge that faced sub-Saharan Africa suddenly confronted me.

'Luckily, Gabamukuni seems to have started some treatment now. If he keeps it up, things should look quite good for him.'

'Oh no, Gabamukuni too!'

'Mmm.' Graham nodded.

Remembering my trip to the clinic with him, I suddenly realised why Gabamukuni had been so reticent about his illness. For now there seemed nothing more to be said. Several more beers later, I manoeuvred the Old Queen Mum somewhat unsteadily out of the car park and set off home down the empty road. So absorbed was I by this dreadful discovery, as well as by the thought of my new responsibilities, that I didn't even feel any sense of surprise when I was forced to come to a halt in the middle of the road just outside town to allow a big broad-headed bull elephant make its way up the hill. Once he was gone, I merely let out the clutch and drove on home.

Somewhat weary the next morning, I still managed to arrive at school in good time. Once the children had been lined up in their class rows and had said their prayers, Graham explained the new arrangements.

'So now we all know that Mrs Johnson will be leaving us to have her new baby.'

Large collective sigh. '*Aaaahh!*'

'But of course we are all very happy for her and we all wish her the best of luck don't we?'

General assent. '*Yessss!*'

'What you will all be pleased to know is that Mr Randall will be taking over the Standard One class, but he will still be able to continue reading with you older children.'

Gasp of astonishment, or possibly horror, from Standard One; thankful murmur of approval from Standard Six.

Explaining that I would be coming to their lessons from now on, Graham told the Standard One pupils that there was nothing to worry about and that all would go smoothly. Looking at the faces of the somewhat shocked little children, I was not entirely sure that they shared his confidence. Not only was I not in any way as beautiful as Mrs Johnson, but I was considerably bigger and rather louder. Some of the little girls were blushing, and at least one, I thought, was beginning to look a bit tearful. All of a sudden I began to think that this might be a rather greater challenge than I had first imagined.

But after that first morning spent with Bothle, Glory, Courtney, Blessings, Olobogeng, Dolly, Happy, Kitso, Skye, Kitty, Hakim, Stella, little Chinese Hui, and Arthur, we were never to look back. The rest of the term spent in their company was to prove not only an unalloyed pleasure and a many-thousand-miled adventure but also produced some of the most exciting footballing moments since they thought it was all over.

9

The Birth of Mr Mango

Tears, a veritable deluge of them, were shed when finally it was time for Mrs Johnson to bid her pupils farewell. Presents were given and a party held in a rather lachrymose fashion. Certainly Janey was much moved by the affection displayed by the children, but unfortunately her tears only served, like a fit of sneezing, to encourage theirs, and poor Elizabeth had her time cut out wiping dirty, smudged faces with one hand whilst trying to console with pats to the head with the other.

Dolly, who it became clear was the leader of the gang, being a little taller and a little older than the others, produced a fit of histrionics that would have impressed a Hollywood B-movie director, and the others, following her lead, emitted such wails of anguish that I had to discreetly remove myself to our little staffroom. Finally, though, Janey was bundled rather unceremoniously into the car by her husband and taken to the airport, leaving a disconsolate Standard One in their classroom designing tear-stained 'Good luck with your baby, hope it's a boy because boys are better' cards decorated with huge, vivid red, love hearts and, in a couple of cases, rather oddly, with what looked like fighter airplanes.

Unkind though it might sound, I was mightily relieved that by the next Monday morning, Mrs Johnson, in the minds of these six-year-olds, seemed to be a distant memory. Even now, however, I needed to re-adjust the rules. Janey had tended to run her lessons along the lines of a cocktail party – a dry one, of course – during which anybody who might have a desire to converse with anybody interesting-looking could simply get up from their desk and wander over amiably to talk to them. Certainly, initially, that anybody appeared to be me.

So it was on that first day, after we had all sat down to work on our adding and subtracting, that within three or four minutes all the seats in the room apart from my own had been vacated and everyone had congregated around my desk. Mathematics seemed to be practically the only topic of conversation not under discussion. The children came from a very wide range of backgrounds, united in this little school by their, or at least their parents' chosen arm of the Christian faith. Almost immediately, I was inundated with information about their lives and a flurry of questions about mine, all delivered at impressive speed.

'We have two big dogs. They are called Kgosi and Tsala. That means "King" and "Friend". We called Friend Friend because he is very friendly, and we called Kgosi Kgosi . . . in fact, I don't quite know why . . . Anyway, Rra, when can they come to school?'

'No, well, we will have to see about that. How big did you say they were?'

'Which do you prefer, sable, eland or kudu?'

'I'm not sure . . . E— what?'

'Eland, Rra. It's the biggest one, but my dad says sable is the most handsome.'

'Where do you come from? My aunty lives in the US. One day we will go and stay there with our cousins. Have you been to US, Rra? I have seen pictures. She lives in Santa Barbara in a condom.'

'—inium?' Condominium, you mean, don't you? I have been to the US but never to Santa . . .'

'Come to our cattle station, Rra. We always go there and stay with my grandad. It is better than US. He has got many, many cattles. Some are called Brahman. We have got many small houses. One for you. And lovely *boma*, you know what it is? Food, delicious food.'

'Look what my mum has got me for my packed lunch! Lovely sandwiches. This one with jam. Look! This one with poloney. This one with jam and poloney. Give it back to me! Rra, Blessings has got my sandwich.'

'I have given it back, Rra. Look!'

'He has eaten a bit. Look, Rra!'

There was a squeal of indignation, but then, this outrage forgotten, a quiet thoughtful question.

'Rra, where is all your hair gone?'

Two blue sandals climbed onto the side of my chair.

'Look, his head is all shiny on the top.'

'Right, that's enough of that. Come on everybody . . .'

With a loud but not unduly harsh instruction for every-one to return to their seats, order was instantaneously and miraculously restored. I blinked and they smiled back at me. Glancing over to the corner, I noticed a warm grin of approval from Elizabeth who was waving a wooden school ruler in a comradely fashion.

What I think are correctly known as 'classroom dynam-ics' have always been a source of fascination to me. Perhaps the same can be found in all human organisations, but never, I think, are they so clearly writ as they are in a school. Within a few days, it became evident which of the children would play which particular roles. Dolly, as I had already discovered, had installed herself in the role of class spokesperson, a sort of shop-floor liaison officer between the workers and the powers that be. She it was who would inform me whether a particular task was to the satisfaction of the class or, occasionally, whether it was not. Any over-sight on my part – forgetting to give somebody a gold star, inadvertently keeping them in when the other children had already run out to play at break time, or failing to hand out sweets to deserving candidates at the end of the week – would be flagged up unfailingly. Skye, Glory, Kitty and Stella were her friends but also her admirers. When Dolly appeared at school with a ribbon in her hair, so then the very next day would the other four girls. If Dolly wanted to play a particular game, then so did they. Individually, these girls were bright and compliant; as a group, they were the closest of companions. Naturally, and I would have been disappointed had it not been so, there was also a group of would-be naughty boys. Unlike the girls, there appeared to be no natural leader, or rather, in a most democratic way, decisions were made by one or another of them until every-body else got bored of taking notice. Courtney, Blessings, Happy, Bothle and Hakim were thick as honest thieves. Much of their time was spent dreaming up adventures on which they were planning to embark; most of them involved feats of ferocious bravery, hunting, discovering, conquering, and above all, of course, killing the baddies. Although they never mentioned it, they were, I think, secretly quite pleased to have a man as their teacher, being possibly slightly fed up with making cakes and useful decorations out of doilies. Needless to say, they were foot-ball crazy.

As was always also the case, there were a few characters who did not find themselves fitting into any particular group at all. I have always identified most closely with the individuals who defy categorisation; those who are not necessarily unpopular, often quite the opposite, but ready, happy, to go their own way. Kitso and Arthur were more than content just to concentrate on their studies. Kitso was impressively, and occasionally disconcertingly, good at maths, to the extent that I found myself practising my times tables on the way home in the car. Arthur was never happier than when he could lie face down on the carpet in the little library and leaf through page after page of picture books full of fantastic fairy-tales, magic and wizardry. Often, too, he would content himself by drawing his own little cartoons, normally alongside his mathematical problems. Perhaps this fantasy world provided an escape from what was undoubtedly at that moment an unhappy home life.

Olobogeng, who had arrived halfway through the term and had lived most of her life in the capital of Botswana, Gaborone, was a silent but sturdy little girl. I could sense her unease as she watched the other friends interact, feel her reticence at getting involved. She, of all the children, required my reserves of tact and patience as I coaxed her into our world.

Hui, a tiny little boy, whose parents were part of the great Chinese diaspora and ran a general store down on the main strip in Kasane, was at a great disadvantage as he spoke next to no English. Yet on that very first day he made a lasting impression on the rest of my stay in Africa.

It seemed to be the habit of the other teachers that before asking the children to sit down they would wish them good morning.

'Good morning, Mr or Mrs such-and-such!' the pupils would chorus in reply before bringing down their upturned chairs and removing their little satchels.

Hui happened to be standing directly in front of me, and I could sense that he was more than a little mystified about what was going on. Kneeling down in front of him I asked him quietly what his name was.

After a little finger sucking he replied that his name was Hui.

'Great,' I said. 'So what is my name?'

'Your name Mr Rango!'

Kitso, standing next to him, giggled. 'What did you say, Hui? Did you say his name is Mr Mango?'

Naturally the rest of the class thought that this was almost certainly the funniest joke that they had ever heard, and from then on nobody ever addressed me as anything but Mr Mango – not just my pupils, not just their parents, not just my colleagues, but everyone in the whole town, strangers, policemen and even one tourist who had been misinformed.

Still, I suppose there are heavier crosses to bear.

Despite the fact that they were comprised of disparate groups and individuals with varied interests, this was really a very homogeneous gang of children who got on, for the main part, extremely well. As well as this, they were remarkably good at entertaining themselves, and so if, as happened several times a week, Elizabeth and I wished to listen to one of them read or help them with various problems, then the rest would happily play any of the numerous games available, either separately or with others.

Normal schooldays were varied enough to remain interesting but retained a format that was comfortingly recognisable. Two or three times a week, once classroom lessons had finished, I would load the children up into the back of the Old Queen Mum and drive them down to one of the largest and smartest safari lodges, Mowena – The Baobab – so called because it was built around a colossal baobab. It was extraordinarily luxurious, built on three floors like a

mediaeval wooden fort. In the grounds were two swimming pools, one built for children and babies, the other a
great expanse of clear blue water. As Botswana is a land-
locked country and the only available water course the
Chobe River, home to thousands of crocodiles, learning to
swim was not a high priority for most Batswana. However,
having negotiated a deal with the owners of the lodge,
Graham – physical fitness being always at the front of his
mind – had insisted that each of his children should be able
to swim before they left school.

My only qualifications in this activity amounted to a
small sew-on badge commemorating the fact that I had
swum two widths of Putney swimming baths, but as even
the larger pool was only chest deep at any given point, I
felt confident enough to supervise. Not that I needed to
have worried, as the children, even if they did not possess
what might be described as recognised strokes, could all
manage to remain on the surface and paddle themselves in
the required direction. Only Hui, who I don't think had
ever seen a swimming pool before, and Bothle, who I don't
think could really see the point of getting unnecessarily
wet, had any problems. Once equipped with a large pair
of water wings, Hui could not have drowned even if he
had wanted to, and Bothle contented himself by standing
in the shallow end slapping his arms up and down against
the surface of the water and occasionally sticking his head
below it. Secretly, I was more than happy to take them to
the pool as it meant a delicious relief from the often
frightening heat of the afternoon.

On other days we stayed at school and practised our
football skills on the uneven but spacious pitch. When the
first session had come to an end and I staggered back into
the shade of the overhanging tin roof, I could not but agree
with Graham's rather unkind assessment that the children

were 'pretty useless' at this sport. Although enormously keen, the boys' and girls' only clear intention was to make contact with the ball as often as possible and boot it as far as they possibly could regardless of the direction. Tactically, their team strategy appeared to be to all chase the ball wherever it then went. Falling over was something that did, on the other hand, appear to come reasonably naturally, and although tears were few, enthusiasm waned in direct proportion to bruises gained.

Bothle was almost always the first to think about calling it a day. Skipping over to me, clutching an injured part of his anatomy, he would look up at me beseechingly. 'Mr Mango,' he would say in his soft, quiet voice. 'Mr Mango, I am now beginning to feel a little bit tired, so I think what I will do is I will have to go off now. I will sit under the tree and have a little rest.' And without waiting for my response he would potter off into the shade and sit down with a sigh. His big round eyes blinking, he would look about for anybody who might be sympathetic to his cause. More often than not, Elizabeth, who had something of a soft spot for him, would scoop him up to her side, where within a few minutes, due to such heroic exertions, he would fall asleep.

Despite their shortcomings in footballing skill the children were all adept in the theatrical department. Final whistles at the end of any of our short practice games would result in loud and exuberant celebrations normally reserved for the winning of an international tournament. As they trooped heavy-limbed from the dusty pitch, sadness, sometimes near despair, would be wrought on the faces of the losing side. Normally, however, they would have considerably cheered up by the time that they received their orange squash and biscuits from Elizabeth, the purveyor of all things sweet.

Fortunately, I managed to find a whistle in the Chinese shop belonging to Hui's parents, and this brought at least some order to the football proceedings. Bit by bit, after I had realised that there was only a certain amount that I could actually constructively teach the children in any one session before they reverted to a rather more rustic approach to the game, small amounts of progress were made. Slowly, too, some of the children began to show a natural aptitude, a real sense of what they should be doing. Surprisingly, little Stella turned out not only to be quite skilful but also able to run like the wind. The boys, not really conscious of any battle of the sexes, just found it fun trying to keep up with her.

'Do you think it will be worth entering them for the competition?' Graham asked me uncertainly during one of the practice sessions.

'Competition?'

'Yes, all the schools that have been set up by the same foundation enter a knockout competition. Gives them an opportunity to play competitive games and visit a few different countries. We never get anywhere because we're so small, but they do love it. Be good for you to visit the region too.'

'Yes, it does sound like fun.' I was quite enthused. 'Hang on, did you say count*ries*?'

'Yes,' Graham laughed. 'It's pretty international. They'll visit Namibia, Zambia, maybe even Zim depending on the political situation. And, of course, we go right across Bots – as far as Tsodilo. You heard of "the hills"?'

I shook my head.

'Then that will be an adventure for you all!'

Graham strolled off shouting encouragement to Dolly, who had just been flattened by a rather over-exuberant tackle from Kitso, leaving me feeling invigorated by the thought of seeing more of Africa and excited by the prospect of the tournament. This was to be our Botswana Adventure.

As I day-dreamed, Hui passed me the ball. Unexpectedly, and without thinking, I booted it in the direction of goalkeeper Happy. It was destined to sail into the top left-hand corner but the little boy stretched his skinny frame as far as he could and tipped it over the bar. With a giant roar of congratulation, we all ran towards him as if he had just saved the last-minute equaliser in the final of the African Cup of Nations.

After our first practice, I had been pleasantly surprised by a quiet round of applause from a collection of parents who, unseen by me as I exerted myself, had gathered under the shade of the mopane trees ready to pick up their offspring. I delighted in the ritual of 'hellos' and 'how are yous', which I discovered I could now just about manage in Setswana, thanks to the personal tutelage I had received from Clever during my brief decorating career.

'*Dumela*, Mma, *dumela* Rra,' I greeted a couple who I recognised to be the parents of our dreamer, Arthur.

'*Dumela*, Mr Mango. *Le kae?*'

'*Re teng!*' I replied, feeling on fine if slightly puffed form.

Mma Kebalakile had all the physical attributes of an earth mother, with ample thigh and bosom to provide succour and comfort to her whole brood simultaneously if need be. This was just as well, I thought, as I contemplated Mr Kebalakile, who looked more thin and haggard, and quite worn out. I had discovered, because I had seen him going about his business, that this modest man cleaned the streets of the little town of the normal litter of tin cans, food wrappers and plastic bottles, not to mention several hundred tons of elephant dung. He smiled at me as cheerily as he could manage and, just as I was beginning to wonder whether perhaps I should ask after his health, he turned away from me and coughed grotesquely and frighteningly into a clear, white handkerchief. As I looked away quickly to the dreamily approaching Arthur, I could not avoid the glimpse of something thickly and richly black being folded into the cloth before it was stuffed into the pocket of his shorts.

'So Rra, we were going to ask you one thing,' his wife asked quietly. 'Maybe you would like to come and drink tea with us one afternoon after school? Now you are Arthur's teacher, we will all be great friends, I am sure.'

Despite the tragic circumstances of this family, I could see that they were clearly doing their best to keep up normal appearances. With pleasure – if a somewhat heavy heart – I accepted their invitation and agreed that I would run Arthur home one day and stay on for tea. With a last smile, Mma Kebalakile led her brood towards the road, glancing back occasionally and waiting for her husband to catch them up.

The poignant sight of this broken man was quickly engulfed by the vibrancy of the cheerful goodbyes of the other parents and the knee-high hugs of the children. Smiling at the pleasure of being surrounded by such personable, friendly youngsters, I then helped Elizabeth clear away the books and pencils, and something unfathomably sweet and sticky that had been spilled on Hui's desk. It smelled strongly of lychees.

Rra Kabalakile's suffering came to mind again a short time later. I had taken up the habit of eating at The Old House a few evenings a week and, eschewing the hunting section of the clientele, had made friendly contact with a number of the regulars. One man who made me laugh more than most was Blessings' father, the Chief of Immigration. It was almost impossible to equate the broad, avuncular figure in a uniform of navy blue and flashes of gold trimming with the man he described as having 'one a hell of a good time boogying down in that nightspot – what they call it – yes, the Crypt!' Obviously, I winced a little at the thought of it – it was in that same Crypt that I had perfected my Mick Jagger routine.

It was fun talking to this friendly man, and he and I had already enjoyed many a St Louis, the Botswanan brew, together before I met him early one evening in the company of a hefty, blond man with side-burns and as many tattoos as scars.

'Mr Mango, my friend!' the Chief of Immigration hailed me. 'Come and meet my other friend Freddy. He is a Belgian fellow!'

I shook the smiling man's hand, which I soon regretted as I removed mine mangled from his grasp.

'*Salut, mon p'tit!*' he rasped.

'I told him you were studying French at our place! When you going to teach Blessings a bit?'

'Oh, sometime soon, I hope. Hello, Freddy. Do you live here?'

'Course he does!' bellowed Mr Blessings. 'Busiest man in town.'

'Oh, I see. What do you do?'

'He's the undertaker! You think he hasn't got enough work. Ha, ha.' But the laughter was hollow and we all stared down at our bottles.

Freddy, I knew, must be doing a thriving trade. HIV/AIDS was thought to affect up to forty per cent of the population, and hand in hand with its sinister partner tuberculosis it was relentlessly picking off its victims.

Sexual mores and cultural taboos were such in this country that AIDS was a subject that was seldom addressed, although the government had dedicated itself to a programme of public health posters. Some comprised pictures of rather wobbly-looking prophylactics, and others depicted in cartoon form a naked man, with a racy magazine carefully obscuring his manhood, enthusiastically promoting what used to be termed 'self-abuse'. The impact of this campaign had been minimal. Botswana was the only country on the African continent that provided anti-retroviral drugs for those determined to deal with the disease in its early stages, but such was the shame attached that few infected dared demand their rightful prescriptions until it was too late. Tebelopele, 'Ray of Sunshine' – a clinic dedicated to treating HIV sufferers, had misguidedly been built in the middle of the main street in town. Nobody who suspected they were possibly afflicted dared to be seen enter. When the victim eventually died, the next of kin would beg the doctor signing the death certificate to note the cause of death as a fever, sickness or TB.

Rra Kebalakile's ruined body flashed before my eyes and his racking cough filled my head. We moved on to the next topic of conversation knowing that only a radical change of cultural attitude, probably over a generation, could redress the critical level of the problem.

Meanwhile, back at school, full of life and positive energy, Graham, his competitive streak becoming more noticeable by the day, was insistent that I should find some suitable opponents for our budding football stars.

'Katima Mulilo,' he explained. 'That's where you want to go. They're only a little school too. Get over there and give them a good thrashing!'

Katima Mulilo, it transpired, was not even in Botswana. It was in Namibia but, because of its geographical location, was actually one of the closest small towns to Kasane. This little outpost was about as far as it was possible to get from Windhoek whilst remaining in Namibia, out on a limb on the furthest tip of the Caprivi Strip. This extraordinary belt of land running artificially between the borders of Botswana and Zambia was carved out in one of the innumerable boundary changes at the end of the nineteenth century. Count Caprivi, an Italian–German, had decided that if he could secure this piece of land, then South West Africa would be able to maintain a connection with the eastern seaboard by way of the Zambezi River. His plan was dashed, almost literally, by the discovery a few miles on of the Victoria Falls. Presumably, the bureaucrats in London and Berlin could not face rewriting all the paperwork, and so this geographical anomaly, in some places barely twenty miles wide, remains today.

Having been told by Graham that I was going to have to go it alone – although I would actually be accompanied by Elizabeth, who was to play the role of assistant coach and physiotherapist, and who would specifically look after the girls – I was a little nervous about this first solo foray.

'You don't have to worry about it,' explained Graham, in his normal bluff but cheerful manner. 'We just have to make sure that all the children have their passports, but they are so used to travelling over the border that it is almost second nature to them. All you have to do is fill out the forms when you get to the border.'

All I had to do!

Our route took us through the park, and the children took a checklist of the various animals that they had seen. As they had grown up in these surroundings, they proved more than useful guides, particularly Arthur, who was sitting up in front with me and Dolly (who clearly believed that was her right and fitting place).

'Look, Mr Mango, that is the fish eagle. You can see many, many, here. It is the best hunter of all the birds. Look, now he's coming in for a kill.' Arthur's solemn little face now lit up with the excitement of the enthusiast.

It was difficult to keep my eyes on the rough track as well as gaze upwards at the soaring bird as it whirled above the world with enviable freedom, shrilling its *whee-ah-hyo-hyo* call. Suddenly, though, it dropped, its wings tucking back to its sides in attack as it sped towards the water, and at the very last second, through some aerodynamic wizardry I did not understand, it braked its descent so that its sizeable claws raked the water with a delicate but deadly stroke. Beating its wings powerfully, it lifted up again off the silver surface of the river, pulling with it a strikingly large, grey-black fish that must have measured some three foot. Almost as strong as the predator, it flapped violently and vigorously but, like some victim in a Greek myth, its death had been preordained the moment the great bird had sunk its talons into it. By the time the eagle had risen as high as the treetops, the fish was still.

So staggering and visceral was this scene played out before us that I failed to realise that I had slowed the car to a stop. As we drove on, the boys, with the exception of Bothle, who, true to form, had fallen asleep, cheered this extraordinary spectacle. Perhaps it was their hunter's instinct, for beyond the immediate confines of the village, they lived in a world that was almost unchanged, witnessing the same cycle of life and death as the very first human settlers here. Somehow, all those barriers built up by an urban society had disappeared. It felt extraordinarily liberating.

My pumping adrenaline was suitably calmed by the time we arrived at the border post at Ngoma Bridge. Leaving Botswana was perfectly straightforward: entering Namibia was not. We pulled up outside a row of low, modern-looking buildings and walked through the door entitled 'Immigration'. All the children's passports were in one bunch wrapped by a thick elastic band, and I handed them over to a smartly dressed lady in uniform sporting a badge which read 'Welcome to Namibia!'.

Counting the passports carefully, she reached for a pad of small forms and tore off the equivalent number.

'Fill these in, please. One for each small child.'

Looking down at the forms, I was dismayed to see quite how many small boxes there were to be ticked and filled.

'Here, Kitso, do you reckon you could fill one of these out?'

With the best will in the world, he studied the slip of paper and then frowned. Shrugging, he looked back up at me and shook his head, smiling but embarrassed.

'No, I know, it's pretty difficult isn't it.'

He nodded, smiled again, and whispered from behind one hand. 'Too difficult for Kitso!'

Elizabeth took the children outside and they went to sit under some trees. Through the open window of the customs office I could hear them singing a song that they had most recently been practising with their music teacher, Mrs Sichilongo. They sang well, their various harmonies competing with each other. At least it made my task that little less onerous.

Ticking the boxes and filling in the information reminded me of the one aspect of teaching in the UK that I had hated most, apart from marking of course, which goes without saying. Report writing was a termly misery. As all the reports had to be written on the same sheet it meant that there was not even the possibility of doing it at home. Strictly marshalled by the deputy headmaster, each form had to be passed from one teacher to the next. We lived in dread of making a mistake because, should we do so, the whole process would have to start again.

Once, when I was a teacher at a boarding school, I had been sent on a refresher course (quite which aspect of me

it was supposed to refresh, I forget) in London, from which
I was to return the night before the last day of term. Rashly,
I agreed to complete my reports last, offering to fill them
out when I got back. Rather happily, or unhappily, as we
shall see, the end of the course coincided with a friend of
mine's birthday party in a very nice Italian restaurant on
the Edgware Road. Celebrations were conducted with great
good humour and any puritanical sense of holding back
disappeared almost as quickly as the first dozen bottles of
Chianti. I had had the foresight, for once, to book myself
a seat on the nine forty-five from Paddington just a few
hundred yards up the road.

Something called Grappa (which I have only consumed
once since, by mistake, and which would be better used to
buff antique furniture) made an appearance at just the
wrong moment, and I ended up accompanying the night
mail westward. By the time I had made it up the high street
and through the school gates, I was intent on tottering in
the general direction of my bed.

One shoe and half a sock off, I suddenly remembered.
The reports.

Working through the night has never been one of my
favourite pastimes but now I had little choice. One hundred
reports needed to be in the filing tray next to the photo-
copying machine by nine o'clock the following morning.
Although I say so myself, I started with some gusto using
elegant turns of phrase, little witticisms and thoughtful
insights, or so I believed. Some children were very easy to
write about. So hard-working or so agreeable, so lazy or so
unpleasant were they that there was no shortage of things
to say. Other pupils occupied the middle path and sometimes my descriptions of them were a little bland; in a
couple of cases I struggled to remember precisely who they
were.

As the night wore on, inspiration began to slip quietly away to bed and I started to resort to the clichés of generations past: 'satisfactory', 'worked well', 'must try harder', etc. Re-reading one particular entry, I noticed that I had somehow managed to include the word 'well' five times in its three or four lines. Still, it was too late to worry about it, I had to press on. Finally, as a couple of sparrows flitted in to have a crack at the ice on the pond in the courtyard below, my task was completed. Feeling, if anything, more unsteady than I had been before, I dumped the pile of reports in the filing tray and staggered to bed.

There was only really time to get in, get out, have a shower and go to assembly. Fortunately, as it was the last day of the Christmas term there was not a great deal to do apart from wish everybody farewell and happy holidays. Tired, very tired, I sought out a quiet corner of the staff room clutching a cup of coffee. Caught in that moment between waking and sleeping, I discovered that I was being spoken to by the headmaster's secretary, a Miss Witherwood, who was as cosy as a broom handle, as attractive as a silage clamp, and who possessed the sense of humour of unpolished granite.

'So where are they then?'

I always expected her to add 'boy' to the end of each sentence.

I knew what she was talking about. Sorry I am to admit that this wasn't the first time I'd been tardy in such matters.

'Ah, yes, yes, Miss Witherwood, they're in the filing tray as they're supposed to be. I think you'll find them there.'

'I think I won't. I've just had a look. Don't think you can start messing . . .'

Leaping up with all the vigour of the righteous, I led her to the tray. It was empty.

'Someone must have taken them!'

'Yes, I expect somebody has. That's the recycling tray.'

Suffice it to say that all my investigations in the school rubbish tip came to nought, the head porter taking great pleasure in the use of his shredding machine.

It was not a merry Christmas nor a particularly happy New Year.

Sick at the memory, I finally finished filling out the immigration forms, including dates of birth, addresses and some not entirely straightforward surnames, and took them to the counter as the children started to sing another round of 'Jingle Bells'.

As it turned out, our little trip into Namibia and our first fixture of the season proved to be surprisingly testing. The school was hidden behind the dusty, shady marketplace and possessed, as ours did, just one football pitch. Everybody from the Katima Mulilo School had stayed behind to watch the game and support the very large children who were supposed to be playing in their team. Elizabeth and I were the only people present on the sidelines buoying up the opposition. Nevertheless, when the first whistle was blown, we did our very best to make up for our lack of numbers. The volume of Elizabeth's encouragement was almost unnerving. At one moment, when Blessings had eluded a great tree trunk of a boy and to his surprise found only a wildly waving goalkeeper between him and glory, she unleashed such a bellow that the poor boy shied and skewed the ball off at a wild angle. Wondering what had hit him, he watched disconsolately as the ball bobbled off into the bush startling a family of mongeese that were snoozing in the shade. Fortunately, I don't think he ever realised that the distraction came from his own camp.

Olobogeng had christened us 'the Kasane Kudus' because she said kudus were strong but fast too. As

Elizabeth and I were supporting a team that was most distinctly not strong or, with the exception of Stella, fast, by half-time our new team soubriquet was beginning to look a little inappropriate. Nevertheless, I put on my most positive face and gave a most cheering 'we will fight them on the beaches', 'once more unto the breach, dear friends', 'snatching victory from the jaws of defeat' half-time talk. When the referee, a rather biased teacher from the Namibian school, blew for the beginning of the second half, I sent the troops back onto the pitch with restored vigour. All except Bothle that was. I caught him tip-toeing in the direction of the Old Queen Mum, no doubt for a heads-down, no-nonsense snooze on the back seat. Yawning widely and rolling his eyes, he tottered back onto the pitch at my behest only to be flattened by a much larger lad. His gaze, when eventually he was stood upright again by Elizabeth, verged on the reproachful.

We lost by a margin of double figures.

Still, the children seemed excited as they drank their lemonade before climbing back aboard the Old Queen Mum (who it seemed, incidentally, was admired internationally). What was certainly true was that it had been a useful dummy run, preparing the children and, more to the point, me, for the rigours of travelling through Africa and for being graceful in defeat. Admittedly, we had not yet had to stay overnight anywhere but nor, more positively, had we encountered any major difficulties.

As we rumbled back up the hill towards Kasane and through the very much more speedy checkpoint on the Botswanan side, I entertained the hope that all our outings would be this straightforward. Sadly, I knew myself only too well.

After the children had finally all been sent on their way home, I drove down to the parade of shops, parked up and, strangely reminded of film scenes set in small-town America, went into the supermarket. Greeting Mma Chika, Bothle's mother, who was having a busy time thumping away at the buttons of a till at one of the checkouts, I made a few purchases. Kudu steak stew was on my menu that night, and I planned to take the ingredients back home, cook them and eat sitting on the small veranda as I watched the hippos stretching their chubby limbs on the Zambian bank of the Chobe. I planned to be firmly behind closed doors before the elephants began their nocturnal wanderings.

Much to my surprise, as I was clambering back into the Old Queen Mum, I spotted Dirk in animated conversation with a much slighter character in the shade of one of the smaller shops' awnings. As he swung his heavy-set shoulders and stamped one heavy boot, I caught a sight of the man that he was talking to so brusquely. Although his face was transformed by the most pitiful expression of unhappiness, I recognised him immediately to be Arthur's father. As much surprised to see him talking to Dirk, as I was shocked by his feeble, decrepit appearance, I could not understand why the two should be communicating at all. Dirk was not, after all, renowned for passing the time of day with local people.

Frowning, I dropped my kudu steaks and one or two St Louis beers into the cool box I now habitually kept in the cab of the Old Queen Mum, and then slowly manoeuvred through the early evening throng.

What could Dirk have been saying?

10

The Road to Pandamatenga

Buzzing low over us as we passed the gates of Kasane Airport was the familiar, beige undercarriage of the four-seater Cessna belonging to my new friend Chris as it came in to make one of its soft, bouncing, lolloping landings. After football practice we were all so exhausted I had promised to drive home those children that normally walked. We turned round and drove into the smart aviation compound which doubled as a civil airport and the airborne wing of the Botswanan Defence Force. Their three camouflaged airplanes were parked in a row on the far side of the field.

Dolly, who had been in something of a sulk after I had told her that she would have to give up her place in the front seat for somebody else, suddenly became very animated. Leaning out of the window she waved at the soldiers on the tarmac.

'Mr Mango, this is what I want to do when I am a big girl. Like my daddy. I can be in BDF, and maybe I will be the first Motswana girl who will fly a plane.'

Dolly had obviously visited the airport on several occasions, but most of the other children appeared to be

speechless with fascination at what they saw. Kasane
Airport was undoubtedly one of the nicest that I have seen
of its size. Spartan but spotlessly tidy, it was run by a
friendly man called Rra Sentle, who waved at me now from
the one check-in counter. Chris, the pilot, came in off the
runway and greeted us. He was a roly-poly, shortish, sandy-
haired man in his mid-forties and worked for one of the
private charter airlines. He was a Zimbabwean, and the
very fact that he did not describe himself, as did so many
others, as a 'Rhodesian', or worse a 'Rhodie', had attracted
me to him when we had first met. Immediately I had
realised that he did not share some of the surprisingly
unpleasant, and certainly deeply flawed beliefs about his
own superiority held by so many others I had met.

He smiled and waved at all the children and punched
Blessings, a close neighbour of his, playfully on the arm.
He was very natural with children of all ages and backgrounds. In fact, it was his ability to get on cheerfully with
just about everybody he met that I had liked about him
when I met first him at the bar of The Old House. There,
he was frequently to be found engaged in ribald conversation with any number of different people.

'Come on then, fellows. Why don't we all go and have
a look at my plane?' he asked. 'Have you got time, Mr
Mango?'

Most of the children giggled when he used my new
soubriquet and pleaded with me to be allowed to go and
have a look. Because I am a kind-hearted and thoughtful
soul, and also because I hadn't yet had a look at his machine
myself, I agreed. Half-fascinated and half-horrified, part of
me yearned to be able to get behind the controls of a little
single-engined plane.

'So, what are you going to do when you grow up?' is a
question that has haunted me to the present day. In modern

Botswana, with its vastly increased range of choices, this was a question that was becoming more commonplace. Where once most of these children would from an early age have worked their family cattle stations way out in the bush, now they were faced with almost as many options as youngsters in the West. Most of them, despite their relatively young ages, had already formed ideas – some rather more fanciful than others. Skye and Olobogeng both wanted to work in the city, to go back to Gaborone and take office jobs. Courtney was interested in the birds and animals around him, and wanted to be a ranger. Happy, to my surprise, had decided that he wanted to be a chef in one of the big safari lodges. He already went to help his uncle in the steely, steaming kitchens at Mowana Lodge. Hui, and I think that this was due to a rather heavy amount of peer pressure to live up to a stereotype, had decided that he wanted to become a Chinese martial arts expert and act in the movies. Kitty and Stella, rather more prosaically, had decided that they were to become doctors and were often to be seen tending stricken dolls at the back of the classroom. Occasionally, they tended to Kitso too, who seemed to rather enjoy the attention. Naturally, these were all dreams to be fulfilled after they had completed their successful careers as professional football players.

Before we were allowed to go out onto the airport runway, we each needed to be issued with a pass. At one stage, I was mightily concerned that some paperwork was going to be involved, but this was waived when it looked as if I might faint. Walking through the smoked glass doors into the bright sunlight, I showed the children how to put their fingers together, invert their hands and place them over their eyes as temporary flying goggles. They learnt to whistle *The Dambusters'* theme tune remarkably quickly as we marched, a bouncy brigade, over to Chris's plane.

All the children were fascinated to sit at the controls, and all of them took the chance to wear the headphones and talk into the microphone, although in Hui's case he would have been better off wearing the headset on his shoulders. Even Bothle, who had started to cry after he had stuck a finger in his eye trying to put on his goggles, was mollified once he was allowed to sit in the pilot seat and fiddle rather alarmingly with all the controls.

When I saw Chris later at the bar of The Old House, where he was 'wetting his whistle' as he liked to put it, we agreed what a nice bunch of children my little class were. 'And bright, and curious and funny,' he went on. 'Shows you what a load of rubbish they used to talk in the old days – you know, about only whites being able to do some things and how Africans would never be able to suss some stuff out. *I* even thought that when I was a kid. Have your lot been to stay with the Afrikaners out there on the farms at Pandamatenga? It's, I dunno, about a hundred and fifty clicks south of here. I know most of them get to go out there because Graham knows those guys very well. You'll find it really interesting the way people are out there. It's all pretty different from the way that either the Whities or the Africans live.'

'Actually, I don't know if they have been out there. Where did you say it was?'

'Pandamatenga. Why?'

'Pandamatenga! No reason, it's just a great name.' I was thrilled by it, and even more thrilled that I could still get thrilled about something as simple as an exotic name.

When I asked Graham about this at school, he looked momentarily blank and then slapped his head in annoyance at himself.

'You're right. No, I've got it all organised. I'm just really sorry I didn't mention it to you before. Truth is, I've been a bit preoccupied with looking after the girls, and Janey has been pretty uncomfortable recently. Anyway, let me just look this up quickly.' He riffled through his desk diary. 'Next weekend by the looks of it. I better see if I can get a message through to them. There's no telephone out there, but I can probably get a radio message through to them to confirm that you're coming – that's if you want to, of course?'

'Well, I don't really know what's involved. What goes on up at Pandamathingy?'

'Well, apart from the football match, of course, the reason for sending the children down there is to let them have a look at how to run a farm. There's not really a history of organised farming in Botswana and the government is very keen to promote it. That's why they invited the Afrikaners in to get things started up. You'll be pretty amazed by what they do down there. Now that they're under way, they get a lot of youngsters down there, and they're hoping that they're going to be able to interest the next generation in agriculture. At the moment there simply aren't any major farms run by Batswana. In thirty years' time they want most cereal foodstuffs to be home-produced. One thing's for sure, they will look after you pretty well – even if you are a Brit! The only problem is that I won't be able to come with you because I have to go to some headmasters' meeting in Maun, so you'll be on your own – apart from Elizabeth, of course.'

He sent his radio message and received one back announcing that the people at Pandamatenga were expecting us. All the children from the neighbouring farms were being brought in to do battle on the football pitch, which had apparently a few days previously been a maize field. With some concern I consulted the map with Graham, and he marked the spot on the straight road heading south to

Francistown where one of the farmers' wives would meet us and guide us to their homestead. We need not take any tents or camping equipment as they were planning to accommodate us and feed us. All we needed to bring with us by way of an offering were two twenty-litre drums of tractor gear-box oil.

When the weekend rolled around, we strapped the drums of oil to the roof and set off on the two-hour journey, expecting to arrive at Pandamatenga by lunchtime. The rains had just come and it had been pouring down regularly for the last week. For once, the pools of water lying in the road were not simply mirages. With astonishing speed the usually moribund bush had burst into a blaze of green picked out with a variety of brightly coloured flowers. The temperatures had tumbled and the ensuing freshness of the weather had filled us all with extra energy, so we must have made a jolly sight as we drove past Maurio's garage and a small industrial estate, and out into the countryside. The children sang songs and played games of 'I spy' and 'Twenty questions', which I had recently taught them. Inevitably, in the game of 'Animal, vegetable or mineral' the popular choice was more often than not 'animal'.

Hui found these games totally mystifying, but learnt astonishing amounts of vocabulary at lightning speed. Unfortunately, Happy, who often took a little time to cotton on to what was going on, had not really understood the purpose of the game. He also demonstrated an extraordinarily fertile imagination when it was his turn to ask a question that could only elicit a 'yes' or 'no' answer:

'So how many legs does it have?'

'No, Happy!' we chorused.

'Oh, OK, shush, quiet please. OK, does it have three legs?'

'Oh, Happy. You're a silly boy. There aren't any animals

with only three legs,' Elizabeth admonished gently.

'Yes, there are,' he declared confidently. 'What about my neighbour's dog, then? He has only got three legs because the other one was eaten by a crocodile when he was only a puppy. His name is Skippy.'

'Yes, but he is not the answer. Anybody else?'

'No, no, let me just ask one more question,' pleaded Happy, and Elizabeth took pity on him.

'OK, wait, wait, wait.' The boy scrunched up his eyes and wriggled his fingers, shaking his body from side to side as he racked his brains for a suitable question. 'Here we go. What about – is it a purple animal?'

'Oh, Happy!' we all chorused again.

'What's the matter? Purple is my favourite colour.' And with that incontrovertible proof of the sensibleness of his question, he folded his arms and stared out of the window.

On the horizon, perhaps some five miles away, stood an enormous grain silo, a cathedral of the modern age, and as we approached it we discovered that it was surrounded by a number of other buildings. A general store, a small bar and a bottle shop stood alongside a garage and café. We stopped and stretched, and I consulted my map. Another hundred and seven kilometres straight on down the road should be the farmer's wife. It all seemed extremely unlikely.

So on we went, and as we cleared the small settlement, I noticed that to my right and left was a long, high, wire-mesh fence, its clear intention being to keep out marauding animals who otherwise would destroy the several hundred hectares of vegetables and cereals that I could now see spread out in front of us. Astonishingly, in Botswana there were some three thousand kilometres of one-and-a-half-metre-high 'buffalo fence', officially called the Veterinary Cordon Fence. It is not a single fence but a series of high-tension steel-wire barriers that run cross-country through some of Botswana's wildest terrain. The fences were first erected in 1954 to segregate wild buffalo herds from domestic free-range cattle in order to thwart the spread of foot and mouth disease. The main problem is that the fences prevent wild animals from migrating to water sources along age-old seasonal routes, and as a result thousands of animals become entangled in the fence while others die of exhaustion searching for a way around them. Perhaps in time it will be decided to dismantle them, for no better reason than that the more animals there are, the more tourists there will be.

That said, the level of cultivation was impressive. On either side of the road, across the flat plain as far as the eye could see, furrows of maize and sorghum stretched away in fantastically straight lines. Some three hundred yards out to our right, a combine harvester was moving at a snail's pace through a section of wheat. From my ill-informed perspective it seemed that it would take the machine a couple of days to reach the end of the line. How strange it must be to see this scene from the sky: a steel-hemmed yellow patch on the great uniformly grey-green canvas of the Kalahari.

It must have taken half an hour to cross this farmland, and eventually we arrived at the gates at the far end. From my odometer I estimated that we would meet our hostess in precisely twenty-three kilometres' time. It still seemed pretty unlikely. Although I had no idea how much further on we would have to travel off the road, I was already quite keen to reach our destination as the children were beginning to fidget. Up until that stage they had behaved fantastically well, but now I could hear the odd inquiry made to Elizabeth about whether we were nearly there. She calmed and distracted them, but soon we would have to stop and let them stretch their legs. I peered down the endlessly straight road and leaned my chin on the steering wheel as the Old Queen Mum chugged on and on.

Since there were no signposts or any particular distinctive features along the side of the road, I was entirely reliant on the distances that I had been given by Graham, and the more the kilometres ticked by, the more I stared about. When we arrived at the prescribed location and found nobody there, should I stop and wait, or should I continue, not trusting the accuracy of my odometer? It was with great relief, therefore, that as the last kilometre clicked by, I espied what appeared to be a horse and rider.

When we slowed to a halt alongside them, I discovered that indeed it was a horse, but in fact there were two riders. A pleasant-looking, blonde-haired woman held the reins of a sturdy bay mare. Behind her sat a young girl about the same age as the children around me, and who was unmistakably the woman's daughter. After climbing down and opening the back of the truck, I went up and put out my hand to the woman who took it in a firm but friendly grasp.

'*Goeiemiddag. Hoe gaan dit?*'

'Yes. No problem at all thanks. Very good instructions, thanks.'

The small girl leaned forward.

'My mother doesn't speak any English,' she explained. 'She is asking you how you are?'

'Oh, I'm fine thanks very much. How do you say that in Afrikaans?'

'*Goed dankie.*'

'Oh, OK. *Goed dankie!*' I replied with a bit of a flourish and smiled.

Turning her horse away, the lady looked a bit baffled but murmured something to her daughter as she did so.

'*Kom*, follow us!' And with that they set off at a rapid trot. 'It is not so far.'

Hurriedly, we piled back into the car, and skidding slightly onto the muddy track we swung and slewed our way after them. Glancing in my rear-view mirror, I noticed that soon, worryingly soon, we had lost sight of the road. We were now travelling on grass and dirt on a path that appeared to have been scythed through the bush. Occasionally, there would be turnings to the left or right that were more or less overgrown, but otherwise we were surrounded on all sides by uniform, unremarkable trees and shrubs. Driving was made difficult by the recent rain, and when we hit occasional puddles of water the Old Queen Mum took off like a tipsy water-skier; wiggling the steering wheel I realised to my great alarm that I had next to no control over the direction she chose to take. Shrieking with laughter, the children urged me on, failing to realise that for much of the time I was the driver in little more than name.

Horseback was clearly a much more suitable form of transport for these conditions, and soon the mother and daughter were some few hundred yards ahead of us. The little girl, one arm around her mother's waist, waved us on with the other, urging us to keep up. Pressing down on the accelerator, I felt the car surge forward and we immediately plummeted into a deeper than normal puddle. In an instant the windscreen was thickly covered in a blackish-brown thin mud. The interior of the car suddenly darkened, and I scrambled around to find the knob on the dashboard that operated the rather ancient windscreen wipers. With a sigh and a rubbery groan, they cranked into action and after two or three scrapes, I could finally more or less see our way.

The horse and riders, however, had disappeared.

Slithering slowly to a stop, I hurriedly unwound my window and leaned out. To my relief, the mother and daughter reappeared from a gap in the bushes that I had not noticed and beckoned us on again. The Old Queen Mum made a leisurely turn and we made our way towards them.

'Not so far to go now. Come on, follow us.'

We pressed on and soon emerged from the thick under-growth, and not before time, as I was now feeling the exhaustion of a rally driver. Before us stood some impressive Western-style gates that were set in the high perimeter fence we had seen on our way through the arable land.

Just inside was a large farmyard, set back from which, behind a small picket fence and flower garden, was an attractive house with gabled ends. On either side of the yard were two large wooden-framed barns behind one of which stood a towering galvanised-metal silo. We parked up alongside a huge wooden cart piled mountainously high with bales of straw and attached to a Toytown red tractor. A group of farm workers was unloading the bales on the end of ten-foot pitchforks and thumping them down on a diesel-powered conveyor belt that delivered them smoothly into the top of one of the hangars, where in turn they were being stacked neatly to the rafters.

Seemingly impossibly, a huge man was carrying two bales at a time, one in either hand and swinging them effort-lessly onto the machine. As soon as he saw us arrive, he strode over, pulling off a greasy leather cowboy hat as he did so. He was enormous, and sported the bushiest beard that I had ever seen. It spread all the way across his barrel-like chest and halfway down his pneumatic tummy. When he stood beside me, I realised that he must have been at least six foot eight. He wore dungarees and a broad smile as he grasped my hand.

'You are Willy? Friend of Graham? My name is Hans. Welcome to our farm,' he said in broken English with an Afrikaans accent that you could have cut with a *panga* – an African bush knife.

All the children looked in astonishment at this giant of a figure as I introduced them one by one. He beamed at them and welcomed them in Afrikaans, calling them, from what I understood, his sons and daughters. He then introduced us to his own children who numbered at least six or seven, and ranged from teenagers to babes in arms. One of the older boys, Marcus, who had a blondish cow's lick, had clearly been volunteered to be the guide for the day. With a friendly smile, he offered to show the children around the farm and introduce them to the children who would make up the opposition. Meanwhile, I was invited to slip away with his parents for a cup of tea.

Immediately inside the front door was a sizeable, almost Victorian kitchen with a large wood-burning stove and a huge table built of heavy timber. The other furnishings were very plain, and the only decoration on the walls consisted of what I surmised to be embroidered texts from the Bible in simple frames. The atmosphere was one of great modesty and simplicity.

With evident pride, Hans showed me the rest of the house. The children's rooms were equally unfussy, consisting only of low, wooden bunks and rush-seated chairs. Hans's wife, whose name I never learnt, had her own small parlour at the back of the house which contained piles of sewing and embroidery, a large Bible and some very ancient-looking magazines.

By the time we returned to the kitchen, a cake and a large pot had been placed on the table, and a bustling elderly lady was laying out plates and knives as she chatted animatedly in Setswana with the lady of the house. We sat down and I felt compelled to communicate, through the offices of the young girl who had followed us into the house, how pleased we all were to be with them. Luckily, I had not formulated my speech, because just at that moment, his hands clasped together and his eyes tightly closed, Hans began to intone, in a gruff but quiet voice, a prayer of thanksgiving – Grace. Biting my lip, I put my hands together and waited.

As soon as he had finished, the solemn atmosphere evaporated and Hans's wife cut the cake into gargantuan slices, one of which was pushed in front of me. Hans stared at me thoughtfully as he took a healthy bite of the jam sponge and mumbled something to his daughter.

'My father thinks you look like a typical Britisher.'

Uncertain whether this was a good or bad thing, I smiled.

'Yes, he says you are thin. A bit weak. You need to eat more, he says.'

After a little while, Hans decided to be a little more confident with his English, and embarked on a lengthy discourse about the history of the Afrikaner people before going on to explain what hospitality they proposed to offer us. First, and my heart sank slightly, the children could play their football game. (Overwhelmed by the complexities of the competition in which we were playing, I had failed to realise that the drubbing we had received at Katima Mulilo had, thankfully, only been a warm-up match. Here, at Panda-matenga, was our first date with destiny.) After the game was over and they had had a wash at the farmyard pump, they could look around the farmstead and then we would take them out into the fields to explain what it was that the farmers grew and how they went about it. In the evening, they would build a big fire in the middle of the yard and cook some nice Afrikaner food. The children could sleep in the barn on the bales of hay and straw. It would be plenty warm enough for them and, thanks to the cordon fence, there was no risk of wild animals. They had made up a room for me, where they were sure I would be comfortable. The next morning, they would cook up a big, special breakfast. Hans, I could see, was already looking forward to it. It would set us up nicely for a trip back to Kasane.

After I had failed to refuse the offer of a third slab of cake, I felt anything but enthusiastic about taking part in a sporting event, particularly as, unbeknownst to me, Graham had volunteered my services as referee. Soon, though, the children's enthusiasm lightened my mood and the game was under way. Although the children of Panda-matenga were in some cases rather older and bigger than the Kasane Kudus, they were very inexperienced. It seemed that they were more used to playing rugby than the round-ball game. This was clearly to our great advantage, although Happy might have disagreed with me when he was flattened by a flying rugby tackle from a large boy in bursting shorts and shirt. Our centre-midfielder looked at me most reproachfully as he dusted himself down, willing me to pull out my red card. Realising which side our bread was buttered that evening, I disappointed Happy by only quietly admonishing the chubby boy. Everything seemed to be pretty evenly matched for the first ten minutes, but just before half-time, Dolly, who had been busy giving Bothle a lesson in how to tie his laces, took her eye off the ball. As a stalwart of our flat back four she was supposed to be following every move of the opposition attack. Instead, she was sitting on the halfway line with Bothle repeating patiently, 'Now over and under, and then a bow, and then another and pull. Yes, nearly . . .'

Indeed, she was unaware of the goal that drifted from deep on the left into the top of the net seemingly several hundred feet above the head of the diminutive Hakim, our goalkeeper, until the crowd roared their approval. Grafting a smile onto my face, I lifted the leaden whistle to my lips. Half-time was spent rather disconsolately in our goal-mouth, Hakim smacking himself on the head with frustration, and Dolly chiding the nonplussed Bothle for having distracted her. Still, some slices of fresh mango and cups of the much loved orange squash revived spirits, and I was pleased to see the children trotting quite cheerfully back out onto the field.

Hardly had I pulled up my socks and blown to start the second half than Stella, who really was extraordinarily swift, skipped and bounded over outstretched legs and, using the outside of her plimsoll, managed to push the black and white ball under the body of the sprawling goal-keeper. Leaping over him, she followed the ball into the net, lifted it above her head and ran back to the centre spot to the adulation of her team-mates. It took all of my self-control not to hurl my whistle over my shoulder and join the celebrations.

Fortunately, from then on the Kasane Kudus had the upper hand. Only a few minutes later, Arthur, his face bursting with pride, came rushing back from the penalty spot having sweetly struck a free kick which had been awarded for a particularly high tackle on little Hui. (There had been a small time-out period after this incident during which I had had to pursue Hui as he pursued his assailant around the pitch administering stinging karate chops.) Once the score had moved to 2–1 we never looked back, and I eventually blew the final whistle with a flourish that I hope was not too triumphalist.

By the time everyone had washed, or at least splashed themselves, at the water-pump in the yard, it was getting quite late and the sun was beginning its descent in the west. Yet there was still so much to do. The children toured the farmyard and were full of excitement about all the pieces of machinery that they were shown. Kasane, despite its location, was by comparison, with its shops, banks and hotels, almost urban, and they had never had the opportunity to fully experience an agricultural environment beyond seeing pictures in books. Although this was primarily an arable farm, the family kept a variety of different animals for their own use. A small dairy herd, pigs, chickens and some beef cattle were all kept in neat fields behind the farm, and strangely to me the children were more interested to see these 'rare' animals than they were to see the exotic animals that surrounded them on a daily basis.

We all climbed into the now empty hay-cart, and tugged by the little red tractor set out into the great wide plains of the fields. Hans, with avuncular good cheer, allowed each of the children to steer the tractor down the straight lines of harvested crops. Amazed, they watched as the combine harvester made its way across the land chewing up the bending wheat, leaving the neatly piled straw behind it as it spewed out the golden grain into a trailer that followed alongside.

By the time we returned to the house the sun was beginning to set over the fringes of the farm. Dragging dead wood from the surroundings, the farm workers had piled up a bonfire that would not have been unworthy of Guy Fawkes' night, and it was just beginning to take light as the children settled around it in a circle. Great piles of coiled boerwors, the hearty Afrikaner sausage, prime beef steaks and silver-wrapped potatoes were set on a trestle table beside the barbecue grate. Home-baked bread rolls and bowls of salad picked from the kitchen garden stood alongside pitchers of freshly squeezed lemonade.

Soon the evening air was filled with the smoky, burning smell of grilled meat as the children cooked their own food and Elizabeth and I attempted to prevent them incinerating either their supper or themselves. Marcus appeared with a huge metal bowl of freshly risen dough and a bundle of sharpened sticks about three feet long. To our general fascination, he demonstrated what I understood to be the ancient Afrikaner art of cooking 'stick bread'. After rolling a piece of soft white dough between his hands until it was about a foot long and two or three inches thick, he speared one end on the stick and wrapped the remainder around it. Holding it carefully over the embers and twisting it slowly he made sure that it did not burn or fall into the ashes. Within a few minutes he had a perfectly cooked bread bun with a cylindrical hole the length of it. Then he produced the *pièce de résistance* – a tin of thick, white, super-sweet evaporated milk, some of which he poured into the hole.

He handed it to Arthur and watched with obvious pleasure as the boy, licking his fingers with delight, consumed it in two gulping mouthfuls. When the others saw how much he had enjoyed it, they all clamoured for a stick and some of the dough. It soon became clear that making stick bread was something of a science and pandemonium ensued. Bothle, who had drifted into a daydream as he toasted his bread, only woke up after his attempt had been completely carbonised on one side and was entirely uncooked on the other. Shrugging wearily, he turned it around and held it back over the flames. Within a few seconds, the stick burned through entirely and dropped off into the fire. Looking at me dolefully, he handed me what was left of it and we started again.

After the meal was finished and most of the sticky evaporated milk had been removed from faces and small hands, Hans produced a guitar and sang what appeared to be Afrikaner country-and-western songs. Initially, the children seemed to be slightly taken aback, but soon they were overtaken by the rhythms and began to clap along. Then, led by Dolly, they scrambled to their feet and danced energetically and impressively in the glowering, dipping light of the dying fire.

Finally, tired out by their exertions, they sat down again, yawning and gazing silently into the embers. Hans swung his four-wheel-drive car around until it faced into the barn and turned the lights on. One by one, the children crawled in under the blankets that had been laid out for them on some freshly tossed hay and closed their eyes. Only Stella and Hui seemed nervous about this new strange environment, and when I realised that they were both on the verge of tears I agreed to sleep in the barn myself. This seemed to placate them and before long they too were sound asleep. As soon as I was confident that they were happy, I rolled myself into my blanket. Some distance away some horses were snorting and whinnying, and with the last notes of Hans's guitar still ringing in my ears, I quickly dozed off to dream of the great Wild West that surrounded us.

Breakfast the following morning was everything that it had been billed to be. Eggs from the hens, crisp bacon (from the pigs, but I left this unmentioned – Skye, Kitty, Glory, Dolly and Olobogeng had declared themselves vegetarian a couple of weeks before to the consternation of their carnivorous friends and relations), tomatoes, corn fritters and sausages were all served around the edge of the fire that had been kept going all night. By the time that we had drunk our tea, made sure that the children had not left anything behind, said goodbye to our kind, friendly hosts and had packed ourselves back into the Old Queen Mum, it was long past mid-morning. Both Graham and Hans had impressed on me the importance of getting back to Kasane before nightfall. There had been a number of disastrous, fatal accidents on the road to Pandamatenga, all of which had been caused by collisions with animals. One lucky man had found himself in the curious situation of driving in slow motion, or so it seemed, on his motorbike between the legs of a giraffe. Sturdy though our vehicle was, I did not wish to consider what it would be like to encounter one of the bigger animals at anything resembling high speed. Still, we had plenty of time as it had taken us just over two and a half hours to reach the spot on the road where we had met Hans's wife, and it had only taken a further half hour to reach the farm.

'My father wants to know if you will remember the way back to the main road. He wants to draw you a map. Just wait a few minutes perhaps?' suggested Marcus.

'No, no, I'm sure we'll be fine. We just go to the end of the track here and turn left, don't we? Then it's just straight on?'

Just at that moment I was distracted by the children. Kitso had started to wail loudly because Happy had just pinched his notebook and thrown it out of the window. It landed at my feet along with his carefully sharpened pencil.

Good timing, Happy, thank you. I picked them up, and instead of handing them back to the little boy, gave them to our host so he might draw me a plan. Stroking his beard carefully, he made sure that I repeated back to him his instructions so as to be doubly sure that I properly understood them. When he was confident I did, Hans raised his worn leather hat and waved us off as we bounced through the fence and disappeared back into the bush.

11

Out There in the Bush

Two zebra jumped out in front of the car just after we had pulled out of the gates, and the children had eventually stopped waving goodbye as our hosts disappeared round the corner. Bucking up their hind quarters, they put on an impressive turn of speed as they galloped up the cutting. Zig-zagging left and right as if they thought I might imminently try and run them down, they pelted the Old Queen Mum with clods of dry earth that their hooves carved out of the ground.

This was the first time that I had encountered these magnificent animals at close quarters; their coats alone, glistening with sweat and sunshine, were utterly entrancing, and the power produced by their muscly, short legs was enough to make us want to follow them further down the track. On they thundered, shaking their heads up and down, prancing and bursting with energy. At one stage they came to a fallen old tree, which they cleared with a simultaneous bound. The Old Queen Mum swerved and smashed through the brittle upper branches without concern and gave chase. Behind me, spending a significant amount of their time airborne, the youngsters shrieked with excitement every time we burst through a puddle or when the branches of overhanging trees poked in through the side windows leaving their green sap splattered on the ceiling.

Finally, though, the two animals veered sharply right and, springing almost abnormally high, disappeared over a hedge and were gone. Panting with exhilaration and laughter, we slowed down almost to a standstill. In the excitement, I had lost my sense of direction. Now, checking my mirrors, I tried to gauge our position but all that I could see was a long, seemingly endless, green avenue. I consulted the map on which Happy had been rather unhelpfully doodling. All seemed well, although I did not really have any clear way of working out how long we had been driving behind the zebra. I had certainly not noticed any left-hand turn-off as we had been in pursuit.

Perhaps the best thing to do was just to continue on our way; it couldn't be too far until we found the turning, then all we had to do was take it and just go straight on until we hit the road. In the back, the youngsters had struck up song again. Amazingly, they seemed to be able to remember some of the Afrikaans words to one of Hans's songs, and although they seemed to have no idea what they meant, they chanted them cheerfully as Dolly conducted.

Humming, I kept on driving, enjoying the great open spaces, the natural world and this fine, charming company. At one stage, I had to swerve quite sharply to avoid a rock about the size of a soldier's helmet, and then another and another, laid out like mines in a minefield. Finally, I had to slow down for fear of damaging the sensitive undercarriage of the Old Queen Mum. As I did so, I peered at one of the lumps closely and discovered to my surprise that I had chanced upon a family, a very large family, of tortoises. Fascinated, having never seen such a creature outside a cardboard box, I stopped and pulled over. We all climbed

out extraordinarily quietly and approached these prehistoric animals, whom I fully expected to retreat into themselves. They did not seem to mind, however, even when I
picked one of them up to test its weight; it just looked at
me in a rather bored fashion. That said, tortoises do have
a limited range of facial expression.

Courtney, who was probably our greatest animal-lover,
lay down on his stomach face to face with his new friend
and fed it choice blades of grass that he had carefully
selected. Talking quietly to it, the little boy didn't seem to
mind that the conversation was all one-sided.

Some minutes later, I did begin to wonder if we shouldn't
be getting back on our way, as I was still not entirely
convinced that we were on the right path. Serving drinks
from the big jerrycan strapped to the back of the car, I
checked that nobody was feeling car-sick or needed to go
to the loo. We drove on.

And on.

And on.

By now we should comfortably be back on the road but
still we found ourselves on this wide grass path. On and
on it went, seemingly endlessly. My relief was therefore
enormous when I encountered a left-hand turning. Partly
because I was so keen to discover that I had not made a
mistake, and also because the countryside was so incredibly
similar, I convinced myself that we were still travelling in
the right direction and that somehow my instinct about the
timing of the turn had been incorrect. My spirits lifted and
I joined in with the nonsensical lyrics of the Afrikaans song.
As we were crossing a huge, wide, graded corridor cut
through the bush, I realised that we had made a mistake,
or rather, as I did not feel that the six-year-olds could be
held responsible for a navigational error and Elizabeth had
taken no part in the map-reading exercise, *I* had made a

mistake. What was of more concern than this was that we were, in fact, completely lost.

Perhaps I should turn right, or maybe left? Would it be better to turn back, or go forward? With trepidation I glanced down at my fuel gauge, but to my relief it was still two thirds full. We drove on.

Fortunately, our generous hosts had provided us with packed lunches, and the children, whose initial enthusiasm for our great adventure was beginning to wear thin, had opened up their packages and were now intent, despite Elizabeth's good efforts, on spreading various bits of food around the back of the car.

Eventually, we had to stop again, and whilst the children milled around, I started racking my brains to try and work out what it was that we should do. Not for a long time had I found myself in an environment that I was totally ill-equipped to deal with. Possibly the closest other human beings to us were our friends, the farmers. I could not even begin to guess how far away they might be as we had been driving for the best part of three hours. Thinking of the welcoming fire and the comfortable hay barn, I began to feel a little down-hearted. My mood was not much improved by the sight of a collection of that most hideous of birds, the marabou stork, picking over the corpse of some much decayed and therefore virtually unrecognisable antelope; bald-headed but for a few stubbly bits of hair, they were squelching around in the entrails like so many out-of-work lawyers.

What worried me more than our fuel situation – thankfully I had a twenty-litre can strapped to the roof – was that it was now mid-afternoon. As I knew only too well, in this part of the world we were so close to the equator that nightfall came very quickly, and with only a couple of hours of daylight to go, I still had no idea in which direction we should be heading. If we didn't find the road within the next couple of hours or so then we would be returning home in the dark. I was concerned that there was no way that I could get a message back to Kasane, but I was even more concerned about where we would be spending the night.

The number of animals that we had seen on our trip through the bush, which included giraffe, elephants and zebra as well as a multitude of antelope, made me quite sure that there were plenty of other creatures out there, and that many of them would only appear after dark and then with healthy appetites. This was certainly no place for four-teen six-year-olds to be spending the night. Luckily, until now, none of them had realised that anything was wrong, and even Elizabeth, although she must have recognised that the return journey was taking considerably longer than the inward one, appeared to have remained unperturbed.

We set off again, but before long, as I began to panic, I began to turn into any available opening. Quite often it turned out that these were dead ends, and I would have to reverse, often with significant difficulty, back out and onto our original track. In what seemed a strangely short space of time the shadow of the Old Queen Mum began to lengthen, and the sun, which seemed to have sat directly above us for most of the day, started sliding down the sky until it began to edge into the trees. Birds that had been flitting industriously through the air now very quickly came to rest. Finally, a strange silence settled about us, so that the clicking of the hot engine seemed to be the only audible noise when eventually we came to a halt, and I turned it off in order to take my muddled mind back through the tortuous list of turns that we had taken. Baboons, which had previously watched us with inscrutable eyes as we passed, had now all but disappeared.

Before long the light could only be described as dimpsy,

and soon after that it was decidedly dark. Only now, having been playing happily in the back, did the children sense that things were not going entirely according to plan. I could feel their restlessness, even their concern. What were we to do? As it was getting dark I was less than enthusiastic about wandering around outside, but I could hardly keep all the children cooped up in the Old Queen Mum until the following morning.

We were now on a particularly rough and narrow stretch of path, and I had had to slow down considerably from fear of encountering an elephant's backside around one of the many and reasonably sharp corners. Their droppings littered the ground, and I suddenly remembered that this meant that it was likely that there was a watering hole nearby – not, of course, that that would be of any particular use to us.

Just then, out of the corner of my eye, I saw something bright gleaming through the trees. But, as we rolled on, it was gone. Out of desperation, I made the sudden decision to reverse, which I did rather jerkily causing a loud chorus of 'ooohs!' from the back. This was followed by a bump in the foot well of the passenger seat as Olobogeng, who had been kneeling with her back to the windscreen, slid off onto her bottom. After she had overcome her surprise, she climbed back up and giggled. I, on the other hand, was very far from feeling like laughing. When eventually I had returned to the spot where I thought I had seen the light, I felt a huge burst of excitement as I realised that it was truly there. Although it was difficult to judge quite where it came from, it looked relatively close.

In the dark it was impossible to work out how to get close to it or indeed, once I had, what exactly I would find there. Still, on balance, some light was considerably better than no light. For want of a better idea I drove on, following the bumpy and increasingly narrow track. It seemed to take us in a tight circle. All was silent now in the back: clearly everybody else had spotted the same chance of salvation – hopefully some not entirely lonely rest spot for the night.

Curving round, the lane swung onto a larger track and then veered almost immediately off it. There was the light again! We disappeared into the bush before suddenly re-emerging as a solitary impala bounced in front of us, its short black horns catching the light of our headlights. My eyes were immediately confused by the sight of uniform shapes in the randomness of this wilderness: geometric squares and oblongs around a waterhole some fifteen or twenty yards wide by thirty yards in length, lit white by the rising moon. It was a small campsite. There appeared to be six or seven large rectangular tents erected on wooden decks along one side of the water. At the far end was a large *boma*, a traditional round African hut with a straw roof, wide open at the front and lit by what appeared to be electric lighting. It was reached by a smooth sandy track that ran along the other side of the pool. I drove down it full of hope and stopped alongside.

'Just stay there for a minute, please, everyone. Don't worry, I'm coming back in a minute.'

The anxiety in the back of the truck was palpable and a few of the small figures behind me slid closer to Elizabeth. The anxiety in the front seat was not vastly different.

I got out.

Silhouetted against the light was a tall male figure. A click and then a flashlight shone in my eyes.

'Howzit?' came the gruff but indubitably South African inquiry.

'Ah, yes, hello, how are you? Good evening. Now, listen, I'm really sorry about this but we are completely lost.'

'Oh, I thought it was Dirk!' came the reply.

'Dirk!'

Not the same Dirk, surely. That would be more than I could manage.

'No, blimey, no, my name is Will. I come from Kasane. I just got really lost on the tracks. Sorry about this. You think it will be all right if we stay overnight?'

'Well, maybe, it might be a bit difficult because you know this is a private camp. I suppose you could put up your tent out there in the bush if you want. So, who are we exactly?'

Somehow, despite the extraordinary situation in which we found ourselves, I had seen this question coming. There was no clear reply that I could possibly give apart from opening the back door of the Old Queen Mum. Out of the back trooped all the children apart from Bothle, who was carried out fast asleep in Elizabeth's arms.

'*Jeez!*' gasped the voice from behind the flash lamp.

'Yes, I know it's a shock. I'm really sorry about this but I'm in a real spot of bother with this lot. You see we were stuck down at Pandamatenga and I got completely lost because I didn't know the way . . .'

I could hear myself mumbling all sorts of nonsense, sounding more and more feeble, and feeling more and more feeble the more I talked.

'Who the hell is that?' a very much less friendly American voice called from inside the large hut.

By this stage the figure that had been asking me the questions had come closer, and I could see in the light of his flash lamp that he was a tall, long-blond-haired man, probably in his late forties.

'Hi, name's Barry,' he introduced himself in a not altogether unkindly manner. He threw the light over the startled but also very tired children. Just at that moment two figures appeared on the threshold of the *boma*.

'Thought this was supposed to be totally exclusive? Where the hell did all these folk show up from?' asked the American voice in a no more friendly fashion.

'Say, honey, don't be so aggressive,' came a fluting female voice. 'These folk are lost out here in the wilds of Africa. You got to have some sympathy. Hey, look at all those really cute little kids. Hi, guys, how are you all? Jeez, you all look so really tired. Look at that little girl – she's just pooped, poor little poppet. Hey, come in, you guys, come in. You got to have some rest here.'

'Hell, honey. We're supposed to be here on some sort of holiday! You can't have any Tom, Dick or Harry walking in here. We've got an exclusive!'

'Hell, honey,' she mimicked. 'You're just here to kill things.'

Already feeling rather disconcerted about our new-found circumstances, this last pronouncement did no good for my general sense of being in control of the situation. Yet I was responsible for these youngsters, so I gulped a couple of times and pulled my shirt down across my chest with both hands.

'We're very sorry for having disturbed you, and we don't want to put you to any trouble. I was just hoping that we could find a place where these children could rest.'

After a little more grumbling, I was invited into the brightly lit hut. Winking at the children and promising them that I would be back in just a moment, I stepped inside. My eyes took a few minutes to readjust, but once they had, they registered a scene of the greatest luxury. To one side was a fully equipped bar complete with ancient whiskies and cut crystal tumblers. The rest of the room was given over to an open-plan living space. At the back was a table laid for a several course meal, and in the front, looking out across the water, were a selection of leather sofas around a low, glass table. The floor was carpeted in animal skins. At a glance I could recognise leopard, cheetah and lion. My eyes sought out the waste-paper basket – it was inevitably made from an elephant's foot.

On one of the sofas sat a wizened, bald man smoking a large cigar. He was wearing an outfit that would not have looked out of place on a baddie in a Tarzan movie. Although it hung off his bony frame, it was made of expensive material and matched that of the woman sitting next to him. Considerably younger than her partner, she was not in the first bloom of youth, although she was making strenuous attempts to battle against Old Father Time, her main weapons of defence clearly being a wide range of expensive cosmetics. Her perfect hair, set in a blonde helmet that towered high above her head, looked absurdly out of place in the wilderness of the bush, but where the man looked callous and cold, grumpy and misanthropic, she seemed to radiate a maternal softness and a kindly, generous character.

They were obviously visitors here, but Barry, the only other person in the room, was clearly made for these surroundings. Like my friend Hans from Pandamatenga, he was a massive man, but lean and strong. He would not have looked out of place as a wrestler in gladitorial games, although he too was wearing safari clothes. Unlike the others', his fitted him perfectly; he looked totally comfortable in his environment. His straight, dirty blond hair fell to his shoulders and over his crinkled, pale blue eyes, and his chin was covered with thick copper stubble. What was perhaps most noticeable about him, however, was that he wore a revolver at his hip. Despite this rather threatening aspect, he, like the woman, exuded an air of trustworthy friendliness.

Having burbled too much already, I decided to say

nothing until I was asked a question. It became clear that the old man was in no way amused by our appearance, but the other two seemed to be more sympathetic to our cause.

'Barry,' said the old man, seemingly perfectly oblivious to my presence. 'You know what I want when I come hunting, don't you? You know what I want, don't you? Exclusivity! Say it, Barry! Exclusivity!'

'Yes, Ritchie, I know that. I know you always look for exclusivity and I can't blame you for that. But hey, man, this wasn't exactly as if I planned it. You know these folk, they just got unlucky. It's too easy getting yourself lost out here, especially if you don't know what you're doing.'

Nobody seemed to take a great deal of notice of my blushing deeply at this.

'Well, maybe we ought to offer them some kind of African hospitality?' suggested Barry.

Ritchie, on the other hand, did not appear keen to be quite so generous.

Turning to me, he fixed me with a cantankerous eye.

'So, you some kind of schoolmaster, or what? Where did all these goddamn kids come from?'

Kitso, who was a curious little boy, stepped into the light and politely held his hand out to Ritchie in the Batswanan style, his left hand held to his right elbow. Ritchie ignored him, and before I could make any introductions he went on. 'Jeez, this is all I need. Some goddamn Limey, Mr Chips, ha, ha, and a whole load of goddamn piccaninnies! Get me another whisky, Shirl.'

'Oh come on, honey. Lighten up, why don't you? There are about four empty tents down there alongside the waterhole. These kids can stay in one of those tonight and they'll be gone before you even get up, isn't that right?' Shirl had stood up and made her way to the bar as she directed this last question at me.

'Absolutely, yes, we've really got to get going in the morning. No, you won't hear anything from this lot. Some of the quietest children in, well, just about anywhere, anywhere in the whole world you can think of,' I ended rather lamely.

Ritchie, whose nose was now stuck firmly back into his whisky, initially appeared not to have heard this exchange. There was an uneasy silence as the four of us looked at each other.

'Goddamn it, woman, why d'you think I'm such an easy touch?' He suddenly glared at us. 'You think I got where I am today by being a pushover?' He drank again deeply. 'Well, I guess as I paid for all the other tents it doesn't matter if they get used for just one night.'

'Look, I am really grateful. Really didn't want to disturb you like this.'

'Hey, Mr Chips.' He liked his little joke. 'Don't thank me, thank my dumbass wife. And if I hear so much as a squeak out of those little varmints while I'm eating my dinner, I'm gonna get myself my gun and blow their goddamn balls off. Can't be disturbed while I'm eating my dinner,' he mumbled into his glass.

Just at that moment a cook, dressed in a full chef's outfit, appeared at the door of the hut carrying a large metal tray piled high with dishes. Barry took this as our cue to leave, grabbing me by the arm and whisking me out before I had the chance to say anything further.

'Get the kids in the car and follow me.'

We drove a few hundred metres up the slope behind the big hut until we came to what appeared to be a kitchen block.

'Okay, in you all come,' he said in a low, friendly voice. 'We've got plenty enough food here to feed you little fellows.'

Indeed, the whole building was made up of one enormous kitchen, in the middle of which was a huge table that reminded me of a bench in a science lab except that it was much wider. Some minutes later, the cook returned and greeted the children in Setswana.

'*Dumela*, Rra,' they replied politely, if somewhat bewildered, and sat down on stools as directed by Barry.

'This is where the trackers normally eat, but because we've only got one client at the moment most of them have gone back to their villages. It's coming up to the end of the season so we're trying to finish everything off. You guys came on just the right evening. We've got enough game stew here to feed an army,' he chuckled.

Richly delicious it was too, and by the time the children had finished off a plate, and in some cases a second plate, they all looked as if they were ready to drop. In Indian file, we all slunk down a narrow path that brought us along the back of the big tents. Unzipping the backs, Barry ushered us in: boys in one, girls in another, and dragging out blankets from metal cases, he made them all comfortable. Elizabeth was absolutely delighted to discover that she had a huge tent all to herself.

'Expect you might like one of those whiskies yourself, Will?' said Barry with a wink after he had shown me my tent. 'Ritchie goes to bed smack on 10 o'clock every evening, so why don't you come down after that? I'll still be around.'

So, an hour or so later, I found myself sitting around a campfire listening to Barry tell me tales of other 'great white hunters' like Ritchie and drinking extraordinarily good Scotch.

'You from Kasane, that's right is it?'

'Well, not from . . . but yeah, that's right. You know it?'

'Yeah, get there about every couple of months for new supplies.' He paused and spat. 'You know, Dirk?'

'Umm, yeah.' I almost recoiled at the name.

Barry must have noticed.

'You're right. He's a complete . . .' He stopped, cocked his ear to listen and grimaced. 'Talk of the devil.'

Listening hard, I could hear nothing but the faint crackle of the campfire that was burning in front of the open-sided hut. But soon, from far out in the bush, came the quiet, almost imperceptible hum of a smooth diesel engine, and some five minutes later I spotted the bright yellow shafts of headlights waving up and down along the rough tracks. As I steeled myself for this new and not very welcome arrival, Barry grabbed my arm and muttered, 'Keep quiet about the kids. Dirk's the professional hunter here. Thinks he runs the place. Let me sort him out.'

Motor whirring, the *bakkie* swung round the back of the building, and we heard slamming doors and shouted instructions. A minute later, Dirk rounded the side accompanied by his two sons, Edwin and Erwin. These two hardly glanced at me as they headed for the drinks trolley, but Dirk looked thunderstruck when he first saw me.

'Er . . . hello!' I said, brightly. 'Was just passing through; thought I would drop in!'

Dirk glared at me, and then clearly decided that he did not sufficiently care about me to pass comment. He, too, headed for the alcohol.

'Barry, my *bru*, I've got a kudu and a nice eland in the cold store. When you come through Kasane, can you drop them by my place?'

'Sure, Dirk, no problem.'

'You can give the camp boys some of that old buff in the freezer if you want, but make sure it's not the best steaks. We got the elephant to the village on the flatbed truck. In the end, Erwin and Edwin had to cut her into six bits and we didn't bother with the head. It's out the back – should have rotted back by next season, OK? Tell you what my *bru*, that chainsaw works just great. Went straight through the backbone. Hey, boys?'

His sons nodded silently and sucked noisily on cans of beer before throwing glasses of Bourbon down their scrubby necks.

'Anyway, we're gonna call it a day. We're out of here at first light. Got to get to Francistown to pick up some more ammo and do a bit of business.' And with that he strode up the wooden decking that ran along the front of the tents beside the moonlit water, his sons following at his heels. Suddenly he stopped, a predator sensing movement. I could see his massive head move as he scanned the bush from his vantage point.

'Come on, follow me,' whispered Barry, and we ran stoopingly across the clearing, the only light the fire and the moon.

We stopped some yards from the three other men, and following their gaze, searched the area below us for movement.

'There,' hissed Barry. 'Tsessebe! So rare, man. Fastest antelope in Africa.' Pointing with a powerful, sunburnt arm, he was clearly excited. 'There must be some others around. Always travel in families.'

The antelope seemed perfectly at ease, standing stock still, mirrored in the water. I looked around for his brothers and sisters. On the low ridge just above the pool I noticed some movement. At first it was almost impossible to make out the shape of the creatures, but quickly it became clear that these were not relatives of the antelope. My untrained eye thought them to be hyena, but as I looked closer I could see that the coats of the twenty or so carnivores were dappled with a carnival assortment of splashes of yellow, white, brown and black.

'Wild dogs,' Barry and I breathed simultaneously, both knowing that this was a rare event. Because of their vicious nature and their ability to decimate livestock wherever they roamed, the wild dogs of Africa have been consistently shot by landowners, reducing them to one of the rarest breeds on the continent. It was late to see them on the move as they were normally diurnal.

As we watched, one of the larger animals peeled away from the group and circled behind the tsessebe, which flinched a little and turned slightly, nervously, to look behind it. Realising that it was at risk, it decided to take flight, but as it turned to scamper up the hill, it became aware of the pack surrounding it. Just as its head began to twitch nervously looking for an escape route, the dog behind it bounded forward.

Caught off guard, the antelope ran in the only direction that was open to it – straight into the pan. Quickly losing its footing, the antelope started to swim, moving surprisingly quickly through the swirling, muddy water. In a single, steel-sprung bound the dog was in the water behind it. I screwed up my eyes and waited for the ensuing slaughter. The dog paddled fast, its eyes bright, its liver-coloured tongue lolling out of one side of his jaws, until it came alongside the twitching creature whose horns bobbed back and forth with the effort. For several yards the two animals swam side by side. Slowly, almost carefully, the dog reached towards the tsessebe with its mouth. Tentatively it grabbed at one of its large ears and once it was sure it had a firm but not biting grip, it dragged the antelope under the water, deliberately drowning it.

Slowly the antelope's head disappeared beneath the surface, and after one flash of legs and belly and a vigorous shake of its neck, it ceased the fight. Very quickly it was all over, and the wild dog turned to swim to the shore pulling the floating corpse. Once back on dry land, it hauled the body, which was probably three times its own weight, up the sandy bank and into the bush. Slowly, greedily, slinking along behind their leader, the rest of the dogs disappeared into the night.

Ahead of us, I could hear Dirk breathing heavily as he and his sons made their way towards their tent. In a voice that was low and slick like blood, I heard him talking to them.

'Survival of the fittest, my boys, survival of the fittest.'

12

Good Morning, Headmaster

Hyenas were still lapping at the greyish water when I emerged silently from our tents at dawn; slinking backwards, they cocked their heads sideways with curiosity before trotting lightly into the bush.

To my relief, Dirk and company had already left, leaving the atmosphere relaxed and light. Barry and a couple of trackers were hunkered down in front of the campfire, frying eggs and bacon and slicing homemade bread. Slowly and noiselessly as they had been asked, the children emerged from their tents, sleepy-eyed and yawning, stretching and scratching. One by one they squatted down and gratefully accepted the food they were offered. Fortunately there was no sign of Ritchie, and Shirl would almost certainly need an hour more to put her face on.

'So don't you just love Dirk?' asked Barry tousling his mane of hair in disapproval. 'You know about his background, don't you? You know the game he was into before, right?'

Shaking my head, I accepted the cup of coffee that he handed me. The youngsters had disappeared up to the camp kitchen with Joseph the cook who had promised them jam on toast to finish off their feast. We sat back in the wicker chairs and watched some elephants wander ghostly through the trees as they headed for the river.

'Well they call it "canned lion".'

'Oh, right.'

Why I imagined that all the dishonest shenanigans of the past had suddenly disappeared because we live in the modern age, I do not know. Perhaps it is truer that as we become more 'sophisticated', so our scams become more refined. Our friend Dirk had, once upon a time, touted himself about as an international hunting operator. He had bought a concession on the banks of the Limpopo just the other side from the Tuli Block and had proceeded, regardless of rule and regulation, to shoot all the big game that lived there. Unready to give up what was a most lucrative enterprise – he stood to earn anywhere upwards of US$30,000 per lion and the same or thereabouts for leopard, cheetah, buffalo and giraffe – he continued to go to the big 'Sporting and Game' shows in the US. Here he would discuss with, generally speaking, geriatric and megalomaniacal wealthy businessmen what it was they would like to kill, and between them they would draw up a shopping list.

I imagined how these conversations ran: 'I guess this year I don't have so much time. We gotta go on to the Bahamas. I really need to get out to my villa there. So I guess this year I'll just go for a lion – male of course – and probably a buff, long as it's got a good head.'

Not possessing these animals on his own land, Dirk would go off on his own shopping outing. Buffalo was easy; he would go to a game fair in South Africa or Zimbabwe and buy one. He even had a converted lorry to bring it back. Suitably tranquillised, they rarely caused much trouble on the journey.

Lions were more difficult. Through the services of a sister company offering retirement pastures for aging zoo and circus animals, he would, for next to no money, purchase an animal from some far-flung corner of the world. This animal would be duly drugged and fed until the arrival of the client. The 'hunter' would then spend up to ten days tracking the unfortunate beast that was, unbeknownst to him, being kept in a cage behind his tent. Miraculously, on the final day they would come across the spoor of the king of the jungle, who would later be conveniently discovered in a ketamine-induced stupor in a clearing in the bush. All the client then had to do was stand up in the back of the *bakkie*, load his huge gun, aim and pull the trigger. Of course, there were plenty of guides, trackers and great white hunters to lend a hand if they were not able to cope on their own.

Dirk had finally given up this game, not because he was sickened by the artificiality of the 'hunt', but because one year a particularly inept Swiss had shot a tracker stone dead and mortally wounded one of the white hunters, who had bled to death at the foot of a thorn bush drinking a last can of beer. Dirk had had to smuggle the punter out of the country and organise the disposal of the bodies.

'Suppose he was finally sick of all the pointless bloodshed?' I mused.

'Not a bit of it,' replied Barry. 'No, he was just really irritated when he got a letter from the client back in Switzerland, complaining that he had never got to shoot a lion and asking for a refund because he had had to leave four days early.'

Still shaking his head, Barry climbed into his pick-up and guided us on a remarkably straightforward route back to the road a few miles north of where we had been met by the Afrikaners what seemed like a short lifetime ago.

Fortunately, Barry had been kind enough to make radio contact with The Old House just before we went to bed, and by now the message would have travelled across Kasane about our predicament. Still, I was keen to get back, and I sensed that the children were also suffering from too much of a good thing. I was silently counting our blessings when, just a few miles outside Kasane, we drove past the carnage of a petrol tanker that had collided with a buffalo. Both were very dead, although mercifully the driver had escaped unharmed; he was looking on unhappily, as even at this early hour there were a number of people busy with machetes carving up this valuable free food.

Luckily, my next meal came from a rather more conventional source. When the children had been collected from the school, all the parents thanked me for a success-ful outing. As they seemed perfectly happy, I didn't think there was much point in making too much of the fact that we were returning their offspring twenty-four hours late. From the middle of the gaggle of parents appeared Mma Kebalakile, who swept little Arthur into her arms, causing me for a second, with a huge lump in my throat, to wonder whether something terrible had happened in our absence. To my relief, she came up to me smiling.

'*Dumela*, Mr Mango, *le kae*?'

'*Re teng!*'

'So perhaps you would like to have tea with us today?' She looked most hopeful. 'I have been baking for you, and I have invited my cousin Pinkie to come round this after-noon about five o'clock.'

Filthy and exhausted, I actually didn't feel much like having tea with anyone, but Arthur implored me so I gave in and accepted, smiling. I would have time to get home and wash, and even have a bit of a sleep. Once everyone had left, and I had explained to Mrs Sichilongo and Mrs

Krantz what had happened, I crawled back into the Old Queen Mum and trundled home. Elephants, or at least I assumed it had been elephants, had leaned against the chain-link fence and gate, and had popped open the chain. I nudged through the opening with the bull bar, climbed down and, after watching two mischievous meerkats play-boxing each other on the front steps of the house, went inside.

Having scrubbed and shaved, I padded about the house dressed in a towel collecting various items of grimy clothing in order to throw them in the bath water and soak out some of the sweat and dirt of the last couple of days. Once everything had been scooped up, except for no doubt one renegade sock, I dumped it in the tub and hunted around for some soap powder. Ten minutes, a few glasses of water, a packet of biltong, a cheese sandwich, a hair-combing session and lengthy consideration of how long it had been since I had had a fringe later, I tracked down the Super Soapy Flakes and returned to the little bathroom. Like a contemplative chef I scooped out the suds and sprinkled them over the surface of the semi-submerged clothes before kneeling down to stir the great big soup that I had created with my arm.

Just as I knelt down to the water, the surface erupted with a furious thrashing and sloshing which sent water up the walls, out of the open window and all over the floor. I rocked back on my ankles in astonishment. Bemused, I fancifully imagined that this bathtub was somehow fitted with a washing machine option and thought how fortunate it was that it had not been set off whilst I had been in the bath myself. Before I could come up with any further ludicrous ideas, a huge scaly green tail rose above the water and then crashed back down upon the surface with an almighty 'splat' which drenched me. As the tail sank, so the front half rose and the prehistoric, leathery features of a giant monitor lizard reared like the creature from the black lagoon out of the tub, tipped and slid itself, all six foot of it, over the side of the bath and onto the tiles at my horrified feet. Making a series of ineffective reverse crablike moves, I desperately tried to get out of the way. The beast on the other hand was intent only on making good his escape. Unable to reach the window through which he had surely made his entrance, attracted by the smell of cool fresh water, he headed for the door out into the sitting room. From there it was only a short scuttle to freedom. Unfortunately, in his attempt to make good his escape, he had cleverly disguised himself in one of my favourite t-shirts and now had the appearance of a reasonably close relative to Toad of Toad Hall in washerwoman's garb.

Acting entirely out of character, I hurled myself bodily across the threshold in order to salvage the shirt. Missing my target completely, I received, for my efforts, a sharp smack on the bridge of the nose from the monster's surprisingly muscled and rough tail. As I watched, squintingly, blood drip over my top lip and off my chin, I counted myself lucky that I had not encountered one of his sharp claws. He was still making his great escape but my desire to pursue had waned, and I wandered out of the French doors to watch the lizard, now advertising a particularly nasty Mexican Tequila, wriggle under the fence and shoot off, bandy-legged, towards the river. Only after a few moments did I realise that during our titanic struggle I had lost my towel. I stood there panting and bleeding just as I had been (fairly successfully) created, laughing like a fool at a passing, mildly outraged family of warthogs.

About an hour later, at the Kebalakile household, much interest was expressed in the patch of lavatory paper stuck to my nose and my burgeoning black eye. Part of me wanted to feign a rumble with ruffians or at least a good close call with a big cat, but finally, I opted for the old favourite.

'Yes, I wasn't looking and I walked into a door. Silly me.'

'*Ee*, Rra,' the assembled company murmured, employing that excellent Setswana expression of comprehension and sympathy. I think they believed me. The assembled company, that hot Monday afternoon, comprised a lot of children, Mma Kebalakile, a number of curious next-door neighbours, and somebody's grandmother. Rra Kebalakile was having tests at hospital but he was comfortable, thank you.

Then of course there was Pinkie. Pinkie had gained her nickname at an early age and for obvious reasons. She dressed only and entirely in pink. Pink toes, pink nails, pink mascara, pink headband, pink bag, shoes, hot pants and crop top. It was really quite disconcerting, almost disorienting. She was, however, most solicitous, insisting on applying a cold compress to my eye and her hot self to my chest.

'At least she did not call you Mr Mango, then?' laughed Chris the pilot, after I told him about the tea party.

'No, but she did insist on calling me Willy and laughing like a loon every time she did.'

The opportunity to sit with the family away from the rush and bother of school had been welcome and, despite the sadness of Rra Kebalakile's illness, I distinctly sensed that our conversation rested on a definite bed of friendship and common purpose. Mma Kebalakile's biscuits had been delicious.

If I had been in for some surprises out in the bush around Pandamatenga, I was greeted by another, perhaps not quite so alarming one, on my return to the school the following day. Graham was his normal bumptious, jovial self in front of the children at that morning's assembly. He had teasingly remarked how pleased he was to see that

Standard One had all returned in one piece from the trip to Pandamatenga, and it was only at break time that I discovered that he had actually been putting on a very brave face. While we were watching the boys boot footballs in all directions from under the flimsy leaves of a jacaranda tree, he dropped his bombshell.

'You know what, Will? I'm afraid I've just had some fairly worrying news.'

His open face clearly demonstrated quite how worrying.

'Janey is just about to have the baby by the sounds of it, and to be honest with you, we think there may be some complications. There is every chance that they're going to have to operate. The problem is that no one seems to know whether they will need to go ahead tomorrow, the next day or in a week's time. To be honest with you, I really need to be there as soon as possible. Will, I think you need to know I've decided that I'm going to go down to Cape Town on Thursday when half-term starts. Believe you me, I'm feeling pretty bad about this. I definitely don't want to leave you guys or the kids in the lurch. And . . .' Here he looked particularly pained. 'You know we've had such a good time here and love Bots, but we've got to prioritise things pretty much now.'

'Oh, okay, I'm sure that absolutely everyone will understand. No, it sounds like a good idea. You should go as soon as you can. So when will you be back?' I asked.

'No, I'm sorry I haven't made myself quite clear. I'm probably not coming back for the second half of term, because even if there aren't any complications, Janey is still going to need me there. So this is probably my lot. I've had a word with the powers that be and they're absolutely fine with it.'

'Crikey, are you serious? I see. Well, look, we'll all miss you. So who will be filling your shoes?'

'Now, Will, that's exactly the point. That's where you come in!'

'Oh, and how is that then?' I asked naively.

'Well, haven't you ever thought about being a headmaster?' He laughed. 'You know, run your own show?'

'No, absolutely no way.'

'Go on. You'll love it. The board of governors have been so pleased to have you here, and they have taken the liberty of faxing your referees in the UK and have given you the thumbs up. You know, if you like it and it went well, chances are that you could have the job permanently. Only person we have to get it passed by is Mma Mokwena! Shouldn't be a sweat!' He laughed cheerfully.

Perhaps I should have been flattered, and the thought of being here permanently stood any of my flimsy plans on their heads. Ironically, and unbeknownst to Graham, one of the many reasons that I had left full-time teaching, packed my bag and gone wandering the world these past five years had been in order to avoid becoming a headmaster. I could still remember the day that my former employer, standing on the side of one of the numerous sporting fixtures that I had attended in my ten years of teaching, had suggested that I might like to start thinking about a job in 'middle management'. Now, I, like most boys, had dreamt of all the fantastic adventures that I might have in later life. I had wanted to be a policeman, a soldier, or an adventurer, an actor or a film star, but I had never ever wanted to be a deputy headmaster. It was not that I didn't see the value of such people, it was just that I did not wish to be one of them.

Surely I had not travelled all the way to Africa, risking life and limb, only to fall into the same pit? Well, as a matter of fact, it turned out that I had. Still, I was not given too much time to consider my lot because events suddenly took a rather unhappy turn.

Ten days after our return from Pandamatenga, I was wishing everyone a safe trip home, and was just gathering my belongings together and shutting up shop when I saw Arthur's mother standing in the doorway. She was silhouetted in the afternoon sun, and behind her I could see her son sitting on a log some distance away by the clamouring football pitch. Although I could not see her face clearly, it became obvious from her heaving shoulders that she was crying.

They were having money problems, she explained, and so Arthur would not be able to go on our next school trip. She was having problems finding enough money to feed her family and extra expenses were not possible. She knew he loved our outings but she was sorry.

I told her, no, no, it was OK and I understood, but would she be able to solve her problems? She answered that no, her husband now definitely could not work, and she thought he was too sick to get better.

But yet more of a problem still was her savings.

Savings?

Did I know Mr Dirk?

13

Rra Mooki, Director of Independent Finance

Dung beetles must be some of the most ungainly creatures in creation. Black and lustrous as ebony, and
twice the size of matchboxes, they normally kept themselves modestly out of sight, buried deeply into any of the
variety of delicious dungs that littered the bush. For just a
couple of weeks a year they made themselves evident for,
I presume, some frantic reproduction while the climatic
conditions were favourable. When they were on the ground,
they were fairly inoffensive. Indeed, some of the little boys
had discovered that they produced the most satisfactory
'crunch' when squashed beneath a small sandal, or that
they could be picked up quite easily to be placed in the
hair or lunchbox of a similar-sized member of the opposite
sex. It was only when the beetles chose to take to the air
that they became a major irritation. Clumsy, and as ungainly
as Chinook helicopters, they appeared to have all the
manoeuvrability of flying juggernauts and all the sense of
direction of a drunken sumo wrestler. This meant that they
did not hesitate to collide with solid and not so solid objects
at every turn. Gabamukuni, the gardener, who seemed to
be regaining his strength daily, had appeared one morning

sporting a puffy black eye sustained after a collision with one of these bruisers whilst on the back of his friend's motorbike.

That oppressive afternoon they crashed like black hailstones into the small, square panes of the classroom windows as I attempted to comfort Mma Kebalakile and get to the bottom of her despair. Although I had always been treated kindly by the people of Kasane, now I sensed a certain feeling of mistrust from this normally jolly, friendly lady.

'So, you know Mr Dirk?'

Something about my expression as I nodded must have suggested that although I had made his acquaintance, we were by no means close friends. She looked more relaxed and took a deep breath. I sensed, quickly, that I was to be taken into her confidence – that I was to be told a big secret, one loaded, I could see, with shame. Although I really wanted to help and we knew one another reasonably well, I felt somehow uncertain how to handle this conversation. Fortunately, I knew that Kibonye was still working in her office so I nipped next door and asked her to come quickly. Soon she had pulled up a chair and taken Mma Kebalakile by the hand, who thanked her, breathed deeply – and out it all came.

Much of what Graham had told me about her husband was perfectly true. He had been a labourer and subsequently a street cleaner working for the municipality ever since they had first met as teenagers at their local church. He had been a strong man and a kind one. They had been given a small house in Chinatown and he had always made sure that he had kept it in good repair. Their rent instalments had never once been a day late. In an attempt to earn a little more he had gone away to South Africa for six months, but a colleague had dropped a grinder on one of his legs and, as he was only wearing shorts, it practically cut it off. It was then that he had received the blood transfusion that would first change and finally end his life. Fortunately, all their children had been already born bar the youngest, and she seemed to have escaped infection. The family had been so happy. Then her husband had begun to get sick.

At first it had been a cough and a cold, or flu and a fever that never seemed to want to go away. They had been to see Doctor Kabala who had given them medicines but none of it worked very well; then he had said he must take some tests and that was when they were given the bad news.

'Tuberculosis.' She pronounced the word carefully, almost thoughtfully.

'You know why, Mr Mango? You know what is the reason?'

Blushing, I shook my head. Although of course I did.

'AIDS.' She looked me in the eye as she pronounced the word quite openly, not emphatically but almost boldly.

'Yes, I see,' was my only, utterly inadequate response.

'Many Batswana say there is no such thing. We don't like to talk about it very much and many of the older people say it is something that the *legowa* has made up to frighten us. But I know it is true. Look at the cemetery alongside the Apostolic Church – it is nearly full! That is not normal.' She paused.

'Of course we are lucky in Botswana. We are quite rich and our president is a good man. You know we are the only country in Africa that will provide free anti-retroviral drugs for the people who are HIV positive.'

Despite my sadness for her plight, and about this epidemic, I could not help but be impressed by her knowledge. She displayed no denial.

'For my husband it is probably too late,' she announced

matter-of-factly. 'He was tested too late, and if it is not the TB then it will be something else that will take him from us. You know how old he is? He is thirty-five.'

'A year younger than me,' I remarked croakily – pointlessly.

'Soon, he will be gone from us and into the arms of our Lord Jesus Christ and he will sing with the angels.' She smiled as this thought gave her some comfort and wiped her eyes again. 'At least we, the children and me, we are all negative. Now I use condoms, and I will make sure my children have all this information before they become young men and women.'

Faced with the stark reality of the Kebalakiles' circumstances, I rose above normal British embarrassment about a discussion of personal matters with a relative stranger. There was much too much at stake to be worried about finer feelings.

What she was to say next, however, was to bring us back with the power of being slammed against a concrete wall to where our conversation had started.

'All the money we have saved for the future. It is gone.' She bent her head down almost until the braids of her hair met her knees and wept.

'Where? What? How is that?'

'My husband, as I have told you, he is a very good father and he always said he had responsibility. We don't have a farm or animals. Our parents have sold everything and they have moved to Gaborone. This is the way in Botswana now, and he always said we should use the modern way. We used to have satellite television and he was always listening to the programmes about money and, you know . . .' She shook her head and frowned. 'Investing. The Botswana Bank in town has investment accounts and we always paid in some of his wages. We know the manager of course. He is my mother's brother-in-law. So, we left it like that.'

There was a long pause broken only by the dopey dung beetles head-butting the walls and windows, and the oppressive swirl of sandy dust against the tin door.

'So what happened?' But already I feared I could have a good guess.

'One day my husband was making our payments. Every week on Friday he would go, you see. One day he was leaving and Mr Dirk was there. He came to my husband and made an offer. He could take our money and he would invest it in South Africa as he said there you can make much more interest. He is allowed to invest there because he is a South African, you see. Also he is a special financial advisor. Like a counsellor. A kind of friend.'

'Is he?' I knew Dirk to be certain things but a leading light in the world of finance was not one of them.

'Oh, yes. He has shown us his papers. But I don't think he is a very fair man. I can tell you why.'

Looking at her, as her tone of voice changed, I suddenly noticed a glimmer of defiance in the depths of her nut-brown eyes.

'Because, of course, now my husband is very sick, he cannot work. Of course he can't. Some days he cannot move all day from his bed.'

Suddenly the woman seemed utterly broken, with all her strength sucked out of her, shrinking her, diminishing her.

'Now, this man says if we can't pay the whole amount in only four more months – we will lose all of it. That can't be true, can it? Mr Mango, say it's not true.'

God. I certainly hoped not.

But I had no idea.

Eventually, somehow, Arthur's mother regained her composure, thanked me for having listened and apologised for taking up my time.

'Let me see if I can find out more? Maybe I can find out something!' My voice trailed off as she waved slightly and walked away back to the road with Kibonye. Arthur was sitting under a tree, his head shielded from the sun by his satchel, and as she approached he took her hand and they headed off towards the plateau, oblivious to the swarms of dung beetles.

Back in my classroom, I moped around until Gaba-mukuni stuck his head through the window and announced it was time for 'lock up'. He grinned and withdrew his head before coughing viscerally, explosively and then spitting loudly.

On my way out, my eye was caught by the bright pink, wet flecks shining in the sand. Oh, that it were not so. But it was.

Any sense of flattery that I might have felt about the new job offer was squashed when I discovered, a few days after my appointment, that the rest of my colleagues had in fact also all been offered the job and had all refused it on financial grounds. Nevertheless, I tried to tackle my new responsibilities, which were not onerous, with good cheer and, carrying on in the tradition set by Graham, I organised a number of extra trips for the children.

Despite the lengthy drive, we had been extended an invitation to play a football match at a small school in Shikawe on the fringes of the great Okavango Delta. We seemed to be embarking on a semi-permanent tour, and training sessions were increased to three times a week much to the joy of the children, who would burst out of the door kicking off their sandals and charge barefoot onto our pitch when Mrs Sichilongo rang the big, brass hand-bell to signal the end of lessons. How much I used to hope, as I drew my Acme Thunderer whistle from the pocket of my shorts and followed them, that they might have miraculously discovered some sort of tactical expertise. However hard I suggested they played in various positions, the magnetic draw of the ball was such that within seconds they were all mauling the ball and tackling anyone who was in possession regardless of whether they were team-mates or not. Occasionally, I sat down on the log bench beside the pitch and put my head in my hands, despairing of instilling any discipline in my lovely class. More often than not, I would discover that Bothle had followed my lead and was fast asleep, his head resting gently on the jacaranda tree that shaded him.

Before we could set off for Shikawe, I determined that I must do something to try to get to the bottom of Dirk's financial dealings. For help I turned to Graham, who was already packing up his home in preparation for his departure. He had, he agreed, heard of various financial scams before but knew nothing concrete.

'You should try Jannie van der Meuwe,' he suggested. 'He is into pension plans and life insurance and that sort of thing. Why don't you go and see him? Down at the campsite, Thebe River Safaris. You know where I mean – down near the rapids.'

I did know the shady riverside campsite with its small rondavel bar and barbecuing area, as I had been there on a couple of occasions with my colleague Kibonye and her friendly English husband Simon to watch the sun set over Namibia and, somewhat dangerously in the gloom, play darts. Yet, it did seem a rather incongruous place for a business meeting.

'When will I find him there?'

'Oh, all the time unless he has gone out door-to-door. He lives there. Pitch no. seven I think, unless he's moved. Only financial genius that I know who lives in a tent!'

Graham laughed but only a little as he unhooked curtains and swatted idly at a pink and green lizard with his ostrich-feather duster. Just recently he had not been his normal bubbly self. Importation and quarantine restrictions had forced him to give away Bambi and Lady, the two hounds from hell. When I had heard the news, I had had to hurry round the nearest corner before dancing a most authentic jig.

When I arrived at the campsite, I parked the Old Queen Mum in a shady corner and asked a grizzled-looking man, who was scooping sodden elephant dung out of the small swimming pool, for directions. Sure enough, he pointed with his dripping net at a small tent with a stripy awning pitched only a few yards from the river bank. Outside it, seated at a camping table on a folding canvas chair, was a serious-looking man with wire-rimmed glasses and a smart but no doubt sweltering suit, tapping away on a solar-powered calculator.

Within a few minutes he had ascertained that I was not going to be one of his more important clients, and just muttered in a muddy Afrikaans accent about how that English pound was so strong it was crazy. When I mentioned Dirk to him, taking care not to give him all the details for fear of compromising Arthur's family, he was overcome with professional propriety and asserted his view that any 'crooks should be stamped out, crushed like cock-roaches' – this he demonstrated with the heel of a smart Oxford brogue – 'bringing us all into terrible disrepute. Ach man, I hate it!'

Had he heard anything about Dirk, then?

No, because he worked on the commercial side of things, but he would ask his colleague Rra Mooki, Director of Inde-pendent Finance, whether he knew anything about him. With that, he picked up a cell phone and dialled a number.

Seconds later, I heard the ringing tone of another cell phone coming from the next-door tent, which was almost identical but a little smaller. The cell phone was answered after half a dozen rings by a voice garbled by sleep. Just at that moment Jannie van der Meuwe began to speak as he wandered along the river-bank. His Setswana was impressive. After a couple of minutes, I could not help noticing activity in the next-door tent, and out of the front in a yawning, somewhat dishevelled state appeared a young Motswana talking on a cell phone. He strode off down the bank in the opposite direction attempting to stretch out the creases in his two-piece, grey suit. The two men then turned and wandered back towards one another, waving a little as they passed each other in an absent-minded fashion before carrying on. It took me a little moment to realise that the two men were engaged in the same conversation. Knotting his tie more soberly, Rra Mooki promised to make delicate enquiries about Dirk's activities. I should come back to them after my return from the Okavango, but in the meantime, perhaps I would like to take a few brochures?

Unable to leave Arthur behind, partly because he was more likely to make connection between foot and ball than practically anyone else, but mainly because none of the rest of the class would have forgiven me, nor I myself, I had a quiet word with his mother. Deciding not to mention the inquiries that I was making for the time being, I assured her that the expenses of the trip were minimal and that I would let her know how much it had all come to on my return. She could pay me back when she was able. Although it took some time for me to convince her, she was there at dawn when we loaded the equipment and children into the back of the Old Queen Mum and headed out to Ngoma gate, across the river and down the straight, straight road that ran the length of the Caprivi Strip above the Okavango Delta.

The Delta sprawls like an open hand across north-western Botswana. The thousand-odd miles of the Okavango River makes it the third longest in southern Africa, and it extends into the desert like a lifeline. It rises near Nova Lisboa in central Angola, flows south across the Caprivi Strip and finally enters Botswana near Shikawe, our destination. The river's annual 18.5 billion cubic metres of water begins to spread in a fantastically complex system, like the veins of a leaf, across the delta plain before being absorbed into the hot sands of the Kalahari or evaporating into the hot, thirsty atmosphere. Not for no reason then is it often known as the river that never meets the sea. This vast maze of lagoons, channels and islands covers an area of nearly 10,000 square miles and, astonishingly, contains ninety-five percent of all the surface water in Botswana.

Our first night in the Delta was spent in comfort at Drotsky's Cabins, a camp hidden in the papyrus of the river-banks, where the owners, a kindly South African couple whose own children had already flown this isolated nest, showered treats on the delighted children. In one of their modern skiffs we investigated the mysterious waterways, tranquil lagoons and labyrinthine channels all overgrown by dense masses of water lilies that bloomed gloriously throughout the night before closing shyly at dawn. In hidden corners we came across old men bobbing content-edly in hand-fashioned *mokoro* – narrow, light, traditional dugout canoes. Supine, they gently jiggled a fishing line as they gazed up at a warm, orange dusk and the intricate pattern created by flocks of knob-billed ducks lifting off the water, disturbed by the snort of a hippopotamus or the sly slither of a crocodile. An African jacana, the lily-trotter, hopped on its spindly, elongated feet and toes across the floating lily pads, annoyed that our passage had disturbed its delicious muddy rootlings. Hundreds of rare lechwe splashed across the marshes – elegant antelope, their red coats burnished by a heavy, lazy sun that sat and yawned on the horizon.

That evening we dined on impala steaks and marsh-mallows, and fell asleep with the smell of wood smoke and lilies wafting around us. We dreamt of victory and of our triumphant return.

Needless to say, a dream was how it all remained. Despite the children's high spirits on our arrival in the small village of Shikawe, a collection of fairly desultory mud huts, I secretly feared the worst. Of course now, and this is only proof of my exemplary abilities as a dreamer, I had, in my mind's eye, been transformed into a football manager of international stature. We had after all toured Namibia. No longer was the Old Queen Mum a charabanc – it was the team bus. Elizabeth had, with my little first-aid kit and a plastic wristwatch pinned to her chest, become the team physiotherapist. Gabamukuni, who seemed to be having a good week and had pleaded with me to let him come along, was assistant coach. He needed a reasonably important role as he was the only person who had any football boots. At one stage, I had thought about giving the two of them one of the camp beds to bring onto the pitch should there be a bad injury but finally decided this would be tempting fate. Water bottles and oranges from one of the large fruit farms outside Kasane and linesmen's flags stitched by Elizabeth had all been stored in the bus, and we even had a huge, rather professional net of new footballs that Graham had brought back from his headmaster's trip to Maun. Of course, I was the guv'nor, He Who Must Be Obeyed, the tactical brains, the inspirational symbol, the carrot and the stick, the best friend, the father, the purveyor of glory, the man with-out whom these players would be nowhere, nothing. It was just a shame it was too hot to wear a sheepskin coat.

Anyway, we got absolutely thrashed. After the full forty
minutes, twenty minutes each way, and the final whistle,
we had nothing to show for all our efforts but a couple of
skinned knees and in Bothle's case a split pair of shorts.
Our hosts were friendly, gracious in victory and very, very
pleased when Kitso presented them with two new foot-
balls. The only one they owned looked like a large, muddy,
badly-inflated potato. They invited us for a delicious tea
which we enjoyed in the shade of their assembly hall, while
poor little Bothle, bursting with embarrassment, sat on the
bonnet of the Old Queen Mum and refused to move. Whilst
the children were entertained by Elizabeth and some atten-
dant mothers, I was taken on a tour of the village.

It was difficult not to be struck by how different the
standard of living was here in the backwaters of the
Okavango. Kasane's infrastructure, its hospital, police
station, offices and banks compared well with any other
centre of population in the world. Here, though, there
seemed to be little more than a fifties-style general store
which doubled as a post office, the small scrubby huts of
the school and a first-aid centre which resembled a roadside booth.

As I watched the donkey carts jangle jauntily up the main
street, sloshing with jerrycans of water from the village
standpipe, I realised Botswana had a long way to go in
ensuring that it's new-found diamond-mining wealth
was distributed across this kind of isolated outpost. Fifty
percent of the population remained below the poverty line
but, and this fills me with great optimism, every year
improvements are made in the standard of living. (Honestly,
I am absolutely flummoxed when people who knew a
developing country twenty, thirty years ago express disappointment when they hear of improvements that have
been made. 'You know in our [*our?*] day there was no road

between Francistown and Kasane. Oh, no, it took a week. A hospital, ho, ho, no nothing like that!')

No, we had not won, we agreed as we drove back over the border and I filled in, with practised ease, the pile of white slips at passport control. Still, five–nil wasn't so bad and it had been great fun on the river.

'And there is one thing you don't know, you boys and girls! Shall I tell you what it is?' I asked as we bounced our way home down the rough ruts of an unmetalled road.

'Yes, Mr Mango, come on please!' Pandemonium broke out in the back and two or three small, smooth arms were thrown around my neck, which caused the Old Queen Mum to swerve and jump out of the tracks before finding her feet again.

'Guess what the coach of the Shikawe side said to me just before we were leaving?' Noisily, very noisily, with Gabamukuni and Elizabeth joining in, they told me that they couldn't possibly guess and that I should tell them immediately. As we bounded along, red-headed guinea fowl gliding away in all directions in panic, trying to keep the excitement out of my own voice, I told them.

'Because their Christmas holidays are starting early and many of the children are going off to their cattle stations for their holidays, and also because it is very far and they have a transport problem – do you know what they can't do?'

More squeals.

'Tell us, tell us! Quickly, Mr Mango!'

'Well they have decided that they will not be playing Victoria Falls Primary School after all, and that means that we will!'

'Shaaarp!' opined Gabamukuni.

'*Au!*' squealed Elizabeth, using that excellent Setswana word to express astonishment or great surprise.

'Hurray!' chorused the children.

We had a very happy trip back to Kasane. Backdoor promotion or not, it's the results what count. Or something like that. I was still grinning at the children's happiness when Arthur clambered into the front seat – strictly against the rules – and shyly showed me his pictures of the delta, of the birds and the animals and a not entirely truthful depiction of him scoring a header from the halfway line. Looking down at his smiling face as he gave me a hug and we trundled back up the hill to Kasane, I realised with a twist in my guts that I would have to look out Jannie and Mr Mooki. Perhaps by now they would have unearthed the truth of Dirk's operations.

Once I had delivered the children back to the school, I drove down to the river and Thebe Camp. To my dismay, once I had got down from the cab, I beheld a scene of utter devastation. It seemed that a huge fight had broken out: cooking and camping equipment, clothes, books and food were spread widely across the clearing. Cheerfully, half a dozen vervet or 'blue-ball' monkeys were picking their way through the debris, sampling a cornucopia of culinary experiences and occasionally, when they bent over, demonstrating where they got their nickname. Lazily, the swimming-pool man was still scooping fitfully at the pool, as if he had not moved since we had last met.

'What happened? Was there a fight?'

'No, just elephant.'

'Oh, just elephants, OK. No problem. So do you know where Jannie has gone and Rra Mooki?'

'Business in Francistown. Back next week.' And with that he just carried on scooping.

On my return to school the following morning, I realised that there was one more very good reason, apart from the incipient birth of his child, why Graham was so keen to make his rapid exit. On a regular basis, the spiky lady school inspector would burst in upon us ready to carry out 'observations' – which unfortunately she was perfectly entitled to do. Much of her time was spent tutting and tapping her pencil on various objects, tables, windows, her knuckles, my knuckles, children's heads, although she rarely, if ever, gave voice to her obvious discontent. At the end of each day she would climb back in her car and bump down the drive in a cloud of angry dust. Her antagonistic attitude stemmed from something more, it seemed, than simply a desire to improve the standard of education in the school. In a village where there were at least a dozen different churches representing various strands of the Christian faith, from the mainstream to the rather more outlandish, friendships and allegiances were founded along religious lines. The foundation of our school did not appear to fit with the views of the school inspector and, it was rumoured, she was set on being able to take on the running of the school herself. All she needed to do was to prove that the leadership of the school was inadequate and she might well be able to supplant it. As that leadership was represented by me, it was possible that her task would not be that mighty a one.

Finally, the day came for my personal inspection, and Mma Mokwena followed my every move for the entire day from morning assembly until I waved the children off at the school gate. When finally I smiled at her weakly, inquisitively, she only screwed on the cap of her fountain pen, put away her glasses and, tucking her clipboard under her arm, strode off to her car. Her irritation puffed from the exhaust as she left. I knew from her silence that all was well. She would certainly not have wasted a moment to tell me if she had found my performance unsatisfactory.

Half-term arrived, as it so often does, at the most convenient moment, and as Jannie and Mr Mooki were away and
I could make no further progress in that particular regard,
I thought I would take these few days as an opportunity
to explore my surroundings further. Chris, the benign,
cheerful pilot of the small sight-seeing plane, offered me,
late one night at The Old House, a trip that very nearly
resulted in a grave delay in the writing of this tale.

'Will, what are you up to tomorrow? Got a proposal,
you're really gonna like it, *mon*.' He sipped his beer with
relish and wiped his steaming brow. 'How would you
fancy a flight over Victoria Falls? You get to go free, of
course.'

'Well, thanks very much. What time were you thinking
of going?'

'Well, about nine. Nothing too early. Coming?'

'Er . . . yes, of course. Of course I am, sounds great,
thanks very much.'

By now, I should have realised that accepting anything
so freely, without further inquiry, is one of the best ways
of getting yourself into what used to be known, rather pleasingly, as a pickle.

Within half an hour of meeting at the airstrip, Chris had
completed all the checks necessary for the flight.

'Put this on.' He laughed as he tossed me a polo shirt in
the colours of his airline. 'You're the co-pilot.'

What he had not told me was that this was actually a
commercial flight. His regular co-pilot had gone to a funeral
back at his village, and as Chris was not allowed to fly
on his own, it appeared that I was doing him as much of
a favour as he was me. He grinned at me and I smiled
back.

Heck. Why not?

'Come on, let's go and find the punters and get their

bags. Then I'll go and get my flight papers sorted out. You just settle them in. OK?'

'Yeah, sure. Not a problem, Skipper.' Sliding on my shades, I leant casually on the fuselage of the plane and burnt my elbow horribly.

Chris skipped into the main airport building and I followed bemused. It was ferociously hot. After a short while, a car drew up at the front. From its size I knew it belonged to Dirk. Sure enough, the driver's door opened and he stepped heavily out. Edwin and Erwin scuttled out of the double front seat and scurried round to the back. When the back doors opened, a couple appeared and with Dirk headed towards me.

Slipping behind a large potted plant, I spied on them. I had no desire to meet Dirk face to face. Still less did I want him to start asking me why I was wearing an aviation t-shirt in front of the two passengers. And what a pair they were! Easily six feet four, the lady was extraordinary. Dressed in a manner that could only be described as skimpy, and reminding me with a certain amount of alarm of Pinkie, she teetered on high heels that sank into the sweating tarmac. She looked a little nervous as she plucked at her vibrant green headband with matching fingernails and wriggled her fake leopard-skin skirt over ample hips. Her fellow passenger, on the other hand, was tiny: five feet and not very much at all. His most striking feature, apart from his wizened liver-spotted face, was a shock of surely false orange hair that stuck out sideways from under a dark green trilby. Despite the heat, he was dressed in a wrap-around brown mackintosh and a shirt and tie. He was carrying a briefcase that to my consternation was handcuffed to his wrinkly wrist. With considerable difficulty, I rearranged my features into some semblance of solemnity as they bid farewell rather stiffly to Dirk.

'Would you be the pilot or is it that chubby feller we just met in there?' An Irishman for sure. 'Just want to know what's going on here now.' He coughed nervously into his free hand.

'Oh yes to be sure. Yes, well you can be sure with us, ha, ha. Yeah, well we both do a bit, you know. Depends how we feel, you know. Dual controls. Know what I mean.' There did not seem to be any good reason to give them anything but the impression that they were in the most professional of hands. 'Let's just get your bags stowed away here.'

I grabbed the bag that the woman was holding and tossed it lightly over the back of the seats.

'Now if you would like to climb in, we'll just strap you in.'

The two of them climbed uncomfortably into their seats and fiddled with the various straps of their seatbelts. They seemed to be having some difficulty.

'Let me give you a hand!' I said, like an idiot. After a great deal of 'excuse me, sorry, would you mind shifting over a bit, ooh sorry did that hurt?' we could not locate one vital strap. Having to think on my feet, I decided I would plug his bit into hers thereby fixing them into one belt which thrust them intimately together.

As I climbed into my seat, I tried fairly successfully to prevent myself imagining them in an amorous encounter.

Minutes went by and I was beginning to worry about the whereabouts of Chris, so in order to underline the role that I was playing, I fiddled nervously with some of the switches and dials on the dashboard being very careful to return them to their original settings. Panic ran through me like a shiver when one button pushed in and then refused steadfastly to pop back out again. When Chris finally returned, muttering something about there being no one at the office but it not mattering, I tried to communicate this to him under cover of my headphones.

'Don't worry!' he announced cheerfully and, I thought, rather loudly. 'It doesn't work anyway.'

And off we flew.

'Lusaka.'

'Lusaka?'

'Capital of Zambia, my *bru*.'

'Oh OK,' I turned in my seat. 'So, off to Lusaka then?'

'You're not telling me you didn't know it? I tort you were de bloody pilot,' came the unnecessarily gruff response from the back seat.

'Oh, yes, of course. You know just checking.'

'Checking what?' He was really not disposed to small talk.

'Oh, just checking. Anyway,' I fumbled around desperately for a change in conversation. 'So you know Dirk, do you?'

'Yeah, why? He a friend of yours?'

'No, not especially.'

'Good, because that man is the most ******* dishonest ******* **** I have ever had the ******* misfortune to *******. ******* ****. Mother ******.' And with that he closed his eyes and groaned.

About forty minutes later we flew over Livingstone, the colonial town on the fringes of the Falls on the Zambian side. Fiddling with the dial on the side of my headphones and nonchalantly fingering the logo on my new shirt, I was beginning to feel rather the part.

Soon it became clear that this was the best way to attempt to grasp the scale of this continent; huge prairies, mountain ranges, Lake Kariba away to our right on the border with Zimbabwe, surprising numbers of waterways, wide and small, sketched fanciful designs across the Zambian countryside. Any fear of flying was swept away by the scale and beauty of the view. I turned to smile at our passengers and give them a complicit, yet professional wink. The curious pair were fast asleep, a packet of pills grasped firmly in one green-tipped hand.

Dodging rain clouds, following the sun, we arrived quickly at Lusaka the capital. I delighted in the bouncing lolloping landing and copied Chris as he flipped up the plastic window by the pilot's seat. Soon we were taxiing towards the airport buildings and I could sense movement in the back. All of a sudden there was a terrible gasp from behind me followed by a string of Irish expletives.

We two pilots turned round and froze when we saw that the two passengers were soaked, absolutely drenched, from head to toe. The ginger toupee had been washed to a curious angle over one ear, and the green headband had now slipped to eye level. Water dripped from two appalled noses. Only a few moments later did we realise that this sudden flood had been caused by the plane rolling through a deep rainstorm puddle. Our open windows had acted as two perfectly aimed spouts. Chris hurried us to the main doors.

So hard were we attempting not to laugh, it was almost impossible for us to apologise to the furious couple who finally stomped off soggily in the direction of their connecting flight. When, finally, they had disappeared out of sight, we both exploded with laughter and headed for the arrivals doors and a cup of coffee, clutching our sides.

Outside the doors were ten African soldiers with Kalashnikov machine guns. At least half of them were pointed at me. Chris had not bothered to get the flight pass, and we had been spotted crossing the border and landing illegally.

We were under arrest and before very long we would be in a cell.

Unhappily, I wondered whether they would release me in time for school on Monday morning.

14

Mr Mango Rides Again

Despite my prognostication that we were destined to grow old in the depths of a Zambian prison, forgotten by the outside world, never to return to the shores of England, never again to see family and friends, and to be fed only on bread and water, Chris remained remarkably cheerful. Even when we were locked into an extremely authentic-looking cell, he insisted we would be released any minute. Chris possessed no proper sense of tragedy, although even he must have thought that his number was up when after a couple of hours he was invited out by two soldiers and I could hear the tramp of their boots on the steel floor.

My fingers in my ears, I waited disconsolately for the cocking of the rifles of the firing squad but I could hear nothing except for the occasional drone of airplanes overhead. When finally Chris returned, he showed no sign of being affected by his short walk in the Valley of Death and described our captors as pretty good blokes.

Then it was my turn.

In fact it turned out that Chris was quite right. They were actually bloody good blokes. When it became very clear that beyond recognising wings, propellers and wheels, my knowledge of all things aeronautical was zero, the group of young soldiers who filled the small interview room with smoke, coffee cups and an alarming number of machine guns, relaxed considerably.

When I was asked what I did as a job, I stretched things slightly by informing them that I was a football manager in Botswana. This elicited intense interest.

'You the manager of Botswana Zebras? Nice team. Beat Zambia too many times.'

'Er . . . no, not that one.'

'What is your team, Mister Randall?'

(I had started to write myself down as Mr Mango on the form and had had to convert the M into an R.)

'Well, I'm not sure you will know them. Umm . . . they are called the Kasane Kudus.'

'I know them; I know them!' a rather impetuous youngster with a too big uniform jumped up with this startling revelation. Then he sat down again, unsure.

'Who is your best striker?'

'Umm . . . well Arthur can be pretty good and Blessings has his moments.'

'And your mid-field? Who is your David Beckham?'

'Well Stella is pretty quick although her passing is a bit shaky.'

'Who else? Who else?'

Fortunately, before Bothle's footballing merits came up in conversation, a sergeant popped his head round the door, and cigarettes were hurriedly extinguished with various 'Psssh's and the odd 'Oww!'. Everyone studiously concentrated on the paperwork and declared me free to go. Did I, they asked, as we walked back out onto the runway, did I prefer four-four-two formation or the Christmas tree?

'Oh,' I declared, with the giddy relief of one reprieved.

'Give me the Christmas tree any day. Chocks away, Christopher!'

Flying like a small free bird, we returned home over the Victoria Falls. Now, I am not really a particularly enthusiastic tourist, but as Chris swung the joystick to the right and the plane dropped sideways, engines screaming down towards what the Africans call 'the smoke that thunders', I knew that all the trials and tribulations of this particular trip, including my temporary incarceration, had been worthwhile.

As the second half of term began life returned to normal. Despite various interruptions by the school inspector, progress continued unabated and I was delighted to watch as the children absorbed with ease the new material that was offered to them. Once the term was back on course, I had the opportunity to turn my attention to the matter of Dirk and the unhappy situation in which Arthur's family found themselves.

So it was at the end of the first week that I returned to Thebe River Safaris. Calm had been restored and all was as I had first seen it, including the man who was still slowly, rather morosely, scooping the pool. Jannie was in a state of some excitement and pulled up a chair at the tin table at which he and Mr Mooki were sitting.

'We haven't seen you for quite a while, Will. We were wondering when you were coming back to see us. Where have you been?'

Not wanting to burden them with the story of my incarceration, I shrugged and muttered something about being involved in a couple of international flying missions.

'Is it? Well I expect you'll want to hear what we have managed to find out about your man?'

Alert to the fact that both men were looking rather

sombre, I nodded. Rra Mooki, given the current wave of enthusiasm for detective work in Botswana, had gone undercover and, slightly to my alarm, had approached Dirk directly, and to my even greater alarm had announced he was coming on my recommendation. Apparently Dirk had suspected nothing and was then surprisingly transparent. At great length, he embarked on what was often a rather technical explanation of what had been happening. In essence, they explained, Dirk was a crook, what he was doing was illegal and he had many more clients than we had at first realised. It would be simple enough to have him expelled from the country but it might be a great deal more difficult to recover the money that he had extracted from dozens of local people. It was, after all, stuck away in a bank over the border in South Africa. What should I do then? How could we resolve the situation? Neither man looked particularly hopeful but only suggested that I did not frighten Dirk off as he would surely just run for Johannesburg.

With a heavy and angry heart, I thanked them for all their efforts on my behalf and determined to leave the situation alone. There was nothing I could do, I realised. Who was I to get involved in the business of people in a foreign country? Perhaps things were not as bad as I had been given to understand. Anyway nobody could leave an entire family destitute could they? Guiltily, of course, I knew perfectly well that they could. Still, I did not know how I could possibly resolve the problem. No, I would be better off concentrating on the day-to-day running of the school. We had several challenges on our horizon: Christmas was on its way and a carol service and final assembly was to be organised. Children from Victoria Falls Primary School, a private, mainly white establishment from Zimbabwe, were coming to play in a couple of weeks' time, and

Graham's parting words were that if we lost that match we might as well 'pack up and go home'. The illogicality of this statement seemed to have escaped him. Just as importantly, the children would have to be tested and I was sure that the spiky school inspector would be casting a very close eye over the results. Fortunately the willingness of my pupils and my colleagues meant that academically at least we could be quite confident.

'Hark the Herald Angels Sing' sounds totally different in a heat that most days topped one hundred degrees Fahrenheit. Yet the children, under the guidance of Mrs Sichilongo seated majestically at her beloved piano, were more than happy to run through this and a dozen other carols a dozen times a day. Occasionally, I would hear them singing the tunes as they made their way home. Apart from one particularly worrying episode, this area of the curriculum was running smoothly.

Carol practice took place just after morning break and as Mrs Sichilongo was more than capable of controlling the entire school – of only seventy children – all on her own, I normally stayed on in our little staffroom sipping coffee and swapping stories and experiences with Kibonye and Mrs Krantz. One morning, attracted by the sweet sounds coming from our school hall, I wandered down the shady walkway and into the back of the room. Shepherds were watching their flocks perfectly satisfactorily when all of a sudden Mrs Sichilongo encountered a technical problem. She suddenly discovered that some of the notes at the top of the keyboard, or was it bottom, no longer seemed to work properly. Instead of resonating clear, sweet notes, they now simply went 'pronk'.

'Sit down, sit down, everyone.' Mrs Sichilongo waved her plump fingers at the rising tide of willing helpers. 'Let us see what is happening here.'

She opened the top of the piano and peered in. Then she screamed. And screamed. Very loudly. As we watched in horror, twisting and undulating rose the head and spread hood of a Mozambique Spitting Cobra. Now the Mozambique Spitting Cobra is so called because there is nothing it likes more than to spit; spit poison at the first person to look it in the eyes; spittle that once it found your eye would blind you leaving you defenceless to its attack and its mortal bite.

Momentarily, I considered what our evacuation routine should be, but then decided to join the stampede. Incredibly seventy children, one large piano teacher and one rather skinny headmaster all managed to get through one small door at the same time.

'Deal with it, Mr Mango, deal with it!' shrieked the now hysterical Mrs Sichilongo.

'Me, why me? I don't know anything about snakes!'

'You must, you are the headmaster!'

'Look, I don't think you'll find that there is anywhere in my contract which says . . . Actually I don't have a contract but . . .'

'Gabamukuni!' Mrs Sichilongo threw herself around the neck of the rather bewildered gardener who had just turned the corner, wondering what the kerfuffle was all about.

'Now listen, Gabamukuni, as the headmaster I wonder if I could ask you a small favour. There is a small, not very big . . .'

When finally I explained, he grinned.

'Just need a stick and a sheet of glass and everyone go away.'

In desperation I picked the still soft putty away from a window pane that had had to be replaced after a rather erratic shot by Hui. Gabamukuni found a cleft stick and we all stood at the window looking on as he went inside.

Holding the glass in front of his face he glared at the snake. Instantaneously a jet of white liquid fired from the fangs of the cobra and splattered on the glass. Like lightning Gabamukuni flicked the stick under the metre-long body and lifted it out of the piano. Turning quickly, he made for the door as the rest of us scattered. Walking, then half-running, he made his way into the bush before flicking his stick and sending the rather surprised-looking reptile far into the air.

'Why didn't you kill it?' I asked as my colleagues nodded furiously. 'It could come back any time.'

'Yes,' replied the young boy sagely. 'But then any snake can come to our school and you can't kill all the snakes can you?'

As I headed home at the end of the day, I smiled cheerfully at the memory of the excitements of the morning. Not least amusing was my ability to get in a terrible panic at a moment's notice. My good humour was suddenly chilled, however, when, just as I turned the corner to head up the hill and out of town, I caught sight of the gleaming white and gold American hearse that belonged to Freddy the undertaker. It stood outside the wood and brick Apostolic Church and was surrounded by a large crowd. As I came closer, I saw with a shock that at the top of the steps was Arthur standing by his mother and younger brothers and sisters. Then it was that I remembered that the boy had not been to school for two or three days. From his expression I understood perfectly why.

Uncertain what to do and not wishing to intrude, I carried on slowly up the hill. As I arrived on the brow of the plateau, I was suddenly overcome with anger. How dreadful this disease was, how insidiously it was destroying a nation that was doing so much to improve itself, to succeed after so many centuries of struggle. Soon, if no medical or social solution was found, Botswana would be populated by only orphans and their grandparents. The workforce of the country would be annihilated. The only light spot in all this was that young Gabamukuni had been given the all clear after his latest TB test. Simultaneously, I was struck by the wickedness of Dirk and his ilk, who had over generations had their fill of the rich goodness of this part of the world but were utterly unwilling to give anything back.

So gloomy did I feel after my return home, that as dusk fell I drove out down the path back to the main road, almost oblivious to three giraffes that crossed in front of me, their tawny elegant legs caught in the yellow of my headlights. Slowly, tiredly, the Old Queen Mum groaned towards town. The Old House was practically empty, but Oliver, the smiling landlord, cheered me up with a few off-colour jokes and a bottle of beer. Watching some warthogs assume their odd kneeling position in order to graze on the lawn, I wondered what on earth could be done to help Arthur's family. Finishing my drink, I was just about to return inside to the bar, when out of the shadows loomed two large but familiar figures. As they came closer I recognised the friendly faces of Hans, the Afrikaner farmer from Panda-matenga, and Barry, the hunter from Bottle Pan. They both greeted me cheerfully. I had been, I understood, the subject of their conversation on more than one occasion. Heaven only knew what had been said. Grimacing at the thought I accompanied them to the bar.

Later, quite a lot later, I found myself pouring out my concerns about Dirk to my two Afrikaner friends. What was I going to do? I asked glumly.

15
Banged Up – Again

Somehow, I managed to put the problem of Dirk and Arthur's family to the back of my mind, this task made easier by the children who, unaware of the magnitude of the difficulties that this little boy and his family were undergoing, went about their daily lives with their normal enthusiasm. When, a few days after the funeral, Arthur returned to school, they comforted him when he was obviously distressed or preoccupied by giving him the first kick of the football or offering him choice snacks from their lunchboxes. Elizabeth, with the innate sense of a mother, would occasionally scoop him up into the folds of her colourful dress and hold him there until he had stopped crying or had dozed off into a fitful reverie. His mother, Mma Kebalakile, arrived silently to pick him up at the end of the day, smiling weakly at me as they went. After they had disappeared into the heat haze of the bush, I sighed and slumped into my chair overcome by the unfairness of it all.

Much needed to be done before the end of term in both footballing and academic terms. Some days before Rra Kebalakile's funeral, I had received a prim printed note from Victoria Falls Primary School explaining what time they would be arriving, that they would not be 'requiring' tea, and hoping that we would be providing adequate changing and medical facilities. I gripped my whistle with determination and took the children out for an extra training session even though the pitch had been temporarily occupied by a tribe of mongeese. On the arrival of the commanding figure of Bothle, ball tucked under his arm, they disappeared into the bush like a mini wriggling magic carpet. Brows, hitherto smooth with lack of worry, now furrowed as defenders, midfielders and forwards alike bent themselves to honing their skills in readiness for the big match with a series of most professional-looking drills. Piggy-in-the-middle practices were now particularly impressive and Dolly's dummy over the free-kick ball, followed by Kitso's strike from just outside the eighteen-yard box would have confounded many a league flat back four. So much had the children increased in self-assurance over the past few months, I was actually rather looking forward to the final match, and started to count down the days with my class/team and the rather bewildered clientele of The Old House.

'Only eight days to go till we give them an absolute hiding! Yup, should thrash them,' I would bellow bellicosely above the hubbub of the bar and the sweet, swinging BoJazz – a peculiar hybrid of jazz born in Botswana – at a rather mystified punter.

'Is it?' he would reply before gazing down the bar in the hope of spotting a spare seat to which he might safely move.

If I was feeling bullish about the football match, I was anything but confident about the return of Mma Mokwena, the school inspector. She alone, seemingly operating in a worryingly autonomous fashion, had decided that she would inspect the progress made by my class in both writing and arithmetic herself.

'I think that the Friday of the week before Christmas would be a most convenient moment to test the children,' she announced to me one afternoon after they had gone out to play and she was sitting at my desk. I was sitting opposite her on Hui's chair, a position from which I most sincerely doubted I would ever be able to rise.

'Oh, I see,' I answered, frowning as my stubble scratched one of my kneecaps. 'That is of course the last day of term and we do, you know, we do have our last football match just after lunch. Do you think . . .'

'Yes, I do. I think that that will be the perfect day. We will do a spelling and tables test in the morning. You will agree that this is a little more important than football.' Naturally I nodded hard. 'Good. First thing in the morning on Friday, and then I will be able to give my verdict.'

And sentence, I thought, but said nothing. Instead, I nodded again vigorously, which was actually as much in agreement as it was just a subtle effort to return to the vertical. After she had finally left, with a snap of her glasses, a poke in a few cupboards and a spin of sedan wheels, I rallied the troops and dispensed new spelling lists and times tables. Packing copies for myself, I hurried home for a practice.

Some of the children, as has been the case in all the classrooms I have ever taught in, were very diligent, some were not. Some were able and some were not. But it did seem that on this occasion, they all sensed the importance of getting everything as right as was possible. Times tables were relatively straightforward and we all chanted them together in the echoing classroom as I picked out various children for solo performances. Even I eventually remembered what six sevens came to . . . Anyway before long I was sure that the children were not going to be bamboozled by even Mma Mokwena's quick-fire questioning.

'Now then Standard One can you spell the word . . . are you ready . . . are you ready . . . can you spell the word "HONEY"!'

Leaping out of my seat like a demented Master of Ceremonies as I uttered the last word, I delighted in them standing too, swinging from hip to hip spelling the word out loud and, all together now, clapping in time.

'Aitch–oh–enn–eee–why! Aitch–oh–enn–eee–why! Aitch–oh–enn–eee–why!'

More often than not, we would end up traipsing in Indian file out of the door; Elizabeth taking the lead and young Gabamukuni, who had little education but was keen to learn, following up behind. We would dance around and around the buildings, shuffling out the same rhythms, puffing up clouds of fine yellowy dust, making up little tunes for each and every word.

'So Standard One, maybe you can spell me the word . . . wait for it . . . wait for it . . . the word "KITCHEN"?'

'Oh yeah, kay–eye–tee–see–aitch–eee–enn.'

On for hours we would go until Elizabeth became so hot and laughed so much that she had to flop down under a feathery jacaranda and catch her breath. Following her lead, the children would do the same, most of them landing on her and me, and there we would sit and laugh some more until we had all cooled down and stopped puffing and panting.

Still, however, I could not rid myself of the spectre of Dirk and his machinations. After a particularly heavy 'spellathon' we were relaxing in the cool of the classroom when the whole problem revisited me. While I gazed, troubled, out of the window, Elizabeth, comfortable in her small armchair, the children at her feet, told them a story from Setswanan folklore. It was called 'The Dove and The Jackal' and it went like this:

Once upon a time Jackal was hungry. He went out to look for something to eat, and soon he found a dove.

'Ah!' said Jackal. 'I shall catch this dove and eat him up.'

Dove had his head under his wing.

'Don't kill me, Mr Jackal,' said Dove. 'Please don't kill me. You can't kill a dove without his head.'

'Where's your head, Mr Dove?' asked Jackal.

'My head is ill,' said Dove. 'I took it to the man who mends heads at the hospital. Soon he will bring it back to me. Then you can kill me.'

'How did you take your head off?' asked Jackal.

'Oh, that was easy,' said Dove. 'I gave Hare an axe and asked him to cut my head off for me. Then I took it to the man who mends heads at the hospital. When he brings it back, my head will feel much better.'

Jackal thought this must be true because he could see with his own eyes that Dove had no head. So Jackal did not kill Dove that day.

The next day, Jackal went out to get firewood. He began to chop down a tree. Along came Dove with his head on again.

'Ah! Dove has his head on again,' said Jackal to himself. 'Now I shall kill him.'

'Good morning, Mr Jackal,' said Dove. 'You see I have my head back on again. It feels much better now. I feel big and strong with my new head. Why don't you send your head to the hospital, Mr Jackal?'

Now Jackal thought this must be true because he saw with his own eyes that Dove now had his head back on again.

'All right, take my axe, Mr Dove,' said Jackal. 'Please chop my head off for me.'

Dove took the axe from Jackal.

Are you ready, Mr Jackal?' he asked.

'I'm ready, Mr Dove,' said Jackal.

So Dove lifted up the axe and chopped Jackal's head right off!

'You won't kill me now, Mr Jackal,' laughed Dove.

For Jackal was dead.

With shrill squeals, the children hid their mouths behind soft small hands and stretched their eyes wide open – all except Bothle of course, whose eyes were closed. I smiled down at them amused, pleased by their unsophisticated astonishment, their frisson of fear. I had no idea whether Dirk might be seen as Jackal or Dove – I had always been hopeless at parables – but what was certain was that someone had to do something to stop his treacherous financial dealings.

On my return home that afternoon, I was surprised not by hippos, elephants or any other four-legged animals, but by a posse of two-legged, uniformed figures who sat on the bonnet of their shiny blue and white police cars. The genial but rather formal Inspector Ramotswe was standing slightly awkwardly on the steps outside the front door of the rickety house, his lapel radio squawking conversationally.

'Oh, William. Good afternoon, Rra.'

'*Dumela*, Inspector,' I replied cheerfully enough, although I immediately sensed that they had not just been passing and decided to drop in. I smiled and nodded at the other policemen, noting as I did so that Stella's father was amongst them. Her mother normally picked her up from school, but I had seen her young father on a couple of occasions doing the shopping with his family. Although we had never spoken I was quite certain that he knew who I was. Stella pointing across the aisles, whispering and giggling into his ear had made certain of that. He looked

distinctly uncomfortable and did not seem able to meet my
questioning gaze.

'Perhaps we can have a quick talk with you inside the
house?' asked Inspector Ramotswe.

'Of course, of course, come in.'

The other officers followed the inspector, not on any security grounds I imagined, but more because they were interested in seeing how this *legowa* lived.

'It is a difficult problem, Rra.' The inspector cleared his
throat and took out his notebook. 'We need to see your
papers please. Your resident's permit and also your passport.'

'Sure, sure,' I happily agreed and relaxed. This was
obviously just a routine check that everything was in order.
I pulled them, somewhat damp and scrumpled, out of my
pocket and smoothed them a little before handing them
over. For some time now, I had decided that I would carry
all my important papers with me at all times, pertinent as
they were to me.

Inspector Ramotswe inspected them at great length
whilst the other men resisted the temptation of opening
cupboards and drawers. Finally, he looked up.

'You see the problem is we have been told that these
papers are forged. This resident permit is not a good one.
We have had some information.'

'What? Who on earth told you that? The resident's permit
is signed by Blessings' dad. You know him, of course: he
is the Head of Immigration. Maybe you can just ask him,
Rra?'

'Well, yes I know this, but there is one problem. He is
on his leave and he has gone away to his cattle post in the
Central Kgagalagadi. He is not back for two weeks.'

'Well, what about Mma Chika? She was there when he
signed it.'

'She is in Francistown. She has gone to a funeral. She is back on Monday. Until we can get confirmation, I am afraid we will have to take you to the station.'

Today was Thursday.

'Perhaps we can wait till then?' Ever hopeful, I smiled. The inspector averted his hazel eyes and said they were sorry but I should just bring a few things.

Suddenly I had a terrible desire to laugh. What a crazy situation. I hoped the cells were comfortable, I chuckled as I wandered vaguely round the house grabbing things and stuffing them in a holdall. Banged up in an African jail twice in as many weeks. Ha, ha, dear, oh dear. Then equally suddenly, I felt absolutely terrified. What would become of me?

We climbed into one of the cars. Stella's dad slammed the door and we drove through the bush, silent in the hot afternoon. Noiselessly a covey of sand grouse flapped golden through the air ahead of us before gliding swiftly out of sight.

'Who told you these things then, Rra?'

'Oh I'm afraid that it is not possible to tell you. It is of course a matter of confidentiality. Rra, don't you know somebody that can tell us that your papers are correct?'

Watching the dust clouds roll away into the distance behind us, I racked my brains for anyone else who had been present when I had been given my permit. As I tried to concentrate on who had been at the sociable interview I had had with the immigration officer, other concerns about the future crept in. Who was going to look after the children the following morning? Mrs Sichilongo and Kibonye would be able to divide up the class I supposed, but who would be able to take on the all-important football practice that afternoon? It might well be the last proper one before the match. Gabamukuni would be there and would help out, but the last time I had left the teenager in charge while I did some marking in the shade of the jacarandas, he had contented himself with dribbling round the children, flicking the ball off his knees and head before cracking the ball into the net away from the reach of the bemused goalkeeper Happy. Then, of course, there was the problem of the tests to be conducted by the school inspector. How delighted Mrs Mokwane would be to discover that the temporary headmaster was incarcerated in a cell under suspicion of being an illegal immigrant, a forger, and heaven only knew what else. I could imagine her grimly taking control of the school, snapping on her glasses, banning football and drilling the children mercilessly day in day out. Meanwhile I would be eking out a sorry existence on water and bowls of pap, writing out my memoirs on sheets of rough paper begged from the unsmiling gaoler.

Of course! Mma Mokwane! So keen had she been to investigate my credentials that she had told me that she had visited immigration to check all was in order.

As we pulled up in the bright yard of the police station, I excitedly explained what I had remembered to the inspector, who looked quite surprised at my forcefulness, particularly when I grabbed his arm and danced a little jig as we went up the steps and in through the glass doors.

'We will see, Rra,' was all that he would say as he sat me down on a comfortable chair in an ante-room outside his office.

Nursing a plastic cup of *rooibois* tea, a singularly uninspiring drink, I waited, watching the to-ing and fro-ing of police staff as they carried out their duties. Hopeful that, however ironically, Mma Mokwena might prove to be my saviour, I concentrated on the mystery of who it was who had attempted, rather successfully it appeared, to land me in hot water.

Until then, I had found my relations with Batswana to be very enjoyable, always cordial and in many cases very friendly. Clever and I still met up now and then for a drink in The Cool Joint, and Pinkie often greeted me loudly and exuberantly in the street, and had introduced me to a number of her equally excitable girlfriends. By now, I knew most of the children's parents and they had always expressed their gratitude for my efforts, and given me advice and suggestions to make my life in Kasane that little bit more comfortable. The ex-pats that I knew had always been civil, and a few, Chris the pilot, Oliver and Boan behind the bar of The Old House amongst others, had become good friends. The only person with whom I had ever had cross words had been Dirk and that had been a long time back.

Unless, unless, and now my mind raced or rather skidded about erratically. Unless Rra Mooki's attempts to get to the bottom of Dirk's business dealings had been a little less subtle than he had imagined. But how had he connected me with his unfortunate clients?

My musings were interrupted by voices inside the inspector's office. He had ushered a guest into his office through a different door and they were now engaged in a vigorous conversation in Setswana. Although I did not understand what was being said, I took no time at all in recognising the less than dulcet tones of Mma Mokwena. What could she be saying? I could not tell from her tone of voice because even when she was at her most calm she sounded frighteningly shrill. At least she had come.

Soon, perhaps ten minutes later, I heard her leave, and then all was quiet. I sat and waited, tapping my feet lightly on the marble tiles.

On my way back home, driven by the inspector who was on his way to a football practice, all became clear. My suspicions were apparently correct. Dirk, or rather one of his sons, had slipped a note to the duty sergeant late the evening before which suggested a number of dubious reasons why I was in Botswana. Many were so outlandish that I did not fully understand them. They seemed to range from ivory trading to the poaching of rare breeds, but they had been dismissed by the police as ridiculous. Perhaps the accusation that slighted me most was that I was some sort of post-colonial agitator trying to claim that the British were somehow more desirable as teachers and leaders of the young than their Botswanan counterparts. I was about to remonstrate with the inspector when he assured me that nobody had believed this. To my great surprise, not only had Mma Mokwena confirmed the genuineness of my papers, she had confirmed that I was competent to do my job.

'We are sorry, but you realise we did have to make sure that your status in Botswana was correct.' The inspector looked at me a little apologetically. I nodded and assured him that I did.

'So why do you think Mr Dirk would want to say these things, Rra?'

'Well, I am not entirely sure but I think . . .'

So engrossed in my story did the inspector become that he missed half his football practice. Undoubtedly, he was taking it very seriously.

16
The Big Match

Perhaps it is that last day of the Christmas term that I will remember most fondly of all my time in Kasane. That morning as I had climbed into the Old Queen Mum, the Chobe River, the life source of this dry country, was bustling with activity. Flamingos, their spindly black legs trailing behind them, flew along the river's course in the direction of the Zambezi. They seemed to move at exactly the same rate as the waters' flow. Hippos that had already made themselves comfortable in the rich black-brown mud of the banks watched their elegant passage before turning their attention to the squawking and flapping of the vultures and marabou storks on the little island mid-stream. Competition was keen to pick out the tastiest morsels left on the carcass of a recently killed impala. The lion, leopard or cheetah that had hunted down its prey was probably lying low somewhere out there under the shiny grey mopane bushes, sleeping and dreaming of the hunts to come.

On the way to school, I passed Clever walking, because he still had no transport, into town. I stopped and asked him if I could offer him a lift. 'No *matata*,' he replied cheerfully. He waved me off until I had disappeared around the corner. Chris was making his way to the airport, and he too waved cheerfully and flashed his lights as I slowed down so that a family of warthogs might cross the road. As I passed some of the children who were walking to school, they recognised the Old Queen Mum and throwing their satchels over their shoulders they started to run after me waving and laughing, excited at the thought of going to school. Excited too at the prospect of the big match.

Of course it would be nice to finish this story with a win for the Kasane Kudus, but sadly that cannot be. I am pleased however to be able to report that the final match of our season ended in a 2–2 draw, with a wonderful header by Arthur that must have gone some way to making life more bearable, and which meant that finally the picture he had shown me became the depiction of a real event.

Our second goal came at the end of the first half and off the end of Hui's nose from a snorting cross by Dolly. The little Chinese boy burst into floods of tears and was inconsolable until someone managed to make him understand that he had put us two goals ahead. Things became more than a little tense when the opposition, resplendent in a specially sponsored football strip, managed to scrabble two goals after half-time. Very fortunately their third goal was disallowed, for uncertain reasons, by the referee.

Just as I was leaving the pitch, Mma Kebalakile disengaged herself from a group of mothers who were giving her some comfort and support. She walked slowly across the dust towards me.

'Thank you, Mr Mango,' she murmured. 'Thank you for saying what you did.'

Slowly the story came out. Dirk had received a visit from Hans and Barry, whose sense of Christian propriety had been outraged, and they had forced him to sign cashable banker's drafts in full repayment to all his 'clients'. This had clearly been something of a physical activity, because when he had been spotted by Chris being bundled into the back of the BDF plane with his foul-mouthed wife and feral sons by the Chief of Immigration, the inspector and his officers, it was noticed that he appeared dishevelled, and was sporting a black eye and badly torn clothing.

Our carol service was a great success, and so moved was I by the children's singing that I chose to join in myself much to the displeasure of anyone in earshot. When we totted up the marks of the end of term tests, even the school inspector could find no cause for complaint. A report of the soccer season written by the coach and read by Dolly to the parents strangely recorded no results apart from the glorious draw against Victoria Falls Primary School. In fact, had you never witnessed our matches, you might have been under the impression that we were all but ready to challenge Manchester United.

Epilogue

Snorting, he managed to turn a sharp corner despite the fact he was also punching numbers, probably entirely fraudulently, into his machine.

'You got to agree though, avencha?'

'Sorry?'

Certainly, fairly certainly, I had been listening to what my taxi driver friend had been saying. Yet somehow the full import of what he had been telling me seemed not to have made it all the way to my beleaguered brain. I had only just managed to return to consciousness after the flight back from Cape Town, which had involved an indecent but free quantity of whisky and an appallingly boring conversation with a huge Icelander, who had talked a great deal about the modern-day dilemmas involved in fishing for herrings.

I knew I was the taxi driver's friend because he had been calling me 'mate' and telling me I was a 'good bloke' all the way down those rather grey roads from Heathrow airport into town. Now, he slid back the partition window between us a little wider, and turned further and rather more illegally in his seat.

'Sorry, you were saying?'

'No, you've got to agree, 'aven't ya?'

Agree?

''Bout the traffic lights. You know, timings and that. Bloody rubbish. 'Scuse my French.'

He leaned heavily on his horn as we came round Marble Arch and headed down Oxford Street, before sliding down his window, with the smack of a gold-ringed hand. In loud and slow English he proceeded to suggest that one of the pinched and cold, hounded-looking Spring sale shoppers went back to wherever she came from, love, comprendes?

'Yeah, got to get these lights sorted out, doncha agree?'

Disagreeing would probably have put me at some physical risk so I decided to change the subject.

'In fact, I've just come back from Africa. It's amazing but the nearest set of traffic lights was something like five hundred miles away from where I was living.'

It was true. Only once you had turned off the dusty dual carriageway to Gaborone and into the sprawling suburbs of Francistown was any attempt made to direct the four-wheeled and four-legged traffic.

Somewhat to my surprise, as we jerked to a halt again, the driver caught my eye in his rear-view mirror.

'Oh, yeah? Been in Africa have you? So whereabouts was that then? Where yuh been?'

'Oh, I've been in Botswana, up in the north-east there.'

'Oh, yeah, I got you. Yeah, I know where you are. Somewhere near, what they call it now, somewhere near . . . Anyway, it's part of Kenya isn't it? Yeah, thought so. You ever been to Melbourne? Piss off! Yeah, my brother-in-law, well, ex now, he's out there. Says the Grand Prix is great. Might get out there sometime . . . you know, don't tell the wife. Christ, did you see that? Muppet!'

Brakes groaned and we stopped with a certain finality.

I sighed and my mind drifted as I gazed into the deep reflection of a smart shop window. Across the savannah of Botswana, floating over a background of cocktail dresses and hi-fi displays, trundled the Old Queen Mum. All about, in the shade of the mopane thorns and mowana trees, grazed and browsed the wildlife that had created the backdrop to my stay in Africa. Animals had vibrantly brought me closer to the natural world, a world which at first had seemed so alien. Now, it appeared, removed as I was, that I could hardly bear to live away from it. Africa like a temptress, as Karen Blixen had also remarked, 'gives itself to you when you are about to leave'. Only now did I recognise how closely I had become involved in the whole fabric of life in Kasane.

Peering closer, I could see in the back of the truck, their faces to the breeze, the Kasane Kudus, my team, my class. There they were, no doubt on their way to another victory, a footballing triumph. Crystallised in the plate glass was each individual face caught at the moment in time when I had last seen them, joyous at the outcome of the match against the imperious Victoria Falls Primary School. Bothle, yawning contentedly, his arms folded comfortably across his tummy, Glory leaping, mad keen, excitable Courtney, the earnest Blessings, the open-relaxed face of Olobogeng, giggling Dolly, Skye, Kitty and Stella, Happy, Kitso and the sadly smiling Arthur, arms around their new best friends Hakim and little Hui.

Although they will remain for me frozen in that moment until we meet again, these children will of course grow up in real time, I have no doubt, to realise achievements that were beyond the realms of possibility for their parents and grandparents. This mainly because they have had the good fortune to have been born into a country and society that exists on the tenet of fair and honest government, and that hopes to afford the populace an education that will allow them to compete on an international stage. Here is a country determined to succeed, a nation eager to buck the template of failure laid down over Africa by the West. These children will, I hope, be amongst the first of that continent to reject the stereotypes of the past, to stand proud.

When the children had disappeared into the dream world of their Christmas holidays, I found myself clearing my desk for the last time. Carefully folding up 'special pictures for Mr Mango' and slipping them into an envelope to best protect them for the journey home, my attention was attracted by the now familiar Setswana call *'Koko, Rra. Koko!'* from outside the door. When I opened it, I found a delegation of teachers and parents accompanied by Gabamukuni and Elizabeth smiling cheerfully at me. Could they come in?

When finally they left again wishing me well, they were, I think, disappointed.

'*Go sentle*, Rra!' they murmured. '*Go, sentle.*'

'*Go siame,*' I wished them in return.

Mma Sichilongo, as the spokesperson, had asked me quietly, Mrs Krantz nodding in confirmation, whether I would consider staying on permanently as the headmaster. Flattery normally has a quite profound effect on me but I had to shake my head and decline the offer. However much I had enjoyed and benefited from this African adventure, I had actually, I now realised, come to Kasane to avoid the sclerotic effects of responsibility – to keep a healthy distance from the desk and the filing cabinet, the rules and regulations, the bills and the forms. Perhaps it was time to keep on the move. My own education was still barely fledged.

Despite their original disappointment, everyone was

delighted to invite a lady from Zambia with twenty years of efficient school management under her belt to become the new headmistress. With her 'old-fashioned African figure' and piercing but kindly gaze, she would be quite able to cope with the day to day running of the little school.

Of course, I have lived to regret my decision. Every day, as I busy myself with 'normal activities' in England, I will be caught off-guard by a memory of life in Kasane, the vast swathes of the Kalahari, the exotic and the familiar creatures that I encountered every day. But it is the people of Botswana that I will remember most fondly and in particular, of course, the children of the Kasane Kudus.

'Course you gotta remember the congestion charge don't really help. Bloody mayor don't care. He gets the tube. They got the congestion charge out there then?'

Groaning, I closed my eyes, but not before I spotted in the main display window of Selfridge's a great, grey bull elephant lift his mighty head, tusks glinting. As we moved on in the sooty traffic, I saw him raise his trunk and trumpet, and the sound he made vibrated in my heart.